About This Book

Why is this topic important?

e-Learning is here to stay, for better or worse. Let's hope it's for the better. The founders of e-learning technology saw a means of improving the quality of individual learning experiences that no other medium offered. They worked to blend what was known about human learning and pedagogy with emerging computer and communication technologies and to study the outcomes to continuously improve effectiveness. Unfortunately, much of today's e-learning fails to build on the vision, the knowledge, and the most important achievements in learning technology. It therefore provides much less learning and performance impact than it could and should, costing organizations immensely and wasting precious learning time.

What can you achieve with this book?

You can improve the quality of e-learning you buy, create, and use. Contributors to this volume openly and explicitly state the lessons they have learned through decades of first-hand exploratory work. The advice and direction so bluntly shared is applicable whether you work in training or education, in corporations, non-profit organizations, military, or schools.

The Pfeiffer Annual Series

The Pfeiffer Annuals present each year never-before-published materials contributed by learning professionals and academics and written for trainers, consultants, and human resource and performance-improvement practitioners. As a forum for the sharing of ideas, theories, models, instruments, experiential learning activities, and best and innovative practices, the Annuals are unique. Not least because only in the *Pfeiffer Annuals* will you find solutions from professionals like you who work in the field as trainers, consultants, facilitators, educators, and human resource and performance-improvement practitioners and whose contributions have been tried and perfected in real-life settings with actual participants and clients to meet real-world needs.

The Pfeiffer Annual: Consulting
Edited by Elaine Biech

The Pfeiffer Annual: Training
Edited by Elaine Biech

Michael Allen's 2012 e-Learning Annual
Edited by Michael Allen

NABEEL AHMAD · CLARK ALDRICH · BOBBE BAGGIO · TONY BINGHAM

JULIA BULKOWSKI · BRYAN CHAPMAN · PHIL COWCILL

ALLAN HENDERSON · PETER ISACKSON · CHERYL JOHNSON

CATHY KING · LESLIE KIRSHAW · TINA KUNSHIER

DAVID METCALF · CORINNE MILLER · CRAIG MONTGOMERIE

FRANK NGUYEN · MARIA PLAKHOTNIK · TONETTE ROCCO

ANITA ROSEN · PATTI SHANK · CLIVE SHEPHERD · MARTYN SLOMAN

BELINDA SMITH · SUSAN SMITH NASH · KEN SPERO · CARLA TORGERSON

THOMAS TOTH · REUBEN TOZMAN · MARC WEINSTEIN

MICHAEL ALLEN'S
e-LEARNING ANNUAL
2012

Pfeiffer
A Wiley Imprint
www.pfeiffer.com

Published by Pfeiffer
An Imprint of Wiley
989 Market Street, San Francisco, CA 94103-1741
www.pfeiffer.com

For additional copies/bulk purchases of this book in the U.S., please call 800-274-4434.

Pfeiffer books and products are available through most bookstores. To contact Pfeiffer directly, call our Customer Care Department within the U.S. at 800-274-4434, outside the U.S. at 317-572-3985, fax 317-572-4002, or visit www.pfeiffer.com.

Pfeiffer also publishes its books in a variety of electronic formats. Some content that appears in print may not be available in electronic books.

ISBN: 978-0-470-91382-6
ISSN: 1046-333-X
Acquiring Editor: Matthew Davis
Director of Development: Kathleen Dolan Davies
Development Editor: Susan Rachmeler
Production Editor: Dawn Kilgore
Editor: Rebecca Taff
Manufacturing Supervisor: Becky Morgan

Printed in the United States of America

Printing 10 9 8 7 6 5 4 3 2 1

Contents

SOCIAL MEDIA

SIMULATION

INSTRUCTIONAL DESIGN

SUCCESS STRATEGIES

Preface

Traditional e-learning is a term that makes me wince. Although it's true that I've been exploring what we now call e-learning for over forty years now, use of computing technology for teaching and learning continues to be an experiment and exploration in my mind. There is no better support for this perspective than the fascinating collection of papers you are now holding in your hands.

As I continue to strive for greater levels of controversy in each subsequent *Annual*, along with a complementary collection of wise perspectives, I marvel at how the number of debates in our field increases over time. It is clear that we have a lot yet to learn about how to use technology most effectively.

NO ONE SOLUTION | If we're looking for a single solution—*one right way*—to use technology, then controversy will reign, and all recommendations will be wrong. There are too many factors influencing the applicability of solutions for a single solution to be effective and appropriate in all instances. As strong a proponent as I am for meaningful, memorable, and motivational learning experiences, I do recognize that there are times when the simple access to information is all a learner or performer needs. My angst comes simply from people not discriminating among situations. Some needs are solved by a simple injection of "the facts," while others are not.

Mismatching the wide range of available e-learning solutions to needs does no one any favors, regardless of meeting budget, skill, and timing requirements. The assessment of e-learning suffers from the misalignment, as does the credibility of those folks who make the error.

Does the proliferation of alternative technology-assisted solutions ease the challenge of fitting solutions to needs? One would expect so. . . . But not so fast. Alternative solutions require different design and development skills. They require different programmatic solutions for rollout, delivery, and tracking. They require a shift in learner expectations and behaviors. As we know, few changes come easily. Sometimes ridiculed as simple fear of the unfamiliar, there can be dire consequences for changing only one component inside a complex program. Nay-sayers sometimes have a point!

The broadened pallet of options does fuel controversy. In the controversy contained herein between various PowerPoint-based solutions, such as those discussed by **Tom Kuhlmann**, **Anita Rosen**, and **Reuben Tozman**, for example, we have two authors feeling the other's approach misses the mark, while the third author feels both need to look to technology for more intelligent solutions such as semantic webs. Interesting, indeed.

In fact, the so-called "rapid authoring" approaches often rapidly develop inappropriate solutions. But they win short-term approval nonetheless, mostly because novices can produce something quickly. But even as one of its staunchest and most articulate advocates, Kuhlmann recognizes that while speed is valuable, success is far more likely in the hands of skilled designers, regardless of the tools.

Rosen concurs that instructional design is more than "nice to have" and substantiates that adding a little narration to PowerPoint achieves far less than advocates suggest. The truth hurts: "When trainers say they used an easy methodology that created a sub-standard experience, what they are saying is that their time is valuable but everyone else's time is irrelevant."

Thomas Toth outlines the challenges facing e-learning designers, introduced by the technology component not found in instructor-led delivery and provides us a tremendous service by cataloging tools available today. He addresses tools of use for graphic design and photo editing, audio and video recording, screen capture, animation, and programming and code development. He provides much additional value by noting prerequisite skill levels and price points.

Allan Henderson would remind us, however, that focusing on tools, whether consciously or by habit, means we're focusing on the wrong things. He suggests that relatively easy solutions abound and that many of those solutions are far more rapid than the touted rapid approaches. And they can be more effective, too. No question, he found methods that were faster and less expensive.

NEW PERSPECTIVES

With respect to today's e-learning, there are issues within issues, perspectives within perspectives, and topics within topics. Some of this year's papers address very specific issues of design or implementation, while a few share thinking at a very broad conceptual level—some in terms of strategy and others in terms of culture.

Peter Isackson's paper pulled me into extended conversations with myself and instigated much reflection. I hope his thoughts benefit you in similar ways. Boldly stated, Isackson says, "The idea of learning, in spite of being around throughout the history of homo sapiens, is undergoing radical redefinition and will take us into areas that are totally unfamiliar to us today." This statement felt like hyperbole to me, but wait until you read his paper. You'll have new, unfamiliar thoughts yourself. Here's a kick start for you: "If the learning process doesn't include the possibility of modifying in significant ways learners' conscious and unconscious perception of their identity, nothing serious can be accomplished."

Bobbe Baggio also addresses the all-too-often ignored importance of learner identities—personal and social identities—and their effects on learning. Anonymity and "pseudonimity" permit learners to explore online behaviors otherwise restricted by public opinion, resulting in unique, but as yet unevaluated learning opportunities. Baggio leads us to contemplate radical possibilities for learning with technology that are rapidly becoming commonplace. You won't easily cast aside Baggio's observations and the possibilities she identifies.

Also in the group of papers that examine the individual's changing role in learning as a result of technology is a thoughtful paper by **Marc Weinstein, Tonette Rocco,** and **Maria Plakhotnik.** The new information ecosystem affords new levels of self-directed learning. Even more revolutionary, however, is the power of "individuals to share, interact, and create new content." In response to the new landscape, HRD professionals will either fetter these productive possibilities or find they need to enact changes at the corporate strategic, technical, and policy levels to enable them.

HAVE LEARNERS CHANGED?

We're all aware that technology has changed radically since early e-learning efforts, and e-learning is no longer either a novelty or a singular instructional approach. But have learners also changed? There is no doubt that learners form expectations from the media they use on a daily basis, and those expectations carry over to e-learning. The controversy of whether or not learners actually learn differently today in the age of interactive media and rapid access to information was introduced in the previous *Annual.* We continue to review the issue within the covers of this book.

Corinne Miller helpfully traces both the history of e-learning technology in parallel to the changing needs of learners and their organizations. She presents twelve "e-lessons" that should be guiding today's efforts and looks seriously at the changes in use of instructional technologies that today's learners demand. Indeed, the learning customer is different from the customer we had only a short time ago.

Gen-Y or the "Net-Gen'ers" are today's fourteen to thirty-four year-olds who have grown up with networked technology. They have no fear of computers or using them. And far from being intimidated by technology, they know what's possible and demand excellence. **Phil Cowcill** challenges our perceptions of this cohort of users and is persuasive in his stance that these learners are, indeed, different. Far from being absorbed in perpetual game playing and watching TV, Net-Gen'ers spend *less* time watching TV than their preceding generation and far more time surfing the web and multitasking. Cowcill delineates specific ways e-learning design must change to accommodate this generation.

Cheryl Johnson points out that technology and learners aren't the only things changing. Organizations that use the technology for training are also changing their expectations and setting new criteria for success. With all these changes occurring simultaneously, it seems quite rational to think in terms of managing chaos. With a recognition of what chaos means, Johnson constructs a plan for success.

GOING MOBILE

In contrast to just a few years ago, no one doubts that mobile devices have an important role to play beyond being just a handy access to information. That's not to belittle timely and convenient access to information, as valuable as it can be, but learning is another solution—a different means of enhancing performance—that carries greater challenges for mobile devices. Are they up to the challenges?

Leslie Kirshaw looks at mobile devices in a blended solution and brings us up-to-date on successful practices already in place. Important advice here: "There will inevitably be some organizations that make the mistake of simply porting over content from already dreadful e-learning sessions that will neither engage, nor motivate, any learner." Content needs to be constructed for its delivery platform. When characteristics of platforms differ, design changes are mandatory.

In an informative conversation, authors **David Metcalf** and **Nabeel Ahmad** debate four key questions:

1. Is m-learning an extension of e-learning or a new way of looking at learning?
2. Is m-learning an extension of formal learning or more like performance support?
3. Are smart phones better to deliver m-learning than feature phones, which provide much broader access?
4. Which is better: web-based mobile applications or platform-based applications?

As with almost all uses of technology, what at first seems simple turns out to have many options. m-Learning is one of those technologies. Author **Susan Smith Nash** points out that even the basics have major design consequences. Are you designing for devices with no connectivity, occasional connectivity, or continuous connectivity? Perhaps this won't be a question some time in the future, but it is very much a question today. Nash provides an informative article complete with itemized approaches to m-learning, screen captures, and case studies.

SOCIAL MEDIA

Presumably we humans began instruction with one-on-one mentorship. Such mentorship carried us through millennia until transportation permitted group schooling. The efficiencies of group instruction began the reign of classroom instruction and the sacrifice of individualized instruction for one instructor to many learners. Technology reintroduced the possibility of individualization, but also isolated learning activities with one computer to one learner. Now we've moved on to possibly the best arrangement of all—many instructors and many learners brought together through technology without the need of physical transportation.

Tony Bingham began his wake-up call to e-learning designers several years ago. "Harness social media or prepare to be left behind." Actually, I think he said, "Prepare to be left out of a job." Social media provides a powerful platform for learning. They don't just repackage the same principles — they offer an arena that supports new types of learning events. Classic models presumed that relevant information was created, packaged, and then transmitted to learners, but now, with information being created at unprecedented speeds, there isn't time for such preparation. Learners can and need to be participants in the whole process, including capturing, packaging, and sharing information with each other.

How do we harness the energy of connected learners no longer tapped in a classroom? Which design principles remain valid and which need reformation? **Frank Nguyen** shares three primary ways to adapt instructional designs for designs for Web 2.0: (1) build learning experiences, not just events,

(2) expand the toolbox, and (3) embrace the masses.

Julia Bulkowski removes any concerns that learner-created content and social learning are unmanageable fantasies far from today's reality. Illustrative examples show how Google's learning and development teams have used social media technologies to save money and enhance learning and performance. This is a compelling piece not to be missed.

SIMULATION

Few would disagree that transfer of knowledge and skills from learning to actual performance is the primary goal of instruction. The more similar the skills practiced during learning are to the skills to be performed, the more likely this transfer will occur. That's what simulations and learning games are all about, but simulations and games are often perceived to be too expensive, inappropriate, too slow, or otherwise just not a suitable solution.

Veteran game and simulation designer **Clark Aldrich** joins *Annual* contributors to share his unrivaled experience in developing cost-effective learning simulations. He explains when and how they fit into an organization's learning programs and, so importantly, identifies roles, responsibilities, processes, and timeframes for creating them.

Ken Spero emphasizes the importance of experience. Experience is a step up from skills. It informs us when to use skills and for what purpose. But e-learning and training in general are often focused at only the skill level, omitting attention to the ability to assess situations and make critical judgments.

Spero outlines practical methods of making experiences part of the learning solution.

INSTRUCTIONAL DESIGN

Many elements come together in the creation of education and training programs. Just content or curriculum identification is a major task, but then, development of objectives, graphics, interactions, text, assessments, navigation, and tracking are also major tasks. Since it's difficult to maintain equal focus on so many elements and tasks, one or two need to draw primary attention while others fall in line to support them. The question is, Which should be the primary points of focus?

Bryan Chapman, one of the most recognized and respected individuals in our field, points out that in corporate settings, critical focus must be on deploying "content-centric learning strategies" as a means of elevating learning "to new levels of mission criticality." He suggests that content-centric approaches based on optimal use of learning content management systems (LCMS) can shorten development cycles, ease updates, and distribute responsibilities across the organization—all of major benefit to the organization. While well-reasoned, presented with vignettes, helpfully complete with specific steps to creating a content-centric learning strategy, this position sparks debate as, indeed, any position singling out a primary point of focus is likely to do.

In response and rebuttal to Chapman, **Carla Torgerson** agrees that the goal of corporate training should be improved performance through responsive training but asks, "Is it most important to save development time or learning time?" Hastily constructed learning activities that have not been well designed can easily frustrate learners. They can be so generally constructed as to serve no specific needs. Don't practice exercises, for example, need to be designed to move performers from their current levels to advanced levels? Isn't it far more important to be learner-centric than content-centric? We might reflect again upon Anita Rosen's comments: Whose time is most important, the designer/developer's or the learner/performer's?

Clive Shepherd enters the fray with concerns that instructional designers just keep doing what they've always done, ignoring variance in actual needs. Sometimes learning just isn't the right answer. If the focus is on performance, then performance support is sometimes a superior investment to learning. Most importantly, Shepherd reminds us that focus should never be on the instructional designer, as too often seems to be the case. Sometimes the best solutions don't involve designers much at all. But far more important than just matching content to learners is matching the best solutions to the real needs.

SUCCESS STRATEGIES There are many ways to find success with technology-assisted instruction and learning. Unfortunately, there are many more ways to be unsuccessful. What's the most expensive form of instruction? Instruction that doesn't work. With ineffective instruction you lost not only all the design, development, and delivery costs, but also all the costs of learner time invested *plus* the cost of all the opportunities lost. Organiza-

tions rarely face up to the costs of poor learning applications.

Martyn Sloman presents data on the usage of e-learning. If anyone doubted that e-learning were becoming a widespread practice, this data will dispel the notion. Enthusiasts will be pleased, but use of technology is neither good nor bad in itself. If focus is on the technology, chances are the use of it is not good. Focus instead on the learner and needed outcomes. As Sloman puts it, learner preferences, attitudes, and motivation must be understood if their learning is to deliver value to the organization. This is a valuable article to have at hand and use in so many situations.

Continuing on this extremely important theme, **Patti Shank** provides a decision matrix for selecting among classroom instruction, synchronous instruction, asynchronous instruction, performance support, or a mixture. Shank is helpfully specific in strategies to apply. "If you are just getting started, [for example] don't run out and buy a learning management system," she says. Be prudent. Keep it simple. Wise advice.

Tina Kunshier treats us to a fascinating look at e-learning development and deployment inside a regulated environment. If the challenges of design, content development, technology, and deployment weren't enough, organizations such as Boston Scientific face additional criteria and federal government scrutiny. Taking a challenge and turning it into an advantage, Kunshier outlines how Boston Scientific has used stringent requirements to refine their processes and achieve "an internal error rate of less than 2 percent of all weekly course completions."

Craig Montgomerie and **Cathy King** bring us up-to-date on instructional videoconferencing, where technologies have advanced just as rapidly as other instructional technologies, creating new possibilities and transforming others. Here again we learn that focusing on the technology rather than the learning experience and instructional design has unfortunate consequences. Major programs intended to fund learning opportunities for those learners otherwise difficult to reach cannot succeed through only the provision of technology. Although learner-created content and sharing have great value, curriculum design remains essential. When done well, however, instructional videoconferencing has immeasurable value.

Adult learners aren't the easiest learners to corral and focus. They are often pressed for time, distracted, and a bit skeptical about whether training programs are going to meet their needs. And today, there's great variance in their comfort with technology. In many cases, synchronous e-learning is the best solution for this audience, but deployment of synchronous e-learning has special challenges all its own. **Belinda Smith** defines these challenges and provides us a roadmap for achieving success with this demanding audience.

READ, LEARN, THINK, AND ENJOY! This is an amazing collection of papers—clearly enough to fuel many courses of instruction about e-learning. I hope this work will receive broad recognition and readership. Contributing authors have invested so much wisdom and considerable effort to bring these important thoughts to you. Every author writes with conviction and a desire to help you develop outstanding learning experiences for the benefit of all. There's no doubt that all of us can and will do better standing on the shoulders of all this experience and insight. Please read, learn, think, and enjoy!

Michael W. Allen, Editor
May 2011

Tom Kuhlmann

Tom Kuhlmann, M.Ed., is vice president, community, for Articulate, where he manages the Articulate user community. He also writes the Rapid e-Learning Blog, which is published weekly to almost sixty thousand readers. Tom has nearly twenty years of experience in the training industry, where he has developed and managed e-learning courses for both large and small organizations. Tom is patient about learning technology, and his core focus is on helping people succeed and grow. He is known throughout the industry for his practical, no-nonsense approaches to e-learning. He's also a frequent speaker at ASTD and e-learning industry events. He has a master's degree in education technology from Pepperdine.

RAPID E-LEARNING REALITY CHECK | Tom Kuhlmann

Superblogger Tom Kuhlmann addresses a topic of importance and one of frequent annoyance to me: "rapid" e-learning. It seems everywhere you go someone's promoting a rapid e-learning application that's going to help build e-learning courses in no time at all and with no required programming. In today's economy, and with increasing pressure from organizations to do more with less, the promise of rapid e-learning is attractive. But what is rapid e-learning? Where does it fit in the e-learning landscape? And can it fulfill the promise? Something isn't always better than nothing, but speed to market is always an important consideration. I appreciate Tom's taking an excellent, frank look at the prospects of rapid e-learning and setting the record straight. Whether rapid authoring is too often maligned or simply called out for what it isn't—well, that may still be the very kind of controversy we invite here. In any case, Tom has undertaken a more substantive analysis and comparison than typically fuels the discussion.

WHAT IS RAPID E-LEARNING, ANYWAY?

Rapid e-learning has been defined in different ways. The most popular tends to be focused on the software. A few years ago the tools to create e-learning courses required specialized programming skills. You couldn't just open up Flash or Authorware and create a course. There was a learning curve. Today, that's not the case. Many tools allow just about anyone to publish e-learning courses with little programming know-how. Now this doesn't mean that everything published is going to be good. That still requires sound instructional design. But it does mean that the tools are available for organizations to efficiently develop and deploy their e-learning courses.

The second most common definition of rapid e-learning involves the simplification of the production process. What used to require a team of people now can be accomplished by just one or two. Many e-learning developers wear multiple hats. They act as the instructional designer, graphic artist, LMS administrator, and course author. The challenge for organizations is to balance their cost-consciousness with course effectiveness. Just because you can create a course doesn't mean you always should. So an ongoing concern is to ensure that the easy authoring is balanced with effective course design. Not everyone with a rapid e-learning tool is going to build a great course. But with the right implementation and focus on instructional design, a rapid e-learning strategy can prove to be an effective and affordable solution for many organizations.

Regardless of how rapid e-learning is defined or what tool is used to build the e-learning courses, the end result is that the courses do exist. My guess is that the learners don't care how it was authored. What they and their organizations expect are e-learning courses that are effective and help the organization meet its goals.

RAPID E-LEARNING TOOLS COME IN MANY FLAVORS

Let's do a quick review of rapid e-learning tools. Many people tend to think that rapid e-learning tools are just rooted in PowerPoint to Flash publishing. But the reality is that rapid e-learning applications are diverse and include more than basic PowerPoint conversions.

When authoring any e-learning course, someone decides what content to add to the screen. This can include text, audio, images, and interactive multimedia. You typically have two types of e-learning tools to author courses. One type is *freeform*, where you start with a blank screen and have to decide how to construct the look and feel of the course and where to place the objects. The other is *form-based*, where the software is built to accomplish a specific function or interaction. Most of the design and structure is pre-built and only requires that the developer add content to the form. Typically, you can insert text, images, narration, and multimedia. Figure 1 compares the two types of tools.

Freeform Authoring. Freeform tools are great because the look and feel of the course isn't defined for you by the authoring software. You start with a blank screen from which the sky's the limit. These types of tools can range from Flash, which it is typically used to custom-build courses, to something as simple as PowerPoint.

Many of the rapid e-learning tools act as add-ins to PowerPoint. Essentially, they provide the course infrastructure and logic and let the developer leverage the easy authoring environment in PowerPoint. Each PowerPoint slide is converted to a single Flash movie. The rapid e-learning software builds the player structure and everything else to play the Flash movies authored in PowerPoint. Examples of freeform tools are shown in Figure 2.

Form vs. Freeform Authoring

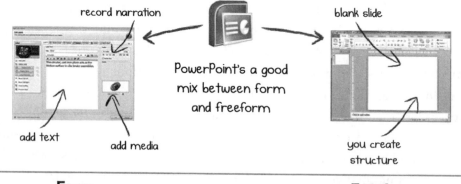

Figure 1. Form vs. Freeform Authoring

record narration

blank slide

PowerPoint's a good mix between form and freeform

add text

add media

you create structure

Form
Fast & easy, but form has constraints

Freeform
Freedom to build what you want; requires programming skills

Example Freeform Tools

All start with a blank screen

Flash   PowerPoint   Quizmaker

Figure 2. Examples of Freeform Tools

Form-Base Authoring. When it comes to building multimedia content, it doesn't get any easier than a form-based application. For the most part, the software does everything—all you have to do is add your content. Because the forms are predetermined, they can be simple or complex. It really just depends on how they're designed. The output can be simple presentations or highly interactive learning activities. The main point is that the form is pre-designed to a specific function. Figure 3 shows some examples.

Both types of tools are effective for e-learning, but they also have their drawbacks. For example, while freeform authoring is highly flexible, it also entails more custom programming. Thus, to build more than simple content, you need to have some programming skills. You're not just going to open up Flash and start building a course. Even building good PowerPoint-based e-learning requires more than a basic understanding of PowerPoint.

Example Form Tools

Figure 3. Examples of Form-Based Authoring

Add content here...   ...to create this in ten minutes

To get away from the programming requirements, you can use a form-based tool. The form makes creating a course or interaction easy, because the structure is predetermined and only requires content be added. But then the form only gives you what the form is designed to give you. Think of it like a Jell-O mold. If you want a crab-shaped chunk of gelatin, you need a crab-shaped mold. Just like the crab mold, the form-based output is only going to give you what it's designed to give you. So it's easy to build content without being a programmer, but at the same time the easy authoring introduces some constraints if you want more than what the form is designed to give you.

Many Flash programmers have their own versions of forms whereby they create a course structure that can dynamically pull in content. All they do is swap out the content. It's really not much different for rapid e-learning forms, outside of the fact that the content is modified by a non-programmer in an easy-to-use interface.

commonly do with it. This is especially true because building e-learning courses is different from building presentations (which is the cause for most of the complaints). Despite the complaints, PowerPoint is a great application to author e-learning courses. PowerPoint 2007 and 2010 have introduced a lot of new features that make authoring e-learning courses much easier and more Flash-like. Figure 4 shows some examples.

PowerPoint doesn't have to look like PowerPoint

Rapid e-learning examples created in PowerPoint

Figure 4. Examples of PowerPoint-Based Rapid e-Learning

POWERPOINT'S A VERSATILE APPLICATION

To some, anything created in PowerPoint sucks. But it's important to separate PowerPoint as an authoring tool for e-learning courses from what people

PowerPoint offers a very rich authoring environment in which you can create interactive and engaging e-learning courses. Because you start with a blank slide, you have a lot of flexibility in how your course looks and feels. You're not limited to any particular template. Essentially, the rapid e-learning software combines all of the graphics, audio, and animations in each PowerPoint slide to create a Flash movie. That published output can be indistinguishable from content created in Flash. And that's the attraction to PowerPoint-to-

Flash e-learning tools—you can create Flash output without learning Flash. Another benefit of PowerPoint is that it is used by so many people, so the transition to e-learning is usually pretty easy. For the most part, anyone can create and publish an e-learning course with minimal instruction. That's not true of more complex tools like Flash. PowerPoint also offers a lot of built-in graphics features that minimize the need for additional graphic design support.

Before rapid e-learning, most organizations had limited access to multimedia development, if any. Even in large organizations, being able to build and deliver e-learning was cost-prohibitive. That's changed—mostly because of the PowerPoint-based authoring.

A lot of the criticism of PowerPoint-based e-learning is misguided. PowerPoint's a versatile tool. Yet there's rarely a distinction between when it's used for presentations, to build graphics, for author videos, or to create e-learning courses. Unfortunately, there are a lot of bad presentations (and e-learning courses for that matter), so it's easy to blame the tool.

With that said, there are limitations to PowerPoint-based authoring. One of the challenges is that, because the tools are easy to use, a lot of courses are built by people with limited instructional design experience. On top of that, they stick to the default PowerPoint templates and essentially take what were bad presentations and make comparable e-learning courses. So there's a need for more focus on instructional design.

Another limitation is the technology. PowerPoint was not really designed to be converted to Flash and used for e-learning. Because of this, the courses tend to be linear.

Although, over the last few years, many of the rapid e-learning tools do offer some interactive branching capabilities, and PowerPoint's own hyper-linking works well. In either case, building interactive content is probably not intuitive to the first-time user and does require more than basic PowerPoint skills.

Like anything, there's always a tradeoff. There's a place where the tools work and a place where they don't. It's just a matter of understanding the tool's capabilities. I've found that PowerPoint's easy to use and capable of delivering decent e-learning courses. To prove my point, I recently built a mockup of an Allen Interactions course previously built in Flash. My goal was to only use Power-Point (for the graphics as well as the e-learning). While it wasn't an exact duplicate, it still maintained the core instructional design components. It demonstrates that, with sound instructional design, you can even use a tool like PowerPoint to build effective e-learning, as seen in Figure 5.

Flash example from Allen Interactions   PowerPoint version

Figure 5. Comparing Flash Courses to PowerPoint Courses

As I noted earlier, different types of tools make up what is known as "rapid e-learning." Many organizations tend to use a combination of tools and do a lot of hybrid development by which they combine the rapid authoring with some custom Flash elements. It's easy to see why rapid e-learning is attractive. It does make content creation easy. However, it doesn't replace sound instructional design. The ongoing challenge for organizations that use these tools is to equip their teams with the resources and means to build effective e-learning courses and not just expect that anything will do.

RAPID E-LEARNING HAS DEMOCRATIZED E-LEARNING

A blog author recently commented on the mainstream media's excuse for lost revenue. The media blamed their losses on all of those pesky bloggers, claiming that bloggers had fragmented the market. The blogger's response was that the market was always fragmented. It's just that previously the technology didn't exist to serve it. I hear similar complaints from e-learning vendors. They say those pesky rapid e-learning developers have fragmented their market.

But my response is the same as the blogger's. Rapid e-learning hasn't fragmented the market. It's only serving a market not served before. In the past you needed money or programmers to build an e-learning course. That's no longer the case. Now, the capability is available to everybody, not just a handful of programmers or corporations with deep pockets.

Many large organizations have formal e-learning teams, yet their resources aren't available to the smaller business units. Some managers may want to train their employees, but these departments are not big enough to warrant any assistance from the formal training groups. In the past, they just made do with what they had. The "learning" still happened. They just ended up with lots of job aids and redundant face-to-face training sessions. However, with rapid e-learning tools they're able to build the e-learning courses they need. They may not build award-winning courses, but they are building courses that help them meet their objectives. This is saving the organization time and money.

NOT ALL E-LEARNING IS THE SAME

e-Learning means different things to different people. Working on a $200,000 e-learning course with a team of Flash programmers provides a different perspective than that of a site safety manager who has to build e-learning courses with no budget. How they see e-learning is different. And considering the disparity in resources, how they approach e-learning is different. If I always had a team of Flash programmers and graphic artists (and a healthy budget), I'd also question how one could possibly build effective e-learning with a simple application like PowerPoint. But the reality is that most e-learning courses built today are built by people who have no resources other than their authoring tools. Is this ideal? No. But it's the reality they work in. See Figure 6 for two types of course focus.

Are you viewing or doing?

Some courses focus on information...

...and others focus on performance

Figure 6. Are You Viewing or Doing?

Objectives for e-learning courses are also different from situation to situation. Not all courses are created equal. Working with an executive who demands an immediate impact to the organization's performance requires a different intervention than the human resources manager who wants to share simple changes to the organization's bonus plan. Some courses are only intended to share information, while others seek to change performance. The main goal is to build a course that is appropriate to the objectives and then to use the least resources to meet those objectives. That's just good business.

In addition to different purposes, not all e-learning centers on corporate training and performance improvement. For example, universi-

ties and colleges don't typically focus on performance in the same way as corporation would. Because of this, they tend to build fewer performance-based activities into their e-learning courses. This makes sense because the e-learning courses they offer are only pieces in a larger curriculum that includes other learning support. Many of them seek to convert lectures and other material to multimedia for online delivery and use that in conjunction with other activities, so they tend to focus more on efficient information delivery.

The examples in Figure 7 shows how rapid e-learning adds value to the curriculum design. Both examples show how organizations are leveraging many of the web's interactive learning opportunities. One is of a Google Map and YouTube mashup as part of learning the Seven Wonders of the World. The other is an embedded virtual world wherein learners can explore and interact with each other—both done in PowerPoint and with no programming.

Higher Ed

YouTube and Google Maps mashup

Embedded virtual world

Figure 7. Example of Higher-Ed Rapid e-Learning

Because of easy authoring, rapid e-learning has spawned a consumer education industry. Consider these two quick examples that weren't possible a few years ago and demonstrate the democratization of e-learning. First, a dentist uses rapid e-learning to teach children how to brush their teeth. He has no programming skills, yet can deliver a rich multimedia experience to his patients. Second, an auto dealership teaches car owners about miscellaneous repairs. The courses are built and maintained by the mechanics. They use it as a teaching experience. The customers love it because, instead of being confused about the repairs and possibly feeling ripped off, they feel empowered and educated.

The main point in all of this is that there is no single type of e-learning or a single approach to how the courses should be built. Instead, there are multiple ways to build the many types of e-learning. Some courses are simple and some are complex. Some are high-profile with a large budget and a full production team. And others are limited and have no budget. And for each situation, there's an appropriate tool. Sometimes, rapid e-learning tools are the right tools and sometimes they're not.

WORKING AT THE SPEED OF BUSINESS

When it comes to the world of business, the organization's overarching objective is not to build an e-learning course. Instead, it wants to meet a specific business goal, and an e-learning course is merely a solution for doing so. Thus, the appropriate thing is to step away from the solution and focus on the business objective. At that point, determine the best solution to satisfy the organization's goals. From this perspective, rapid e-learning can be a very effective solution to meet the organization's e-learning needs.

Here's an approach that I've found works. I start with a rapid e-learning tool to build courses. The tools are capable and can meet most of the organization's e-learning needs. This lets you take care of the low-hanging

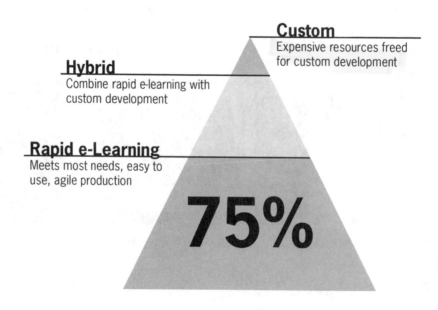

Figure 8. Rapid e-Learning Hierarchy

fruit and many of the simple, information-based courses. From my experience, you can probably build 75 percent of your courses with this approach. (See Figure 8.) Although this obviously varies based on the types of e-learning courses you need, the main point is that you're not committing expensive Flash development resources to projects that can be satisfied with the rapid e-learning software.

While the rapid e-learning software can do quite a bit, it can't do everything. Many courses require some custom development. In that case, the next step is to do some hybrid development where the course's infrastructure comes from the rapid e-learning application, but is augmented with custom Flash pieces. This lets you leverage the rapid e-learning tool's easy publishing and still create the custom programming that might require variables or other logic-based interactivity. This is a popular production strategy for many organizations that want to leverage both the rapid authoring and the custom Flash skills of their developers.

However, there will always be some courses that require more. For example, you're not going to build flight simulator training in PowerPoint. So the next stage is to commit your resources to custom development. Using this strategy, your resources are used in a manner appropriate to the organization's objectives. You don't want your resources or multimedia developers committed to content that can easily be created with rapid e-learning software. They are expensive resources and you want them working on the types of projects that warrant them.

One of my favorite e-learning examples is of an organization that had a weekend fatality. The safety team scrambled. They shot

some onsite video detailing the accident, interviewed the CEO, and pulled together a refresher training program. All of this content was assembled by the site safety manager using a digital camera and rapid e-learning tool. And it was delivered to all of the production facilities in less than twelve hours. If the corporate e-learning team were involved, it would have taken three months of back-and-forth meetings just to perform a needs analysis, let alone deliver anything. The course met the organization's immediate needs. They needed to document the incident and then swiftly communicate with the other production facilities. And that's operating at the speed of business.

As we noted earlier, there are all sorts of demands and use cases for e-learning. There's not a one-size-fits-all approach. It's important to be agile and flexible, and that means having the right tools for the right job at the right time. You need rapid e-learning tools in your tool chest to be agile and responsive in today's business.

THE FUTURE OF RAPID E-LEARNING

Years ago when looking for work, you went to a commercial printer who printed your resumes. Once computers arrived, you hired a desktop author to design and print your resumes. Soon after, you bought your own computer and created your own resumes. Today, you just go to a website and fill in a form.

This doesn't make you a rapid resume builder. You're a job seeker who's using technology to find a job. But over the years the technology has changed and made it easier.

It's the same for e-learning. There's really no such thing as rapid e-learning. It's all just e-learning. The only difference is that, just like creating resumes, creating e-learning courses is getting easier. We've gone from Authorware to Flash to rapid e-learning. And soon we'll have a next generation of tools that will require no programming, yet produce complex multimedia content that not only will look and perform well, but will also offer more programming sophistication. Many critics of rapid e-learning want to blame the tools for bad e-learning. But as I like to point out, *Michael Allen's Guide to e-Learning* was written in response to crappy e-learning that existed way before rapid e-learning. So while there may be some bad courses out there created with rapid e-learning tools, they're created by people who don't know how to build good courses.

In some ways, the critics are like the typesetters lamenting the introduction of electronic resume creation. It makes sense because there's a shift in how the industry does business. But like any industry, technology changes—and our roles change as well.

Here's where I see opportunity. Course authoring is only going to become easier and more feature-rich as the technology advances. But easy authoring doesn't replace sound instructional design. There will always be a difference between good and bad courses. And those who can build good courses will flourish despite the changing technology; probably more so because of the movement by organizations to take their training online.

Another opportunity is in supporting organizations that do use rapid authoring tools. Someone has to show them how to use the tools to create better learning experiences so that they get the most out of their investment.

Something that is often overlooked about rapid e-learning (but that has benefited the industry tremendously) is that we no longer are spending time discussing how to program our courses. Instead, a lot of the conversation has shifted to how to build better courses and learning experiences. Previously, instructional designers were often cut out of the conversation, because it all centered on the technology and programming. However, now that the tools take a lot of the production conversation off the table, they've made room for more conversation about effective learning. (See

Today's tools make it easier to focus on instructional design rather than programming.

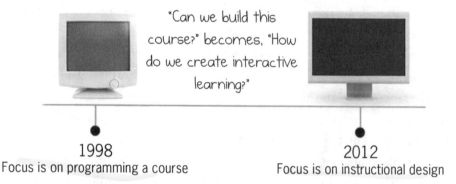

"Can we build this course?" becomes, "How do we create interactive learning?"

1998
Focus is on programming a course

2012
Focus is on instructional design

Figure 9. 1998 to Today Timeline

Figure 9.) And that's something that hasn't always been the focus in the past.

Here's the deal when it comes to rapid e-learning. The tools are going to become more sophisticated and easier to use. We need to shift our attention to better equipping our instructional designers. They need a broader understanding of graphic design and visual communication so that those can be coupled with sound learning theory. We also need to equip our subject-matter experts. While they may not always be the best ones to develop e-learning content, the reality is that, as social media and rapid e-learning tools advance, there will be more pressure on them to create content. And if that's the case, we want their courses to be good and effective.

There's a lot more to be said about rapid e-learning. Hopefully, this is a good start.

Anita Rosen

Anita Rosen, MBA, is a successful trainer, speaker, and author on Internet-related topics, including e-learning and e-business. She has appeared as a guest speaker on many business radio programs and Internet shows. She has been a contributing editor to the *IT Times* and keynote speaker for a number of conferences, including conferences given by the eLearning Guild, ASTD, Country of Singapore, French Telecom, and the American Management Association.

Anita has written four books published by AMACOM: *eLearning 2.0, Effective IT Project Management, eCommerce: A Question and Answer Book,* and *Looking into Intranets and the Internet.*

As a consultant, Anita has worked with a number of companies, assisting them to integrate current business goals and objectives into a successful Internet and e-learning strategy. She has worked with companies such as Digital, The Depository Trust Company, Global Village, Oracle, Matrixsoft, Netscape, Novell, Unilever, and 3DO.

She brings more than twenty-five years of management experience in e-learning, high-tech marketing, project management, and sales. Currently she is president of ReadyGo Inc.

AN ARGUMENT AGAINST VOICE-OVER POWERPOINT FOR E-LEARNING | Anita Rosen

PowerPoint clearly appeals to a broad audience of users for creating presentations. Once having learned to use PowerPoint, comfort and familiarity with the tool often lead to efforts to develop e-learning with it as well. This is an especially attractive path when PowerPoint presentations exist as a starting point for e-learning development. But author Anita Rosen asks, "Should we use these PowerPoint presentations with voice-over narration for e-learning? What do the stakeholders think? Are these courses meeting their needs?" These are important questions addressed by Anita's case studies.

WHAT WORKS?

Most trainers know how to organize their thoughts, prepare a PowerPoint presentation, and present to a classroom full of adults. But can the same presentation be used on the web to create an effective learning situation? Taking the presenter out of training is not as simple and straightforward as we would like. To have content stand on its own on the web takes careful consideration.

This article is about why I believe Power-Point is not an effective tool for creating web-based training. To determine whether or not an approach is effective, I feel it is important to know who is measuring effectiveness, what they are using to measure results, and how they identify what is not effective. For adult education in the workplace, it is not an academic person who measures course effectiveness; it is the organization's management who decides whether or not training is meeting their needs. The employees who are taking the training identify whether the experience was one they are willing to repeat.

ABOUT ORGANIZATIONS

When I speak with organizations about e-learning, I find there are multiple stakeholders who are interested in training. Each has varying needs and wants. The main stakeholders are upper management, managers, trainers, and learners. For a training program to be successful, these stakeholders must have their needs addressed and met. Over the past ten years, I have worked with many different organizations and have come in contact with all of these different stakeholders. I have worked with corporate, government, military, and not-for-profit organizations located throughout the world. Interestingly, even though these organizations have very different organizational goals, responsibilities, and structures, I find their needs and wants align based on the roles individuals play within their organizations. That is, upper management, managers, trainers, and learners typically have a similar response to what they want and expect from training. I am neither an academic nor a researcher. I am a business person and have asked my questions to better focus my company's products, features, and services so that they can better address our customer's training needs. Of course, I also ask these questions to satisfy my own curiosity.

WHAT DO YOUR STAKE-HOLDERS WANT?

When I work with an organization I make a point of asking stakeholders what their goal is in having a training program.

What do executives want?

When I talk with upper management to discuss their goals when implementing e-learning, they typically tell me they want to be assured that their employees can demonstrate that they understand the material. I find few in upper management who have a clear idea of what a good e-learning course looks like or how it should behave. They are very clear on the results they want. Most upper managers want their training organization to provide the implementation strategy.

What do managers want?

Managers have a more operational view of training. They want their employees trained so they can better perform their jobs or can meet organizational requirements. More importantly, I find that managers want to have their employees available to do their jobs. Managers articulate this by saying they want their employees to be out of the field for as short a period of time as possible. When I discuss with them what this looks like and how long an e-learning course should be, most managers want to allocate fifteen-minute timeframes for employees to train. They tell me that fifteen-minute modules make it easy to fit training into an employee's work schedule.

What do learners want?

When I talk to learners about their experience with e-learning, I typically hear similar feedback. Most learners start by telling me that they prefer e-learning over classroom training because it's convenient. When I ask them about a specific experience, I repeatedly hear that it is very hard to maintain concentration for more than fifteen or twenty minutes. They appreciate having courses chunked so that they can be easily taken in that timeframe. When I ask learner to critique e-learning, the most popular comment I hear is "Don't waste my time." The time-wasters I hear most often, cited in order of importance, are:

➢ "I'm literate; don't read to me."
➢ "If a multimedia application (Flash or movie) does not clarify an idea or bring a thought being explained to life, please don't make me watch it."
➢ "I don't mind if a course is entertaining or not; I don't have time to be entertained for the sake of being entertained."
➢ "It's really hard to read a manual online; please write in an approachable style."
➢ "Make the navigation intuitively obvious."
➢ "Don't hide necessary information in mouse-overs."
➢ "Don't make me play a game in order to finish a training course." (The more senior the learner, the more often I hear this.)

What do trainers want?

When I speak to trainers or training managers, I am usually told how many hours of training they have provided to their constituency or how many hours of training material they have produced. When asked about what methodology they use and why they use this specific methodology, I find trainers fall into one of two categories. One group likes to tell me how easy the tool they use is. The other likes to tell me about the methodology they use for product training. They seem to want something easy to use that fits their methodology.

Because this paper is on why I don't think PowerPoint creates good courses, we will focus on those who use this methodology.

What do course creators want?

When I talk to course creators who use PowerPoint, I ask them why they chose this methodology. Inevitably I hear the following responses

> ➤ "It's easy."
> ➤ "I don't want to learn another tool."
> ➤ "I want to replicate the classroom experience."

I've been shocked on how self-serving their responses were. What surprised me even more was what they were not saying to me—specifically, how the training they are producing meets their stakeholders' needs. When I ask course creators about the learner's experience, they reiterate how easy the tool they use is for them and how they don't want to learn another tool. They then go on to defend their voice-overs.

WHAT IS THE OPPORTUNITY COST FOR TRAINING?

I don't hear trainers or their management correlating the number of hours they take building a course to the number of hours of organizational time spent taking the course. Training costs organizations money. It is costly to build a course, but it is even more costly to have employees take a course. If a trainer builds an hour-long course that five hundred employees take, and the average cost per hour for an employee is $100, the corporate opportunity cost to take the course is $50,000 (500 x $100 = $50,000). This equation puts training in a different perspective. When trainers say they used an easy methodology that created a substandard experience, what they are saying is that their time is valuable but that everyone else's time is irrelevant.

Training's Cost/Benefit Ratio.

There is a excellent cost/benefit ratio if a trainer spends only eight hours creating a course (say $800 creation cost), even if the organization spent $50,000 taking it. It would be a great scenario if creation of a very effective course cost only $800. But if the number-one goal is making it easy for the course creator to build a course, I question the motivation and what it leads to.

How Course Creators Should Spend Their Time.

Trainers think that if it takes them time to learn a better methodology and use a more appropriate tool, it will take them longer to create the course. The trainers may not see any benefit in working harder or longer, and frankly, if the organization is complacent, why should they?

But these cost metrics are strong. Even if it took a trainer a full week to create a course, the organizational cost would only be $4,000 of development time to $50,000 of everyone else's time. If it cost $3,200 more to avoid wasting $50,000, wouldn't you spend it? If five hundred people benefited from a better experience, I believe that spending extra time to learn how to create an effective course is worthwhile, and we should not forget that an effective course better meets critical stakeholders needs.

I was brought into an aeronautics company by an engineering executive to provide e-learning direction. His division had been a recipient of e-learning for a number of years. The e-learning training group had been moved recently from human resources to his responsibility. While the training department was under human resources, his people had taken e-learning courses. The courses were voice-annotated PowerPoint with a test at the end. His people quickly figured out how either to let the course play in the background while they worked or how to skip ahead to the end and take the test. He said, "Now that training is my responsibility, I want courses that aren't a joke." He was looking for direction on how to turn their learning experience into one that was effective.

CASE STUDY: POWER POINT VS. INSTRUCTIONALLY SOUND WEB COURSES

So why do I say PowerPoint doesn't work? One of my customers is a telecommunications company with 100,000 employees. Their e-learning division was asked by senior management why they were spending so much time creating courses when they could just take the existing PowerPoint presentations, save them as Flash applications, voice-annotate them, put a test at the end, and put them online. The training group management was made up of instructional designers who had been on the cutting edge of e-learning. They felt that repurposed PowerPoint would create a sub-optimal experience and wanted to convey this concept to their management. I recommended that they conduct an experiment and use the results to tell the story.

The Course. We chose a compliance course that the training group had been tasked to create. Approximately 20,000 employees would be taking this course. We asked two different course creators to develop the course using the same PowerPoint presentation as their source document. We also created a test and survey that would be used by both course creators and placed at the end of each course. One course creator used a PowerPoint-to-Flash tool and annotated the slides with audio. The other course creator used ReadyGo Web Course Builder, a tool that creates a structured web course. The course creator using ReadyGo Web Course Builder was encouraged to deploy effective instructional design and web design methodology. Both course creators were familiar with the tools they were using. It took both course creators a similar amount of time to create a course.

The voice-annotated PowerPoint course was given randomly to 10,000 employees, while the ReadyGo Web Course Builder course was given to a different random set of 10,000 employees. The results were astounding.

Measuring Effectiveness. To properly measure effectiveness, we developed a test that would measure how much an employee retained from the material, rather than measuring how much they knew when they started the course. The employees who received the ReadyGo course scored, out of a possible 100 points, 20 points higher than the employees who were given the voice-annotated PowerPoint. Additionally, the employees who received the ReadyGo courses gave 40 percent higher satisfaction feedback in the post-course survey. We made sure our questions were not nebulous. For example, we did not ask a question like, "Did you like taking this e-learning course?" We asked insightful questions, such as "On a scale of 1 to 10, compared to classroom training that you have taken in the past, how do you rank this learning experience?"

The Results. Training management believed that web design and instructional design would make a difference; however, they were surprised on how much of a difference it made. From a corporate point of view, the ReadyGo course met the requirements of upper management, managers, and learners. What manager wouldn't want employees who score 95 percent on courses over employees who score 75 percent? Put another way, an executive is assured that her employees understand the material when they score 95 percent. This demonstration showed that instructional design and web design make a difference when creating e-learning. If an organization is serious about creating web courses, it is very important to build these courses using the appropriate tools and appropriate methodologies.

WHAT WORKS? So why doesn't voice-annotated PowerPoint work?

Audio. The quick answer is audio and PowerPoint visuals. More specifically: Adults don't prefer or don't learn best by hearing someone read to them. A defense contractor asked me to critique their current e-learning courses. When I presented my thoughts on audio, I received a lot of negative reaction from their trainers. Specifically, I contended that audio is very passive. Their courses would be better received and generate higher retention if they provided the information in a text format. I have found that when adults take an online course with audio, most people will move their eyes away from the screen within four to eight seconds. Adult learners figure that if you are going to read to them, they can multitask. Unfortunately, we are not very effective learners when multitasking.

Another point against using audio as the focal point of a course is that the average adult reads two to three times faster then most people speak. If a learner is given two courses, both covering the same material, the audio course will take forty-five minutes and the text-based course will take fifteen to twenty minutes. How many adults will choose the longer course?

The point becomes even more heightened if the target of the course is not a native English speaker. Most people who know English as a second language learned English in school. Schools outside of the United States teach in their native language while using English-language textbooks. Non-native English speakers who know English usually are proficient at reading and writing in it, but find it much harder to learn by listening to someone speak English.

Back to the defense contactor. Even after these arguments, the trainers were still resistant to my theory that voice-overs are not effective. We decided to let the learners decide. We also agreed that wanted them to answer two questions: (1) Do learners prefer audio tracks? and (2) Do learners learn more from audio tracks or from reading? We set up an experiment.

We took a course already produced, provided the audio track, and then added text that reflected what was being read. We gave the learners a choice: they could be read to or they could read the information themselves. We connected a cookie to the audio track so that we could monitor which path learners chose. We found that over 95 percent of the learners chose to read the material rather than being read to.

Instructional Design.
For the second question, "Do learners learn well?" we took one of the PowerPoint with audio track courses and created a new course to which we applied the appropriate methodology, which included instructional design and web design. The new version did not include an audio track. We created a test that required the learners to have taken the course in order to correctly answer the questions. Again, learners who took the course with the appropriate web course methodology scored over 20 percent higher than the learners who took the voice-over PowerPoint course. This exercise convinced management and trainers that they wanted to produce courses using good web course methodology.

Visuals.
As a visual point, PowerPoint is not effective on the web. Specifically, PowerPoint in a classroom is not the class; PowerPoint only represents a portion of the course content experience, since most presentations are meeting notes with some graphics. I have never left a class or presentation after which a fellow attendee has said, "Boy, that was a great PowerPoint" or "that PowerPoint made the session so interesting." It is usually the instructor who makes a course interesting, not the support materials. Instructors create learning events with their knowledge, understanding, delivery, and the hands-on experiences they facilitate within the course. If you went to an organization's website and all they had up was a PowerPoint presentation, you would think the company was a loser. That is because PowerPoint is not inherently web material. PowerPoint was designed to display information on a screen with a person standing in front of it, bringing the material to life. PowerPoint is not designed for web viewing. Web pages typically have a white or light background with small (10- or 12-point), dark fonts. Most PowerPoint presentations consist of a page with a few words, maybe a picture, a schematic, or a moving graphic. PowerPoint works well as a memory jogger for the instructor and as notes for the learner. PowerPoint was never designed to be a website. PowerPoint has a linear structure, whereas the web is designed for people to access content in a non-linear way. For e-learning, a non-linear design would include optional drill-down elements, links to supporting resources, and information organized into chapters.

Reusability. Furthermore, I find most organizations cannot use their existing e-learning content effectively if the courses were produced using PowerPoint. Courses should be a resource, not just a one-time event. After taking a classroom course, I rarely use the material I just learned within the first few weeks. And after a few weeks, my memory of the material has started to fail. When I need to use the information, I want to be able to pick up my notes and review a section or page that I think is important or that I want to apply to work I am currently performing. After I take an e-learning course, I also want to access the course material in the future. I want to apply what I learned when it is convenient for me. I do not want to be forced to take the entire course or listen to the speaker go on about something I find irrelevant. I want all the course pages accessible from a course map, and I want to enter key words so I can be taken to the page where that information was presented.

If necessary, I want to print out the page(s) I find important. A PowerPoint presentation saved as Flash file with most of its message contained in an audio track does not give me instant access to information I need, when I need it. And it cannot be printed out.

SUMMARY I contend that if trainers built courses that were designed to work well on the web by incorporating e-learning instructional design and web design, all stakeholders, including upper management, managers, and learners, would have their needs met. Once trainers took the time to learn the skills necessary to create effective e-learning courses, they would find it does not take them any longer than producing poor courses with familiar tools like PowerPoint. The intrinsic rewards of building effective courses are great and professionally fulfilling.

Reuben Tozman

Reuben Tozman, M.A., is the chief learning officer and founder of edCetra Training. Reuben graduated with a master's degree in educational technology from Concordia University in Montreal, Quebec, and has worked as an instructional designer, a project manager, a consultant, and product manager within a variety of organizations. As CLO of edCetra Training, Reuben steered the company to provide niche services around the use of semantic web technologies in the e-learning space. Reuben speaks regularly about the semantic web and instructional design at key industry events. He is a former member of the board of directors of CeLEA, a former member of the OASIS DITA for Learning Subcommittee, and a contributing inventor to sLML, an open source markup language for learning.

WHY E-LEARNING MChange:
MUST CHANGE: | Reuben Tozman
A CALL TO END RAPID DEVELOPMENT

Reuben Tozman stirs up the rapid authoring debate with a frank assessment, alternate perspective, and fresh solution. "Rapid development allows organizations to build out e-learning while compromising quality for speed and cost. Although an acceptable tradeoff to some, rapid development addresses an antiquated notion of learning and development that is entirely event-based. Outside e-learning, technology is providing consumers with access to content on demand at lightning speed with greater and greater precision. The same technology holds tremendous promise for e-learning, but requires the industry to shift its working paradigm from supporting event-based training to something more along the lines of 'performance-centric learning on demand.'" This article discusses why we e-learning professionals should be looking outside of our industry for innovation and replacing rapid development practice with one more in tune with semantic web technology.

The February 27–March 5 issue of *Economist* magazine printed a special report it dubbed "The Data Deluge." In one article titled "Handling the Cornucopia," the writer notes "And whereas doctors a century ago were expected to keep up with the entire field of medicine, now they would need to be familiar with about 10,000 diseases, 3,000 drugs, and more than 1,000 lab tests." The article goes on by saying "A study in 2004 suggested that in epidemiology alone it would take twenty-one hours of work a day just to stay current." In the same special report, an article titled "Data Data Everywhere," the writer says "When the digital sky survey started work in 2000, its telescope in New Mexico collected more data in its first few weeks than had been amassed in the entire history of astronomy." What does all of this mean-and more importantly what does it mean for us in the learning and development industry?

These issues are at the core of why we need to revolutionize how we build learning environments. To date most learning and education programs in both the corporate and academic sectors have been and are delivered in an "event" type format. The event format includes both online and offline learning and implies a formality in a program requiring some form of attendance. That attendance is usually away from whatever one's current tasks are. Even online learning playing out in a learning management system is learning that must be taken away from what a person is doing. Students must go to the system, log in to the system, enroll in courses, and so on. The preparation for the design and development of a learning event varies, but suffice it to say that, when it comes to e-learning, the design and development of quality online learning is a significant undertaking.

RAPID DEVELOPMENT

The term *rapid development* is a catch all phrase in the e-learning industry that represents both a suite of tools and a set of processes that are meant to sidestep conventional practices in the design and development of online learning. Rapid development is a response to the need for shorter design and development times, the need to do so at a reduced cost, and the need to allow for larger volumes of work to be accomplished. Rapid development pundits point to the volatility of content, the volume of content and return on investment (ROI) as key business drivers around rapid development.

Regardless of the benefits believed to be gained through rapid development, it is widely recognized that there is a compromise made in the quality of a product, but that this loss is acceptable due to the volatile nature and life expectancy of the content.

As Sheperd (2006) says: *"Are you seriously suggesting that a mere SME could possibly produce a piece of training material that anyone in their right mind would want to look at? The answer is 'yes, when the need is urgent, the shelf-life is short and you're prepared to take the time to provide them with a little training."*

The very mention of rapid development to a professional group of e-learning specialists immediately polarizes friends and foes alike, with one group of professionals believing that, although rapid development practices and tools generally don't produce the best results, there are examples of it working extremely well and that the blame doesn't lie with rapid development itself. The other side believes that the fault does lie in the very meaning of rapid development, that its essence is misguided and that the failure of the e-learning industry to produce consistently good materials lies entirely with rapid development.

Briefly explained, the process of rapid

development short-circuits the heavy use of instructional designers, programmers, and graphic artists and instead creates a direct link between subject-matter expert (SME), raw content, and e-learning authoring/publishing capabilities. There are many rapid development tools in the market, and they share very similar characteristics. Some key characteristics are:

➢ A short learning curve
➢ Do not require the course developer to know how to create a course's look and feel
➢ Built-in navigations ensures that all navigation works
➢ Do not require any programming or HTML knowledge
➢ Integration with LMSs is built-in—no advanced skills necessary
➢ Deploys easily—do not require any plug-ins
➢ Support learning objects such as Flash, graphics, and clip art in a straightforward manner
➢ Support short learning events

It's safe to say, whether you believe that rapid development has successfully addressed the business drivers for its emergence or whether you believe it has not, the end products resulting from rapid development, for the gross majority of organizations, has been well below what most experts would call "quality e-learning" (as elusive as the definition may be). The one factor that determines the success of the rapid development initiative is simply whether the compromise of quality was worth it, given that the content within a course was volatile and changing anyway. This argument, and the arguments over who is responsible for the loss of quality (rapid development itself or those using the tools) isn't really the BIG problem.

The real problem with rapid development is that the innovation within rapid development circles runs completely contrary to the innovation in web technology that is emerging everywhere outside of e-learning. Ironically enough, the innovation in web technology that the e-learning industry is choosing to ignore is perhaps the most promising technology that can resolve the issues around volatility of content and can also completely change the paradigm of event-driven training.

CHANGING EVENT-DRIVEN TRAINING

Let's focus on this notion of event-driven training. As previously mentioned, event-driven training is training that learners must attend separately from their work or play. They must leave whatever it is that they were doing and either physically go to or log into a separate environment from the one they are currently in. For the most part, the training event that they attend is built with the assumption that the content within it will remain valid for a period of time. Sustained validity of content is a premise for the period of course design as well as when the training is being attended and some time after. From the time someone starts to prepare the training up to and including the time it's delivered, the content needs for the most part stay as is. It's probably fair to say that event-driven training is intended to leverage the cost spent developing the training over a period of time and over a number of learners.

Rapid development claims to resolve some

issues for those situations in which the content in event-driven training is volatile. In other words, if you want to prepare event-driven training and the content is extremely volatile, then the costs for planning, preparing, and delivering the training may well exceed the benefits of the training itself. The reason for this is that the content will have changed significantly before enough people have seen it and a rewrite is necessary.

OUTSIDE E-LEARNING

Outside of the e-learning world, the web is evolving to service globalization and the massive amounts of information that is being posted to it. The next generation of the web, coined Web 3.0 by Tim Berners-Lee in 2001, is a web that can read and understand itself. According to Berners-Lee:

"The semantic web will bring structure to the meaningful content of web pages, creating an environment where software agents roaming from page to page can readily carry out sophisticated tasks for users."

In other words, the future of the web will allow machines, not humans, to make sense of information on a web page. If machines can make sense of what is on a web page, then they can process that information for human consumption. Right now when Google provides a link to a web page, it doesn't "know" the actual content on the page; it only reads specific pieces of information within the source code of the page—the metadata. A web page can show or say anything and have information within the metadata of the page that runs contrary to what's actually on the page. In such cases, search engines will refer people to the page based on the information in the coding of the page rather than the content in the page itself.

What Web 3.0 promises to be is a web that understands the content within the pages. The words are no longer just words on a page, but are themselves the links to the actual things they represent. "Montreal, Quebec" on a web page right now isn't known to the web; however, Web 3.0 will know that Montreal, Quebec, is an actual city within Quebec, with a longitude and a latitude and people who speak both French and English.

If this seems implausible, consider Wolfram/Alpha. According to Wikipedia, "It is an online service that answers factual queries directly by computing the answer from structured data, rather than providing a list of documents or web pages that might contain the answer as a search engine would." In other words, rather than a search engine pointing you to pages that may have the information you need, Wolfram/Alpha hopes to understand your question and provide an answer to it. The answer is created based on pulling data from structured sources and reasoning with the data to provide an answer.

Another example is a project called Open-Cyc, according to Wikipedia an artificial intelligence project that attempts to assemble a comprehensive ontology and knowledge base of everyday common-sense knowledge, with the goal of enabling AI applications to perform human-like reasoning." Ontology, as it is used here, is very similar to the example above and the reference to structured data. OpenCyc enables machines to process data in a manner comparable to human reasoning. OpenCyc has a database of structured information that any processing agent or program

logic can understand and applies rules similar to human reasoning and logic.

As an example consider the following:

Typical pieces of knowledge represented in the database are "Every tree is a plant" and "Plants die eventually." When asked whether trees die, the inference engine can draw the obvious conclusion and answer the question correctly.

PERFORMANCE SUPPORT

In the place of event-driven training, performance support can in many cases offer the same or better learning results for the end user. Performance support is information delivered at the time of need, targeted to the context in which the person is operating, and helping the person perform a task. The format of performance support material can range in complexity from printed text to computer simulations.

Recalling the examples of Wolfram/Alpha and OpenCyc, we see examples of a web that can use the data contained within it to provide meaningful information at the time of need. If we tie this capability back to the notion of performance support–driven training and consider the one operating system that is ubiquitous to the majority of people's lives (the web) being able to execute queries and answer questions for us as practitioners, we can readily see a huge opportunity for us to leverage this.

Not only are the innovations in web technology helpful to the e-learning community, but so also are innovations in hardware. Consider that a new manufacturing technique "will enable manufacturers to produce

25-nanometerchips, which is a huge leap considering that late last year, Intel Corp. made its first move from a 65nm process to 45nm" (Gaudin, 2008).

The shrinking computer chip brings a dramatic increase in processing power. With amazing power and chip sizes shrinking almost to atomic levels, it will be possible to place chips within many objects and communicate with them. Once again, daring to think about this in the context of performance support, one can only imagine the opportunity for support through communication with actual objects.

THE DIFFERENCE

There is a significant difference between innovation occurring outside the e-learning world and within the e-learning world. Innovation within the e-learning world is still focused on (1) providing a learning environment through events and (2) providing learning for stand-alone machines. It's true that the e-learning world has been focused on learning 2.0 for the last several years with a re-energized focus on informal learning. However, structured data has not been given much consideration at all, and there has been no significant movement away from event-driven training. Even informal learning is something that practitioners want to "structure" into events.

Key software manufacturers remain focused on using machines as stand-alone units rather than trying to harness the power of networking. We have long since surpassed the value of computers as stand-alone machines. The value of a computer today is its ability to network. Imagine owning your computer today without using it to network.

It is worth noting the findings of the North Central Regional Education Laboratory survey that within education "effectiveness is not a function of the technology, but rather of the learning environment and the capability to do things one could not do otherwise." It further highlighted that "technology in support of outmoded educational systems is counterproductive" (Hampton, 2002).

Although written in 2002, the message remains very poignant today. To support outmoded educational systems or theories through technology is counterproductive. Isn't that true of rapid e-learning that supports event based training?

What does the alternative look like? What would innovation consistent with innovation outside of e-learning look like in the e-learning world? With the possibilities of incorporating Web 3.0 technologies or semantic technologies into the learning environment, e-learning should be moving to support performance based learning or performance support. The platform is a system that is ubiquitous to the modern age, an operating system that is always on, and machines that do the work for us.

In 2009, The Library of Congress released a new tool for educators in the United States under their main website www.loc.gov/teachers. The new tool provides educators in the United States the ability to generate their own curriculum, at run time, based on a set of topics relevant to their classroom ambitions. What's interesting is that the content is generated either as a classroom-ready package, including instructor guide and student materials, or as a SCORM 2004 e-learning package.

The content doesn't exist in any format until the teacher says, "Create it for me." It takes about two minutes for the system to generate the materials, but the materials include up to the second revised content and are built by the teachers. There are no pre-existing combinations of topics, HTML pages, or PDF documents.

Consider the amount of preparation and man hours required to produce hundreds of classroom-ready packages and hundreds of SCORM packages if you were to try and do it using conventional authoring tools. With the Library of Congress, no such work is necessary because the machines do everything. The application reads user input and then generates what's required. New content can be added to the application at any time; old content can be modified at any time; and all changes are reflected the moment they've been made. Users are always provided with the latest and greatest. No development team required.

How does the Library of Congress application work? How is it different from what might be produced using a conventional e-learning authoring tool? The big difference is the ability for a machine to understand and read content so that it can process that content itself. In the Library of Congress application, all content is structured using an XML schema that helps the web application itself understand what each piece of content is, when the content needs to appear in a deliverable, and what it should look like when it does appear. By setting the rules of engagement, so to speak, any content that is added to the application's database using the standardized markup can be understood by the application and can therefore be processed by the application. Conventional authoring systems gen-

erate a black box of content that is dumped on a server and wrapped with meta-tags. The web can only display that information as it was prepared, but cannot itself process it. In other words to create more content, you need to author a new package.

The big change required in e-learning is to foster innovation consistent with global innovation outside of e-learning. First and foremost, we must move away from event-driven training to performance support. That does not mean that event-driven training will go by the wayside. It does mean that event-driven training would be a performance support tool when appropriate. This also means that our conventional way of building online learning, most noticeably through rapid development, must also come to an end, as the tools and processes support an antiquated learning model. Not only that, but they also fail to deliver content that is transparent and structured in a way that allows the web to process it. Conventional rapid development tools find a way to build e-learning more quickly and with fewer dollars but fail to deliver something consistent with the evolution of web technology.

Semantic web technology can produce faster results than conventional rapid development tools, simply because computers can build their own training packages for us. In addition, the use of semantic technologies and structured data means that we will be able to deliver custom-tailored learning in the format most appropriate for the context (including user decisions).

How does this paradigm shift affect design and development? Currently, our design and development teams create multiple deliverables one at a time. A typical example is the redesign of existing paper-based learning modules into e-learning and mobile learning. Every time an existing paper-based product is converted to e-learning or m-learning, the design and development process starts afresh. Not only do we start again, but the e-learning, m-learning, and print all contain the same content (or variations thereof) in three separate files. If content changes, changes must be made in three places.

In the new paradigm, design and development are very different. Initial design and development aren't concerned with packaging and formatting any specific content whatsoever. They are concerned with setting up the rules for web applications to package and format content. The first step is to create a taxonomy that will help a computer understand what content is, what it means, what formats are appropriate for display, what contexts the content is used in, etc. These rules all form part of a schema in which content during its creation stage is marked up with the schema language. Very similar to the Dewey Decimal Classification System for library sciences, the schema provides an algorithm that enables different technologies to query and extrapolate information.

The next step in design and development is the creation of rules for output herein referred to as a processing agent. During this stage, authors create the processing rules around the different elements in the schema. These rules tell the computer to process content of a specific type into a defined format. The rules for output must conform to and be entirely dependent on the schema. The processing agents can be integrated into various technologies and be used for a wide range of purposes and needs.

CONCLUSION The transition away from rapid development to semantic web technologies is a massive gap that will most certainly be overcome, but is far from fruition. If truth be told, the transition isn't nearly as cumbersome as was thought and can be made by simply investing corporate dollars differently. Instead of investing in one piece of learning at a time, dollars must be invested in infrastructure that will enable learning to be produced on demand. Google was never intended to be an e-learning solution, yet I don't think any other application has done more for learning than Google.

REFERENCES

Berners-Lee, T. (2001). The semantic web: A new form of web content that is meaningful to computers will unleash a revolution of new possibilities. *Scientific American.*

Gaudin, S. (2008, July). MIT uses nanotech to shrink chips to 25nm. www.computerworld.com/s/article/9108318/MIT_uses_nanotech_to_shrink_chips_to_25nm

Hampton, C. (2002, November). *Innovation and e-learning: iB4e.*

Sheperd, C. (2006, January). Rapid e-learning gets the job done. www.cedma-europe.org/newsletter%20articles/IT%20Training/Rapid%20e-learning%20gets%20the%20job%20done%20(Jan%2006).pdf.

The data deluge: A special report on managing information. (2010, February 27–March 5). *The Economist.*

Thomas A. Toth

Thomas A. Toth, MAEd, based in the Denver, Colorado, area, is a designer/developer with almost twenty years of experience in the training and e-learning industry. Thomas designs and programs traditional and e-learning training courses using Adobe products and has created more than two hundred websites for corporate clients since his career began in 1996. He is the president of dWeb Studios, Inc., a web design firm, and the Catapult Training Group, a training and e-learning design and development firm in Parker, Colorado.

Thomas wears the hat of web master, instructional designer, leadership consultant, project manager, HTML programmer, graphic designer, Flash programmer, executive coach, and stand-up trainer. Thomas teaches Dreamweaver, Fireworks, Flash, Photoshop, and InDesign at local area training centers, bringing his students real-world knowledge and experience on how to use these products.

Thomas is the author of the book *Technology for Trainers,* published by ASTD in April 2003. *Technology for Trainers* is an e-learning primer, written for the learning and development professional who is faced with the task of developing e-learning for his or her organization. He is also a contributing author to the *ASTD Handbook for Workplace Learning Professionals,* published in 2008.

Thomas has his B.A. in human communication, his M.A.Ed. with a focus on educational technology, and belongs to several professional organizations such as ASTD, the American Marketing Association, eLearning Guild, and Toastmasters. Thomas is also a published and performing magician, a trained chef, and musician.

THE RIGHT E-LEARNING TOOL FOR THE JOB | Thomas A. Toth

Multiple perspectives help in the search for optimal solutions. While Allan Henderson's article alludes to what I might call a tyranny of tools, Thomas Toth sees the same problem but suggests that embracing the richness of a broad tool pallet is a way to take command. Thomas says, "Instructional designers are often frustrated when designing e-learning because it involves much more than just writing activities and content. To actually get great e-learning off the page and onto the screen takes a skill set usually not found in the training department." This article highlights and catalogs development software. It provides instructional designers and training managers with information about basic roles and functionality of alternative tools to help them build a software "toolbox" for creating e-learning projects.

Creative training programs require fantastic instructional design, engaging activities, and a real desire to improve the learners' performance. Great facilitators use their presentations skills and mastery of the content to create a real environment for people to learn. They have a set of tools they use to add excitement to the classroom setting—toys on the table, snacks in the back of the room, clay, construction paper, and Lego™ bricks. Facilitators continually use techniques like this to take their training to the next level.

Suddenly and with little warning, the World Wide Web arrived and changed the way e-learning was to be delivered and experienced. Techniques for delivering content had to change for compatibility with the new technology medium. Computers emerged as a prime method for the distribution of content. Instead of being "wowed" by a well-designed class or instructor, learners were in front of a glowing computer screen for hours at a time, clicking buttons and interacting with computer-generated people.

The tools that the instructional designer uses to develop a course are very different from those used by an e-learning developer to actually build it. Many of the same design skills instructional designers use to create stand-up training can also be used to design amazing e-learning; however, the actual delivery of the content requires a completely different skill set. Previously, instructional designers passed their content to a facilitator, who would bring it to life; but in the e-learning world, it's not that easy.

The skills of the e-learning developer are very similar to those of a web programmer/designer. If web distribution is the chosen delivery method for the designer's e-learning project, the developer needs to understand browser technology, web-safe color formats, graphic design standards for the web, and other web-centric techniques. This is a huge challenge—instructional designers are frustrated when designing e-learning because it goes much further than just writing activities and content. To actually get great e-learning off the page and onto the screen takes a skill set usually not found in the training department.

Many people believe that good e-learning programming falls into the bailiwick of your company's IT or web marketing group rather than in the training group. I disagree. In my experience, I find it much easier to teach training people about e-learning technologies than it is to teach IT folks about training. Training groups should consist of an instructional design team, a facilitation team, and an e-learning programmer. I don't believe that training groups should outsource their e-learning work to other, more technical departments within the firm. I think that the end user benefits so much more from a programmer who has a training background, rather than a programming background.

So this puts our training groups in a train/hire situation. Should we hire someone specifically to build and program e-learning programs? Do we do enough over the course of the year to support this role? Should we train one of our facilitators or instructional designers to build e-learning?

Then, after you decide whether to hire or train, you are faced with the challenge of deciding which software tools are necessary to build the programs. A popular myth is that a single piece of software will allow teams to build e-learning projects. That simply isn't true. There are some fantastic "all in one" pieces of software that will put the e-learning project together, but what about the graphical content? The multimedia content? Video? Audio? Screen capture and recording?

Developers need a suite of software with a variety of capabilities in order to create engaging and interesting e-learning projects. There is no single software solution that will

accomplish all the tasks necessary to create and distribute e-learning. Having access to the right software tools for the job is important for the development of e-learning.

The development tools are vast and varied, but they fall into generic categories. If developers have at least one piece of software in each category, they will be able to create high-quality e-learning so your organization can offer another way to receive training.

Building an e-learning project from scratch can seem like a daunting task. There are so many moving parts that it can be difficult to know where to begin. The next sections highlight each of the software categories and provide you with information about basic functionality so you can make good buying decisions and help your team use the right tool for the job.

GRAPHIC DESIGN AND PHOTO EDITING Surf to your favorite websites, and you will notice a few things about the pages you like. Generally, they are made up of two key elements: text and images. As you look at the page, you will notice that the interface is made up of buttons, colors, lines, and photographs. When talking about graphics, people often visualize the full-color images and "clip-art" images that appear on a web page. However, the buttons, color spots, navigation bars, gradated swirls, background images, and even the background color are all examples of graphic elements that someone had to design and create for the web page.

All of these additional graphical elements that appear on the web page come together to create the interface. In e-learning, the interface is the method for the learner to interact with the training program. Think about the radio you have in your car. There are buttons and slots, knobs and dials, all designed to allow you to interact with the radio. One button advances the CD to the next track, another changes the volume, while yet another stores your favorite radio stations. You tell the radio "what to do" through these buttons and dials. They are your interface to the radio.

Graphic design software's primary function is to create and edit graphic elements, but it also allows you to draw your own images or clip art. Paired with a digital tablet, more expensive software can actually simulate the stroke and pressure of a paintbrush or charcoal pen and produce amazing-looking digital artwork.

Of course, the visual appeal of the custom artwork is in the hands of the artist, not the software, so be aware that purchasing any software solution will not turn anyone into an artist. Many great graphic designers have an art background and use digital tools to create, rather than canvas and watercolor.

In addition to editing photos and creating clip art, e-learning developers use graphic design programs to design the interface for your e-learning program. Good e-learning interfaces have next and back buttons, graphical framing, and miscellaneous elements that bring the training program to life. Without a good interface, your program can be frustrating to users. These interface elements can all be created using graphic design software.

Photo editing software's primary function is to edit and manipulate photo-realistic images or images from a digital camera. Most images that come out of a digital camera are set at a very high resolution. They are designed to be printed and shared like film-based photographs. The resolution of these images is much higher than necessary for web use. In fact, most digital cameras produce images at 300 dots-per-inch (dpi) and higher. High-end digital cameras can produce images up to 1200 dpi! That's a lot of dots!

Computer monitors can reproduce 72 dpi or even 96 dpi, at best. A 300-dpi image would be much larger in file size than needed for the web. Good photo editing software has tools that allow the higher resolution photographs to be optimized for web distribution, reducing the file size, the resolution size, and saving it into one of three web-safe image file formats: .JPG, .GIF, or .PNG.

There are several great software packages that combine the elements of both a graphic design program and photo editing program; Adobe Photoshop and Fireworks fall into this category. For strictly graphic design, CoreFX, CorelDRAW, and Adobe Illustrator are good choices. For browser-based photo editing and optimization, you may want to consider Picnik or FotoFlexer. Both offer web-based solutions for editing graphics at inexpensive prices.

The matrix on the next page compares some of the more popular software packages for creating graphics and editing photos. Review this list to help you choose the right tool for the job.

Tools for Graphic Design and Photo Editing

Software Tool	Level of Complexity	Learning Curve	Primary Function	Platform	Cost
Adobe Photoshop	Advanced	Steep	Photo editing Graphic creation	Mac and Windows	$699
Adobe Fireworks	Intermediate	Intermediate	Photo editing Graphic creation	Mac and Windows	$299
Adobe Illustrator	Advanced	Steep	Vector graphic creation	Mac and Windows	$599
CorelDRAW Graphics Suite X4	Intermediate	Intermediate	Vector graphic creation	Windows	$399
Core FX	Beginner	Easy	Vector graphic creation – Art projects	Windows	$59.99
Picnik	Beginner	Easy	Photo editing	Web Browser	$24.95 per year
FotoFlexer	Beginner	Easy	Photo editing	Web Browser	Free
Serif Photo Plus 9	Beginner	Easy	Photo editing	Windows	$9.95
Picasa	Beginner	Easy	Photo editing	Mac and Windows	Free
Xara Xtreme	Intermediate	Intermediate	Photo editing Graphic creation	Windows	$49
PaintShop Pro X2	Intermediate	Intermediate	Photo editing	Windows	$69.99
Poser	Advanced	Steep	Human 3D model creation	Mac and Windows	$249
Bryce 5	Advanced	Steep	3D landscape modeling	Mac and	$99.95

AUDIO AND VIDEO RECORDING Incorporating audio and video elements into e-learning projects used to be an expensive affair. The creation of good audio and video required expensive microphones and cameras, sound studios, mixing boards, and a mess of other technical hardware. The bandwidth requirements necessary to run audio and video through the web were very high. Users could wait sixty minutes for a two-minute video to download. The value/benefit proposition for incorporating video and audio into your web-based e-learning project didn't make much sense as recently as three years ago.

With the advent of high-speed connections, new video and audio file formats and a slew of high-end computer editing tools available, producing your own audio and video projects for web distribution is much easier. A quick trip to your local electronics store and less than $500 in hardware and software means that your learners can enjoy video and audio media that have been produced by your e-learning developer in-house.

Essentially, audio recording software digitally records voice-over tracks, sound effects, music, and other audio spots. Good audio software allows you to cut and crop the audio track, loop the music track, bring up or down the volume levels, and clean up the overall recording. Higher-end audio software allows you to alter the voice tones and pitch, as well as export these final files into a format for use in your e-learning program.

A conversation about audio software requires a comment or two on microphones. No matter how good your audio recording software is, you will be unhappy with the results of your finished product if your microphone is low quality; low quality microphone equals low quality audio. Take the time to research and find a microphone that fits into your budget. If the voice-over track is to be the main learning point of the e-learning project, having rich clean tones makes all the difference to the learner.

Then again, you are not going for broadcast-quality audio. Your learners are probably not listening to your audio on their THX Certified Surround Sound system at home. Odds are the audio will be coming out of tinny little laptop speakers, inexpensive desktop speakers, or earphones worn in the workplace. Be sure to get a microphone that sounds good, but you don't have to break the bank, considering how your learners will be listening to your audio. I use a $30.00 Logitech USB microphone and it works like a dream.

QuickTime Pro and Windows Sound Recorder are software tools that provide an easy way to record audio, and both have simple editing features. Adobe Sound Booth and Audacity are more robust audio software studios that allow you more control over your audio content and allow you to tweak a variety of variables to make your audio sound fantastic. And the fact that Audacity is free makes it a first choice for anyone wanting to start with audio software in his or her toolbox.

Video editing software allows you to take your digital video content directly from the camera and allows you to manipulate it. You can cut scenes, merge scenes, and apply a variety of special effects to your video to give it that professional look. Good video software will also allow you to save to a variety of web formats so you can skip the additional converting step.

Tools for Audio and Video Recording

Software Tool	Level of Complexity	Learning Curve	Primary Function	Platform	Cost
Audacity	Intermediate	Easy	Audio recording Audio editing	Mac and Windows	Free
Adobe Sound Booth	Intermediate	Steep	Audio recording Audio editing	Mac and Windows	$199
Garage Band	Beginner	Easy	Audio recording Music creation Audio editing	Mac	$79.99
QuickTime Pro	Beginner	Easy	Audio recording Audio editing Video editing	Mac and Windows	$29.99
All Recorder	Beginner	Easy	Audio recording Audio editing	Windows	$29.95
Pyro Audio Creator	Beginner	Easy	Audio recording Audio editing	Windows	$34.99
RecordPad	Beginner	Easy	Audio recording Audio editing	Mac and Windows	$38
Multitrack Studio	Intermediate	Intermediate	Audio recording Audio editing	Windows	$119
Overdub	Intermediate	Intermediate	Audio recording Audio editing	Windows	$26.95
iMovie	Beginner	Intermediate	Video editing	Mac	$79.99
Final Cut Pro	Advanced	Steep	Video editing	Mac	$1299
Final Cut Express	Intermediate	Intermediate	Video editing	Mac	$99
Movie Maker	Beginner	Easy	Video editing	Windows	Free
CyberLink PowerDirector 7 Deluxe	Intermediate	Intermediate	Video editing	Windows	$199.95
Ulead Media Studio Pro8	Intermediate	Steep	Video editing	Windows	$399.99
Corel Video Studio X2	Intermediate	Intermediate	Video editing	Windows	$79.99
MAGIX Movie	Intermediate	Intermediate	Video Editing	Windows	$89.99

Video that comes right out of the camera is designed to be viewed on a television screen, not in a browser window. Good editing software will reduce the file size, the pixel size, and save it in a web-safe format, making it easy to use in your project.

A good video production requires good camera equipment, but don't think you need to spend a ton of money on hardware. The best thing to invest in is lighting. A consumer camera recording can be transformed to something near a professional video if the proper lighting is used. Don't think that ambient light from the overhead fluorescent bulbs or open window will be enough to light the scene. Visit your local camera shop and look for a simple lighting kit. It will really take your video segments to the next level.

There are very expensive video editing software programs designed for use by professional videographers, but those would be overkill for the purpose of a simple e-learning video segment. Apple Final Cut Express and iMovie are both excellent inexpensive programs, but only work on a Mac. Windows Movie Maker, Corel VideoStudio, and Adobe Premiere Elements are inexpensive software tools for your Windows-based machines. All offer excellent video editing capabilities at a low price tag.

The matrix on the previous page compares some of the more popular software packages for creating audio and editing audio and video. Review this list to help you choose the right tool for the job.

SCREEN CAPTURE

Using e-learning to teach people how to use software is an excellent match; using a computer to teach people how to use the software on their computers is a natural partnership. Various of software packages are available that allow you to easily record or capture screen interactions for use in e-learning projects.

Screen capture software should be able to capture both still screen shots, as well as record mouse movements and any animated content on the screen.

Some screen capture software has been designed with e-learning developers in mind, allowing for the recording of audio while simultaneously recording screen shots. This software actually provides visual tips and hint "bubbles" on software buttons pressed and links clicked as a part of the development environment. Also, the recording can be purely visual or highly interactive. During playback, the learner could be required to click on the screen and simulate using the software. These additional bits can help your team dramatically reduce the development time for software training production because much of the annotation and many direction notes are automatically created while recording the screens. Also, some software allows for a single-click export, which builds a simple interface that wraps itself around your captured presentation.

Screen capture software can also be used to add interactivity to PowerPoint presentations and turn them into a kind of "Franken-e-learning" project. Imagine building your entire e-learning project in PowerPoint, and then using screen capture software to record

Tools for Capturing Screens

Software Tool	Level of Complexity	Learning Curve	Primary Function	Platform	Cost
Adobe Captivate	Intermediate	Intermediate	Screen capture Screen recording e-Learning components	Windows	$699
Camtasia Studio	Intermediate	Intermediate	Screen capture Screen recording	Windows	$299
Snag It	Beginner	Easy	Screen capture	Windows	$49
Snapz Pro	Beginner	Easy	Screen capture Screen recording	Mac	$69.99
Screen Hunter 5.1	Intermediate	Intermediate	Screen capture Screen recording	Windows	$29.95
FullShot Professional	Intermediate	Intermediate	Screen capture Screen recording	Windows	$59.99
Screencast-O-Matic	Beginner	Easy	Screen recording	Web browser	Free
Jing	Beginner	Easy	Screen capture Screen recording	Web browser	Free
MW Snap	Beginner	Easy	Screen capture	Windows	Free
!Quick Screenshot Maker	Beginner	Easy	Screen capture	Windows	$39.95

the presentation as you narrate the slides. While I don't feel that this is a true e-learning project because it lacks some of the key interactive elements designed to help your learners understand the material, it can be a quick, satisfactory solution in some situations.

There are several good Windows-based capture software tools available, the most robust being Adobe Captivate. Camtasia Studio does a good job of recording and packaging as well. If you are looking for a browser-based solution, Screencast-O-Matic and Jing both offer simple screen capture functionality that you can manipulate and drop into your e-learning program.

The matrix below compares some of the more popular software packages for using and editing screen capture. Review this list to help you choose the right tool for the job.

ANIMATION/ MOTION GRAPHIC — Animations and motion graphics play a key role in any e-learning project. From simple effects that move text around the screen to more complex graphic piece that users interact with and manipulate on the screen, the level of interactivity is greatly enhanced when things are moving around the screen and can be "played with" by the user.

Today, most animation software does much more than just play simple, animated sequences over and over. Advanced functionality and interactivity can be programmed using these software tools. Interactivity helps the learners really grasp the concepts you are trying to teach. Interactivity can take the form of a simulation learners work through or a diagram they assemble, all tied to the course's learning objectives. These types of complex interactions can be created using current animation software.

Animation software allows developers to create and draw elements from within the application in addition to importing elements from your graphic design software programs. In fact, there is usually a tight partnership between the animation software and graphic design software, allowing many different image formats to be swapped back and forth.

Adobe Flash is the standard for interactive multimedia creation and, at a bare minimum, it creates simple animated sequences. Also, Flash has become a standard for the creation and distribution of online learning. From within Flash, you can take video, audio, and visual graphic elements and combine them to create a single e-learning file for distribution on the web. Flash can become a central hub for the entire e-learning project.

If you are just looking for animation software, then SWiSH is a good option. It has many of the robust qualities of Flash, but focuses mainly on creating animated sequences. It can be a less expensive solution if your developer just wants to create simple animation.

The matrix on the next page compares some of the software packages for creating animation and motion graphics, including 3D animations. Review this list to help you choose the right tool for the job.

Animation Tools

Software Tool	Level of Complexity	Learning Curve	Primary Function	Platform	Cost
Adobe Flash Professional	Advanced	Steep	Multimedia Animation Motion graphics Interactive capabilities	Mac and Windows	$699
SWiSH Max	Intermediate	Intermediate	Multimedia Animation Motion graphics Interactive capabilities	Windows	$149.95
Pencil	Intermediate	Intermediate	Animation	Mac and Windows	Free
MS GIF Animator	Beginner	Beginner	Animation	Windows	Free
Animo 6.0	Intermediate	Intermediate	Animation 3D animated graphics	Mac	Free
Toon Boom Animate	Advanced	Intermediate	Animation Motion graphics	Mac and Windows	$999
Animate Pro	Advanced	Advanced	Multimedia Animation Motion graphics	Mac and Windows	$1999
Ulead GIF Animator	Beginner	Easy	Animation	Windows	$49.95
Ulead Cool 3D Production Studio	Intermediate	Intermediate	Animation 3D animated graphic	Windows	$129
Swift 3D	Advanced	Intermediate	Animation 3D animated graphics	Mac and Windows	$249

CODE WRITING/ APPLICATION DEVELOPMENT SOFTWARE

Everything that appears in a browser window is there because a mesh of code has been created behind the scenes that provides instructions to the text, graphics, and multimedia on where to appear on the screen. The application development software is the "engine" behind the scene. All the miscellaneous elements that make up the content on the page are powered by this engine.

Code writing software will create HTML or XHTML and will give you the opportunity to write code by hand if you wish. If your developer doesn't write HTML, some software tools allow users to work in a WYSIWYG (What You See Is What You Get) environment, where elements can be created and moved around the screen as desired and generate HTML automatically.

Software is available for e-learning developers specifically designed for web programmers. These tools are very robust and offer a limitless opportunity for web-based creation. Other tools specifically designed for e-learning development offer a smaller set of options, but the tools and templates are targeted specifically for the development of web-based training.

Adobe Dreamweaver, Microsoft Expression, and CoffeeCup HTML Editor are all designed for web professionals, but can be used by e-learning developers as well. These tools all take the content created in other software tools and arrange it for display in the web browser. While not e-learning-specific, they do offer more choices and more flexibility for any content to be displayed in a browser.

e-Learning development software that provides a great solution includes Lectora from Trivantis, ProForm from Rapid Intake, and Knowledge Point from Atlantic Link. These software applications can import images, audio, video, and multimedia created in with other tools and create the engine that drives browser-based delivery. They also come with a variety of graphic and interface templates for you to use to ramp up your development time and extensive e-learning specific functions like question types, button coding, and navigation tools. The important thing to remember is that none of these applications stands alone. They all require images, audio, video, and multimedia created in other applications to create a rich user experience.

The matrix on the next page compares some of the software packages for creating web code and specific software for creating e-learning. Review this list to help you choose the right tool for the job.

Tools for Application Development

Software Tool	Level of Complexity	Learning Curve	Primary Function	Platform	Cost
Adobe Dreamweaver	Advanced	Steep	Web programming	Mac and Windows	$399
Coffee Cup HTML Editor	Intermediate	Intermediate	Web programming	Windows	$49
Taco HTML Edit	Intermediate	Intermediate	Web programming	Mac	$24.95
HTML–Kit	Beginner	Intermediate	Web programming	Windows	Free
EditPad Pro	Intermediate	Intermediate	Web programming	Windows	$49.95
1st Page 2000	Beginner	Intermediate	Web programming	Windows	Free
KompoZer	Intermediate	Intermediate	Web programming	Mac	Free
Microsoft Expression	Advanced	Intermediate	Web programming	Windows	$149
Trivantis Lectora	Intermediate	Easy	e-Learning programming	Windows	$2790
Articulate	Beginner	Intermediate	e-Learning programming	Windows	$1846
Rapid Intake ProForm	Intermediate	Intermediate	e-Learning programming	Windows and web browser	$499 - $1799
Rapid Intake Unison	Intermediate	Intermediate	e-Learning programming	Web browser	$49 per month

STRATEGIES FOR CREATING

Each of these software tools can be an important asset in the development of e-learning programs. Let's walk through a series of scenarios in which each of these tools is used in conjunction with another. These are real examples of the high level of dependence these tools have on each other.

Scenario 1: Web-Based, Text-Focused.

This project is a simple, multi-age online document—a human resources new employee guide. It is text-driven and will be distributed via your company's corporate intranet. Your developer uses Photoshop to create the simple user interface and then exports the images to a web-safe format. Then she takes the images and puts them into Dreamweaver to layout the HTML pages and links. The instructional designer provides content in a Microsoft Word file, and the developer cuts and pastes the text out of each MS Word page into the Dreamweaver-designed HTML.

Scenario 2: Web-Based, New Custom Software Training.

Your IT team has just completed a new contact management application that all the sales reps in the company need to learn. You use your digital camera to take a snapshot of the development team, which you then drop into Fireworks to optimize down to a web-safe format. You use Captivate to walk users through the initial knowledge sections by showing them the correct procedure and then having them click through the simulation themselves. At the conclusion of the program, you show a picture of the IT team responsible for the software creation, bringing in the picture you edited in Photoshop.

Scenario 3: Web-Based, High Multimedia.

Your company is offering new managers a series of leadership development courses distributed off the company intranet. You decide that it will be highly interactive with high levels of multimedia. You use your video camera to record senior managers in the firm talking about leadership and edit them in VideoStudio. You record the audio track yourself, editing the audio in Audacity.

Because of the highly interactive nature of the design, you choose to use Flash as your main development platform. You design the graphical skeleton of the interface in CorelDRAW and import it into Flash. You use Flash to animate the content, and you link the audio to the animation. You import the video segments into Flash, which allows the user to view them easily. You program the complex personnel simulation in Flash, using images created in CorelDRAW.

As you can see by the three simple scenarios above, each piece of software in the toolbox has a very specific and needed role. They all play together in a dance that can help you create amazing and impactful e-learning. Don't try to put a square peg into a round hole. Use the right tool for the job, and you will be amazed by the quality and speed of your in-house e-learning development.

Allan Henderson

Allan Henderson is the author of *The E-Learning Question and Answer Book,* which focuses on the major concepts for e-learning in the workplace, especially the way that tradeoffs play a central role. Allan has held a number of management, technical, and training positions at IBM for the past thirty-five years and is currently the e-learning manager for business analytics in IBM's Software Group. He lives with his wife Meg in Marietta, Georgia, and can be reached at hender@us.ibm.com.

DON'T GET TRAPPED BY YOUR E-LEARNING TOOLS | Allan Henderson

I have a particular fascination with e-learning tools, so I'm especially grateful to Allan Henderson for contributing this article. Allan says, "When creating e-learning for the workplace, the e-learning tools you have at hand will usually determine a lot about how you design the e-learning itself." My colleagues and I discuss this very point often, wondering mostly whether tools can actually lead designers to better designs (we hope so). But the danger, as Allan points out, is that the tools you plan to use will limit your thinking; in fact, the workplace business problem that the e-learning is addressing can easily get lost as you work within the capabilities and constraints of a particular e-learning tool. Allan sets a proper perspective: Don't let yourself be trapped by only thinking within what your tools are obviously designed to let you build. Don't ask, "What can I do with my tools?" Instead ask, "What is the business problem I need to solve?" And then ask, "What tools, even simple tools, can I put together to solve that business problem?" When looked at this way, your design process can generate surprising and creative solutions.

Trainers can select from a variety of e-learning tools to carry "training" to their target audiences. The variety of options is apparent by just looking on the Internet.

Many e-learning managers and designers, however, become trapped by their e-learning tools. Once they have a comfortable tool, they don't consider the variety of other tools and sometimes don't even notice that a variety exists. They use the one or two tools they have at hand to do everything they are asked to do. They fail to ask, "What tools can I put together to accomplish my goals?"

While my interest is applying e-learning in the workplace, you might be interested in e-learning for schools and universities or e-learning for self-improvement. These other areas differ from workplace training because they are focused on improving the individual person. (Although I can pretty convincingly argue that people really attend universities in order to receive a diploma, not to get an education.)

Workplace learning, on the other hand, exists primarily to solve near-term business problems. For example, it's common that a company's sales personnel need to learn the details of a new product release so they can explain its value to their customers' value and increase sales. The end goal is improving the business, not improving the salesperson, although it's true that the salesperson will know more after the training.

There is no end to the deficiencies in knowledge and skills that you could address in a worker population. But only those that apply to near-term business problems are likely to be addressed by a company.

The goal in workplace learning is to improve the business.

In workplace applications, the "I will build it and they will come" approach does not get results. Few people in the workplace think, "I don't know something well enough, so I should look in the online training catalog and take an e-learning course to learn how to do it better." More typically, they attend training because they know they were required to do so.

Let me present two "thought experiments" to better express the salient points. The business situation for these two thought experiments is this: Your company has two hundred sales personnel around the world. They have laptop computers and cell phones and are, of course, connected by the Internet. They are very busy people. Their time during the day is already 99 percent filled with making their sales quotas.

THOUGHT EXPERIMENT ONE—LEARN THE NEW PRODUCT RELEASE The business problem here is that the entire sales force needs to learn about a new product release coming out in a few months. The solution designer might consider creating a collection of self-contained learning modules for the sales force to download and play on their laptops, although it would need to be done very quickly, with everyone being trained within three weeks. And there isn't a large budget. We could record a series of videos on which the product development experts explain the product in a lecture format. The sales and marketing experts could lecture about how the new features affect ways the product should be sold. We could put the recorded lectures in our learning management system (LMS) so that we know who watched the recordings. But because this is an important release with some critical new product features and because it's important to know how well they've been learned, we could create a multiple-choice assessment in the LMS for each person to take after watching the set of recorded videos. Then we can use the results of the assessment to see how much of the population learned what they were expected to learn by the due date.

But what if there is no learning management system? Worse yet, what if there is no easy way to create video lectures? What can you do?

You can do more than you think. Instead of video lectures, you could create screen casts with one of the free or low-cost screen cast tools you can download from the Internet. The screen cast captures a "video" of what's on your computer screen along with an audio of someone talking about what he or she is doing. Alternatively, you could just record the audio in a free tool like Audacity and ask salespeople to open a text or PowerPoint file while playing the MP3 audio file on their laptop computers. (In fact, my phone connection at IBM lets me press a few buttons to record the audio as an MP3 file.) You could email the audio and PPT files to each salesperson. To create the assessments there are free or low-cost online tools for creating and delivering simple exams on the Internet.

What can we learn from this thought experiment? First, there are a variety of different tools you can use to achieve roughly the same effect. Second, your choice of tools will depend on your constraints and other forces pushing on the project, such as available time, budget, and subject-matter expertise.

MY FIRST E-LEARNING EXPERIENCE

Let me tell you a personal story. My first experience with e-learning used almost no tools or budget at all. Years ago, my job was to deliver live training courses on a hardware product. I was asked to put together a class for twenty new hires who worked in one of three geographically dispersed sales centers and who contacted customers exclusively by phone. The class was to teach them enough of the product details so that they could start making the sales calls. I didn't have the right product training materials, nor did I have the budget to run three separate live classes with only a few people in each class, but I did have an experienced instructor. I was about to declare I couldn't deliver the training when I discovered that all of the new hires had been issued published books about the hardware in question by their managers. So I suggested we do an online "correspondence course" class via email. Each week the students were assigned parts of chapters to read and they were sent an email with about ten essay-style questions to answer and send back to the instructor, who read the responses and sent back feedback by email to each student. The course lasted six weeks. By our measurements at the time, it was as successful as any live course we were running.

THOUGHT EXPERIMENT TWO— CONSTANT LEARNING

In the first thought experiment, the business problem had a deadline for everyone to learn something quite specific. This thought experiment is fundamentally different.

Here's the business problem: Your company's sales management team is concerned about the skills and knowledge levels of the entire sales force, and the stated business problem is to instill "constant learning" in the sales personnel. There's too much to learn to run classes on it all, so the salespeople need to start to teach themselves. "Constant learning" here means that the salespeople will look beyond their immediate customer situations and will begin on their own to teach themselves more about the product features and about how to sell the product, even if the formal training doesn't exist for it. They will begin to do this "constant learning" as a normal part of the work week.

This looks like a tough business problem to tackle, but let's think it through a little bit.

We could run a series of webcasts, where experts speak live to the salespeople about how to do "constant learning." We could record those webcasts so that people could replay them later. Better yet, we could deliver a series of weekly webcasts on topics that they need to know. If we have enough budget, we could even build self-contained e-learning modules to be downloaded and played each week, with built-in questions and flashy animations.

However, the business problem really expresses the need for active learning, and so far our learning solution isn't very active. Listening to lectures doesn't cause learners to combine facts and come up with solutions. It's so easy to let your mind wander while attending a virtual lecture.

Instead, we could run a series of live virtual classrooms wherein the content could be much more interactive. The students could collaborate on projects in small teams and could interact with a live instructor remotely. Learners could even work collaboratively on case studies. We might have a virtual classroom tool just waiting for us to use, but this wouldn't solve the real business problem because we would be hard-pressed to run sessions regularly—even assuming the salespeople would attend regularly. Each session would require a commitment of hours at a time. Further, the solution doesn't really reinforce self-directed learning.

COMBINE WHAT YOU ALREADY HAVE | Let's consider a completely different approach—a variation on the technique used by chess enthusiasts who teach themselves to become better at chess by studying the games of chess masters. They work move by move through a chess game from a grand master and, for each move, they tell themselves what move they would do next and then compare their answers to what the grand master actually does.

Of course, we might not have a tool that handles the automated delivery of the sales process step-by-step.

Let's see what we would do that way by lashing together some tools we might have at hand.

Instead of a big case study with multiple moves to make one after the other, let's break the content up into smaller pieces. We could send an email to every salesperson every few weeks with what we'll call "the new sales puzzle." It could be a situational puzzle that could be answered in ten minutes. The situational puzzle could put the salesperson in a real-life situation and ask "What would you do next?"

For example, you are talking to the CEO of Company X with a certain history of dealing with you, and he asks, "What do you do next? We could provide learners multiple-choice answers to select from. Or better yet, we could use an active-learning approach so that learners would have to write out their responses. That way they could say *why* they are taking an action, not just what the action is. They would have to think, not just select. They would only need to write a few sentences—no more than a paragraph or two. Along with the puzzle itself, we could include a short list of online training and reference web pages that could help learners solve the puzzle if they wanted to look up answers. We could do that all in email, except for the web pages that already exist.

Obvious pragmatic concerns include where learners would write their answers. Do we have an automated tool for correcting essay answers? Or if we don't have a tool, who's going to read and evaluate all those essay answers? What about the non-English-language learners?

If we don't have an automated essay-correcting tool, we could have learners just email answers to a central mailbox. We could have them enter their answer into a wiki—if we weren't worried that everyone would just copy someone else's good answer when they found it there.

We wouldn't have to read all the answers for correctness if a recognized subject-matter expert answered each puzzle and sent that to everyone when we emailed everyone the next puzzle. Everyone could check their own answers against the experts' answers.

How would we know that everyone would actually act in good faith in regard to answering the puzzle if we were not looking at each response? Looking closely at the business problem, we find we are not really interested in tracking each person, but in improving the population as a whole. Our evaluation could therefore just sample a small group and extrapolate. If we selected a handful of answers at random and found that those answers were good, we could feel sufficiently confident that everyone's answers were acceptable. Over time we could watch to see whether response accuracy trends upward or downward. Non-English answers could be translated with the free text translation tools on the Internet.

There is a risk of the clever salespeople realizing that all the answers are not being read and trusting that their poor answers (or no answer) will not be noticed, but we can solve that problem by passing some randomly selected answers to upper-level sales managers, highlighting the ones that seem to be poorly done. A salesperson is not likely to take the risk of being embarrassed in front of his bosses by sending in a poor answer or no answer.

For people who don't like to type, we can provide options to record their answers verbally using the free Audacity audio capture tool from the Internet. We could even find an audio-to-text conversion tool.

The solution here demonstrates the use of a simple tool (email) to do something for which a comprehensive e-learning tool does not yet exist. Many e-learning managers and designers are overly biased by their e-learning tools and fail to consider what they want to do and what tools they could put together to accomplish it.

DON'T GET TRAPPED

What do you need to consider so you aren't trapped by your tools? First, make sure you have the business problem clearly in mind. The business problem addresses what the company needs, not what the individual needs.

Each e-learning job is different because each has different constraints. You have to work within constraints. You have to make tradeoffs. The only question is whether you make tradeoffs well or make them poorly.

Here's a quick checklist of constraints that will help you identify some of the major tradeoffs to make as you look for the right set of tools for your e-learning job (Henderson, 2002, Chapter 8).

- ➢ Budget: big, small?
- ➢ Number of students: large, small?
- ➢ Student time available: How many hours can the student spend on what you created?
- ➢ Student familiarity with the e-learning tool: Will students need to learn the tool as well as the material you want them to learn?
- ➢ Time to build/develop: How much time do you have before delivering?
- ➢ Expert availability: How much time can the subject-matter experts spend?
- ➢ Ease of development: Does the tool make content development easy?
- ➢ Deadline: Do you have to train a population in a fixed amount of time?
- ➢ Shelf life: Will this training stay available, or is it a single-use application?
- ➢ Skill levels? How large is the gap you want to close?

➤ Need for interaction: Do you need to build in collaboration among students or with an instructor?

➤ Measurement and tracking: Do you need to track individual performance data or do you just need overall counts?

Let's draw an analogy. Depending on the e-learning problem you're trying to solve, you can think of the constraints in the list above as individual agents arranged around the perimeter of a circle. Each agent on the perimeter is attached by a rope to a single agent in the center of the circle. The agent in the circle's center represents your e-learning solution. Now the individuals on the perimeter start to pull on their ropes, but each has a different strength. What happens is that the agent in the center is pulled toward the strongest puller on the perimeter, but since everyone's pulling, he winds up somewhere off-center, inside the circle, but nearer to the agent pulling him the hardest.

Taking the constraints into account can look complicated, but there are typically only a few big constraints for each new business problem. Once you understand the number and strengths of your constraint and what that means to your solution, you can think about lashing several tools together that take those constraints into account. As the thought experiments showed, you really have more tool choices than you think you do.

Finally, consider the tools you can use. Different e-learning tools will let you implement different building blocks of e-learning (Henderson, 2002, Chapters 2 and 7). There are only a handful of basic building blocks for e-learning, including:

➤ Self-paced learning (and self-play lectures)

➤ Virtual interaction with people (in a virtual classroom, wiki, and so on)

➤ Simulations and games

➤ Virtual reference library (such as documents to download and read)

➤ Measurement and tracking

Some tools address only one of these building blocks. Others address two or more, while others will address them all.

The pace of technology improvement is relentless. Tools become out of date very quickly. Try to avoid putting all your eggs in a single basket. The tool that looks so good today may be inadequate in just a few years.

THERE IS NO PERFECT TOOL

Each tool has its advantages and disadvantages. As you put together an e-learning experience, you will need to make tradeoffs. Some tools are functionally richer from the user point of view, some are easier to use for content development, some are very expensive to operate, and some are unfamiliar to users. In IBM we have lots of tools that can be used inside the company for e-learning, but even we don't have tools that can do everything we want to do. We try to make tradeoffs consciously, instead of relying on habit.

When faced with an e-learning job in the workplace, the key questions I ask are these:

➤ What's the business problem? What business improvement is the company looking for?

- ➤ What are the constraints? What are the relative strengths of each for the job at hand.
- ➤ What e-learning tools can I lash together to solve the problem?

The worst thing is to let yourself be trapped by your tools. Don't ask: "What can I do with my tools?" Instead, say, "What do I want to do and what tools can I put together to solve the business problem?"

As one of my colleagues recently said, "Wait! There are simple and effective solutions. Think—How do you solve the problem? not: How do you use your tools?"

You have tool options. You have more options than you think.

REFERENCE

Henderson, A. (2002). *The e-learning question and answer book.* New York: AMACOM.

Peter Isackson

Peter Isackson, a native Californian with dual U.S. and French nationality, was educated at UCLA (BA) and Oxford University. He has worked in France for over thirty years, acquiring a reputation as an innovator in the use of technology for learning. Although working in multiple areas of knowledge and professional skills, he has specialized in the intercultural field as a consultant, trainer and coach, and trainer of trainers.

He has spent most of the past twenty-five years developing learning strategies, methods, and content that integrates audiovisual, information, and telecommunications technology. A prolific author, producer, and publisher of a wide range of multimedia and e-learning products for management, language learning, and other subjects (including helicopter maintenance), he has managed several small multimedia publishing companies and collaborated with multiple publishers: BBC, Heinemann, Macmillan, Pearson-Longmans, Cambridge Digital, EuroTalk in the UK; Les Editions Didier, Hatier, Auralog, and the Editions Albert René in France; and Cultural Detective in the U.S.

He is currently CEO of a Paris-based company, Learnscaper, that is launching a new range of interactive products—in particular, "full video serious games"—as well as training and consultancy services.

LEARNING IN THE QUATERNARY ECONOMY | Peter Isackson

I'm grateful to Peter Isackson for making me think about societal, technical, and behavioral changes in a new and potentially more productive way. I've reread this article multiple times, each iteration gifting me new actionable ideas. As we are all aware, the growth of the role of technology in our daily lives has already begun to have a strong impact on human behavior. The economy itself is undergoing massive change too. For many of us, the certainty of uncomfortable changes is great, but undefined. In the "quaternary economy," built on the principle of relationships rather than simple transactions, new forms of behavior are evolving not only for buying and selling, but also for learning. The implication is that learning will increasingly be recognized as fundamentally social, defined by a purpose not just of acquiring knowledge, but rather of evolving the learner's "identity," which includes both the sense of one's social and professional roles—as felt by oneself and seen by others—and an increased mastery of a range of complex and interrelated skills. While a fear of change is natural, the ability to adapt makes humans resilient. With the help of technology, we may find our best abilities yet to adapt to new realities.

I designed my title as a teaser bringing together two terms, one most people find only too familiar and another that probably sounds hopelessly obscure. The terms themselves are far less important that the historical moment we are now living through. I hope that we can collectively begin to realize that:

> ➤ The idea of learning, in spite of being around throughout the history of homo sapiens, is undergoing radical redefinition and will take us into areas that are totally unfamiliar to us today.

> ➤ There is a real observable trend concerning the way we do things in our daily lives—a trend I link to the notion of an emerging "quaternary economy"— and this trend should provide the key to the new definition of learning and its goals.

The idea that we might be entering a new phase of economic transformation, following the seismic shock of the industrial revolution in the 18th century and its evolution toward an economy of services in the 20th century, has been bandied about in academic circles for at least a decade. In spite of the ongoing debate, no simple accepted definition of the new quaternary economy exists. A quick Google search reveals lists of new style services related to information technology, education, and R&D, which innovative economists dare to call the "quaternary sector." The idea of a quaternary economy, initially launched by French sociologist Roger Sue (1997) gives us a dynamic macro view of the question, taking us beyond the description of particular professions. The quaternary economy represents a major cultural mutation that will have a transformative impact similar to that of the industrial revolution, possibly with a more global impact.

To situate the importance of this change, let's review in the simplest terms the evolutionary stages of the Western, and ultimately, the world economy over the past three hundred years. The *primary sector* of the economy applies to the production of food and raw materials, the *secondary* to manufacturing and the *tertiary* to services. Miners in a primary activity extract metal; producers of steel transform the metal, and others manufacture cars, activities typical of the secondary sector; the dealer who sells or leases us the car represents the tertiary sector. Of course, each stage of development incorporates and refines the contribution of the previous one. Manufacturing depends on the availability of raw materials. Services are built around the supply, management, and exploitation of manufactured goods. The *quaternary economy* builds on the other three but significantly transforms the notion of service by adding the radically new bottom-up notion of personalization made possible by the emergence and democratization of two key technologies: mobile devices and cloud computing. The quaternary economy turns around the notion that information cannot only be accessed and shared everywhere, but can also be created by everyone. It seems obvious that learning is one of the key human activities that will be significantly affected by this mutation.

Rather than categorize these phases of the economy as "sectors," as if they were isolated areas of concentrated activity, I propose to look at them as interacting in complex ways as each retains its basic principle of organization. This should

enable us to construct a vision of their impact on society as a whole.

Humanity has lived through a succession of cultures that have determined most of our social roles. Each one of those phases has produced a general way of thinking about and dealing with the world around us: as a source of food and material, as a social and political framework for organizing the production of goods, as a milieu for transferring ownership or permitting the use and management of goods. One of the particularities of the quaternary economy is that it will have a further effect of actively breaking down the barriers between existing sectors.

Figure 1 is my highly simplified illustration of the quaternary economy.

Over the past two centuries the market economy has developed and evolved around transfers among the first three sectors, all requiring precise physical conditions of supply and delivery:

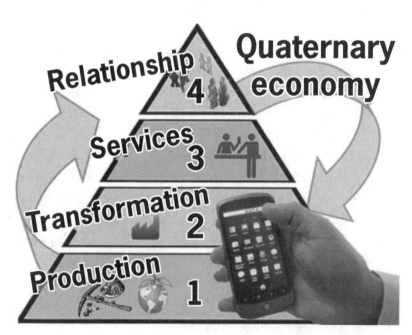

Figure 1. Quarternary Economy Pyramid

- Finding and extracting resources in order to sell them (the primary sector)
- Transforming them into new products (crafts and manufacturing, the secondary sector)
- Cataloguing sets of controlled actions that can then be made available to customers and charged at standard prices (the tertiary)

The emerging quaternary economy will be based on the infinitely flexible notion of relationship rather than that of transfer of property or the supply of a set of discrete actions packaged as a catalogued service. It will be built on real-time relationships of need and exchange between human beings, who may be more than the simple owners or custodians of identified goods and services. Access and interaction rather than purchase become the chief organizing principle determining where value is perceived and how new value can be created, delivered, and rewarded, whether through payment, recognition, or the creation of value within the network—value from which everyone benefits. The notion of access itself will no longer be strictly individual, but will frequently involve collective phenomena, a social presence in which sharing—both physical and intellectual—and co-managing will become a standard reflex and contribute to the perception and remuneration of value. This is a real and deep cultural change and will take time to play out. The emerging quaternary economy is the prelude to a quaternary culture in which our perception of the world and our relationship with it will have changed.

The trend has already begun. The short history of Amazon.com can be used an example of this trend. Initially designed as a virtual bookstore replicating the supply of service and goods of a shop on Main Street, by implementing networking technology its innovative appeal appeared merely to be the streamlining of purchasing processes and stock management. In other words, Amazon began as an attempt to duplicate an existing tertiary model, innovating in three areas: scale of marketing, customer management, and logistics. The model focused on the automation of traditional in-shop services. The dialogue with the salesperson was transformed into a flexible and easily accessible database with space for customer comment. And, of course, Amazon used information technology to rationalize its stock management and delivery. In so doing Amazon created a model that redefined a book distributor's relationship with publishers, customers, and logistical partners.

That was Amazon way back when. But what has Amazon become in a world that is already moving toward a quaternary economy? Almost imperceptibly Amazon has morphed into something totally different from a book supplier by taking on the role of a complex relationship manager, hosting and overseeing myriad micro-relationships and dealing with an infinity of goods, the whole thing masquerading as a bookshop! There's still a lot of the tertiary culture built into the current Amazon model, and as a powerful global supplier, that is bound to remain true. But Amazon will undoubtedly keep evolving toward a model increasingly influenced by the notion of relationship as the quaternary economy grows up around it.

LEARNING IN A QUATERNARY CULTURE

The one thing that radically differentiates the quaternary economy from the tertiary, taking us well beyond the Amazon model, is its shift from a traditional focus on the simple and definitive transfer of property to the integration of complexity, thanks to the availability of infinitely variable benefits provided by intricate and continually optimized networks, saddled with fewer and fewer hardwired time constraints (transfer, delivery, payment). Thanks to the new technology, human networks (people) consciously or unconsciously turn the technical networks they work through into an infinitely flexible infrastructure of constantly reconfigured relationships. As the emergence of the social web has shown us, under the right conditions a technical networking structure will be spontaneously mobilized by its users to create unpredictable and, to a large extent, uncontrollable human networks. Creativity, variability, and flexibility become the basis of all the new forms of productivity, leveraging energies that were formerly dispersed or actively repressed. This is true whether those energies are directed toward consumption, production, play, or the development of knowledge and skills. The quaternary culture is bound to be richer than the tertiary.

What this means is that today's technologies—in particular mobile access to interconnected networks, increased bandwidth, cloud computing, and eventually virtual worlds—coupled with the cultural transformations already visible with Web 2.0 and also reflected in Gen-Y's lifestyle—will inevitably transform the economy itself as we move beyond the one-way, "one and done" model of the typical tertiary transaction and enter a quaternary economy based on a diversity of manageable relationships with people, things, and cultural artifacts. Whereas the tertiary economy assigned simple roles to its actors who fell into one of two roles—service providers or service consumers (and that includes teaching)—the quaternary economy will not only allow for but also encourage shifting and multiple roles.

In the quaternary economy the notion of acquisition, ownership, and individual control will be replaced or significantly modified by access to goods and services mediated through relationships, emphasizing the role of connectors. This will have an impact on people's sense of identity within an expanding variety of communities that each person in the multiple networks may belong to. I have always maintained that transforming the learner's identity is the central but strangely neglected issue in both training and learning, whose institutions traditionally focused on something much more abstract: knowledge and skills. From my experience in domains as divergent as language learning and helicopter maintenance, I long ago realized that if the learning process doesn't include the possibility of modifying in significant ways learners' conscious and unconscious perception of their identity, nothing serious can be accomplished. This basic fact becomes more obvious in a quaternary perspective. More than that, for the first time it becomes a manageable process.

THE LEARNER'S IDENTITY IN A QUATERNARY CULTURE

The industrial revolution ushered in the triumph of the secondary economy, which had previously played second fiddle to the primary, but now found itself conducting the orchestra. At the same time it created and solidified a philosophy of learning that was increasingly utilitarian and voluntarily limited in scope. A focus on productivity led to an extremely narrow understanding of what skills were needed for any given profession. The fewer and more focused they were, the better, because that made teaching and managing them easier, saving time and money. Anything that couldn't be reduced to a teachable formula or "essential knowledge" was considered not worth knowing.*

The uncomfortable truth, however, is that actual performance skills go far beyond "essential knowledge," both in depth and in complexity. Although this is beginning to sound obvious in a world that has rediscovered complexity thanks to our renewed awareness that we are all dependent on networks, for several centuries we seemed very happy with a model based on the idea of the simple transfer of established knowledge modeled on the same pattern as our simple commercial transactions: you get what you pay for, neither more nor less.

The quaternary learning economy will function in a totally different way. To start with, it's all about dynamic relationships and the use of an expanding diversity of resources, both material and human. This means that it's eminently social. It's more a culture than a practice. The immediate corollary is that every question relating to knowledge and skills turns around the notion of the learner's (or the subject's) identity, which can no longer be seen as some sort of static position in the hierarchy—an interchangeable cog in the system—but as the embodied result of a complex, multifaceted set of relationships. Identity—the sense of who I am for myself and others—founds my belief in my capacity to act effectively, not only on my own but in conjunction with others.

Traditionally, professional skills for a particular job profile have been described as lists of actions and attitudes ("key skills," sometimes referred to as "job referential") that qualified operators are expected to be good at. But when we look more carefully at how people actually work, we discover that the successful execution of all of these critical actions depends on a sense of identity that is both professional and social. Identity, in its true philosophical sense, is about *being* before it is about *doing,* and it's what makes effective doing possible.

I see five complementary and essential facets of being that contribute to our sense of identity that define the space and scope of professional competency:

➤ *Personality,* which describes our modes of interaction with others and which is developed over a lifetime of interactions;

---

*Oscar Wilde, perspicacious and ironic observer that he was, highlighted the error of his era with his comment, "Education is an admirable thing, but it is well to remember from time to time that nothing that is worth knowing can be taught." (from *The Critic as Artist*)

➢ Appropriation of specific work skills as a qualified *operator*, mastery of processes and practices, both tacit and explicit;

➢ Our role as a *team member* in a corporate team, project team, department, community, population with a particular professional profile, etc.;

➢ Our role as a *cultural actor* adapting to and contributing to the evolution of the cultures and milieus of our various teams and communities; and finally

➢ Our role as a *cultural connector*, transmitting values and knowledge between the multiple contexts of one's identity and making the link between social and professional identity.

Figure 2 demonstrates the dynamic relationships of these facets. Identity occupies the gravitational center of a person's being, represented here as a spiral galaxy. The sense of identity both feeds into and is nourished by the contexts in which relationships are developed and managed, only part of which is the workplace (the broken line circle). The sphere of work appears here as slightly off center because, for all the importance of one's professional image, identity is built on much more than one's job profile and professional relationships.

Translation: "My *identity* is that of a *personality* who *operates* (does his job) as a *team member* acting within one or more cultures and helping each of them to *connect* with the others. If I learn something, all of these aspects are simultaneously enriched. And if I sense that they have been enriched, then I know I have learned something."

True learning—quaternary learning—means tweaking the learner's identity in ways that will allow him or her to deal with new areas of experience and new contexts rather than just adding to an existing store of operational knowledge. It means readjusting each facet of identity, changing one's relationship with the various elements of a complex environment. In comparison, our traditional training policies can be seen as neglectful of everything but the officially designated skills of an abstract operator, with occasional forays into team membership. This leaves personality and culture out of the picture. Quaternary learning, on the contrary, will allow us—and should even incite us—to leverage all five of the interacting dimensions, effectively enriching our identities. One of the immediate benefits to be expected will be increased flow between life-embedded and work-embedded skills.

This would appear to violate the traditional corporate obsession with focused objectives

Figure 2. Complementary and Essential Facets of Being
Copyright 2010 by Peter Isackson.

and controlled productivity. But a simple and increasingly common example illustrates the advantages this kind of cross-pollination can produce in the workplace. Someone who maintains a blog, participates in discussions groups, contributes to wikis, or participates in a community of practice will, in most cases, thanks to these activities, develop both a stronger sense of identity as well as continually refine a wide range of communication skills, including writing style, logical reasoning, emotional control, and the art of interpersonal dialogue, to say nothing of expanding areas of knowledge and interest that could equally have an impact on the quality of work. In other words, identity works in the same way as a powerful gravitational force for producing order from chaos. And identity is at the center of every significant event in its universe. Who would you expect to contribute more to the development of your business—the person who aligns all the listed skills and can pass tests to prove it or the person who continually invests in reflecting on those skills and learning from interplay with others? Traditional employers see personality and autonomy as sources of potential risk. Quaternary employers realize that they are the attributes that create value.

QUATERNARY LEARNING ACTS ON THE LEARNER'S SENSE OF SOCIAL AND PROFESSIONAL IDENTITY

Organizing effective learning in the quaternary culture will therefore require recognizing the multiple facets of the learner as a professional and social being. For designers of quaternary learning it means going beyond the goal of defining and representing officially recognized learning objectives. It also means redefining the roles of everyone involved in implementing learning. But most of all, it means respecting and encouraging a balance within the learning process between input and output by providing the occasions for both spontaneous (informal, experimental) and less spontaneous expression in multiple professional and social contexts. This is perhaps the most significant and dramatic innovation of the quaternary economy for learning: multiplying the contexts for the expression of output as well as accepting a reduction of direct control while stimulating real productivity. In the secondary and tertiary economies, relinquishing control was deemed an unthinkable paradox. For the quaternary, it's the way the game is played.

Thanks to recent breakthroughs in technology and real shifts in human culture, the quaternary economy is beginning to emerge. We are still living in the old culture and it would be easy to point to much of current practice to prove that nothing much has changed. We don't see many leaders ready with coherent plans for harnessing the energy that is visibly being generated. But as always in times of rapid change, professional culture lags behind not only the advances in infrastructure but also the spontaneous activity of those individuals who know how to use it to achieve their own personal goals or simply have fun with it. Culture is the way people behave collectively on the basis of the values they share coupled with their understanding of the world and their immediate environment. We are still a long way from achieving a quaternary culture, but there is little doubt that it's on its way.

Corporate training has consistently lagged

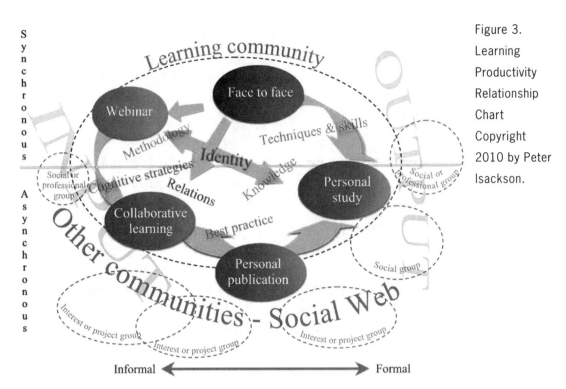

Figure 3.
Learning
Productivity
Relationship
Chart
Copyright
2010 by Peter
Isackson.

in evolving its culture to take advantage of the changes in infrastructure. Figure 3 shows how it would be possible today to organize and exploit optimally the tools we have for maximized learning productivity.

The central concept is the recognition of social complexity and the existence of communities. Whenever a community comes into being, a culture is born. The old model of learning stressed individual performance in a competitive environment in which cooperation and collaboration were seen as anomalous. It also put excessive emphasis on input, as output was limited to allowing or obliging learners to prove that they had processed input in the most predictable way or simply remembered the discourse associated with it. The traditional learning model not only did not encourage creativity, it excluded it. It's difficult to imagine a more inefficient and less natural system of learning, but our institutions rose to the challenge and imposed a set of values that did more to stifle than encour-

age the kind of learning that leads to true productivity.

Web 2.0 has already shown that vital knowledge—the knowledge we use, evaluate, apply, and transform—can no longer be constrained by its representation in the form of fixed and objective facts and principles, but instead functions flexibly as an object of continual research, negotiation, and redefinition as it is applied to real and varying contexts. It marks the difference between static and dynamic learning and heralds the shift from the secondary-tertiary model of finite transactions to a quaternary model of potentially infinite reconfigurations. Ever since Piaget and Vygotsky, we know that authentic learning, the learning that has an impact on identity, is by definition dynamic and social. Bateson (1968) identified four levels of learning (0, I, II, and III) and pointed out that most learning models rarely aim above level I, rote learning, whereas learning to learn starts at level II and the highest form of learning, a form of enlightenment with an impact on the learner's identity. What these 20th century researchers discovered long ago we are for the first time in a position to begin to apply.

The first practical step in implementing a quaternary culture of learning is to recognize two basic principles:

- ➢ Communities are our basic reality for accomplishing anything, that is, learning is social and rooted in context.
- ➢ Input and output must exist in a state of relative equality, which is to say that input should never restrict output.

course, it also elevated static, passive learning to the status of universal norm for learning behavior.

The quaternary economy promises the creation of different relationships between the receivers (learners) and those who were formerly designated as the exclusive transmitters of knowledge: author, teachers, trainers, and mentors. In their collective intelligence, communities will know where to look for the resources that allow them to build and restructure critical knowledge. Instead of seeking designated trainers and mentors as

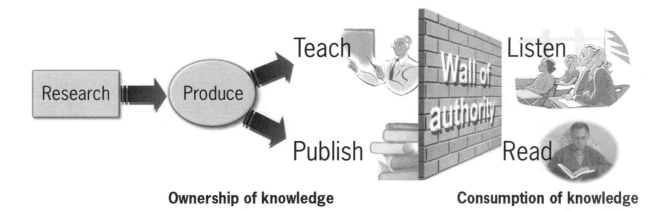

Figure 4. Traditional Model for Production and Delivery of Learning Content

In traditional teaching and training, recognized "authorities"—experts, authors, and teachers—were paid to produce, manage, and deliver input (see Figure 4). Learners (or their employers) paid for the right to absorb whatever was transferred over the wall of authority. Creative output was restricted to the left side of the wall. Learners on the right side of the wall processed it as input. This made things easy to manage according to the transactional logic of the tertiary economy. Of

their unique source for the transmission and transfer of knowledge, they will integrate a new and much more flexible category of operator, which for want of a better term may be called "enlightenment coaches." They will be familiar with both background and foreground issues, skilled in informal constructive dialogue, and capable of influencing group dynamics in positive ways. Even more radically, unlike the class of coaches that have invaded the corporate landscape over the past twenty years, they will work from within the communities and increasingly focus on helping group culture evolve, both in terms of its methods and results.

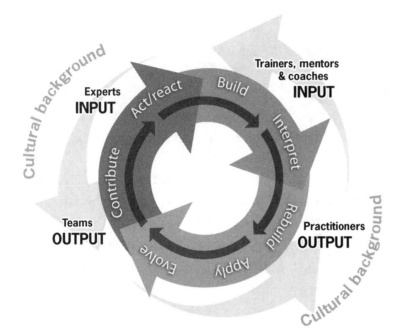

Figure 5. New Model: Balanced Dynamic Input and Output

In the new configuration shown in Figure 5, the wall of authority has disappeared, input and output become cyclical, feeding into each other against an equally dynamic background of cultural evolution, which includes both organizational and social culture (for example, the practice of the social web and other quaternary habits). Specific actions and events (*programmed learning activity*) can be planned, but they must be subordinated to the overall dynamics. The dominant verbs are no longer *research, produce, teach* on one side and *read, listen,* and *reproduce* on the other, but rather *act and react, build, interpret, rebuild, apply, evolve, contribute*—with the order of actions always adapted to the context rather than set in a standard sequence.

Will such a model become the norm? There are plenty of forces of resistance in its path. But the initiative will no longer be in the hands of training professionals, who, as a class, are the most likely to resist. The spontaneous practices generated by the quaternary economy will most likely impose a new organizational logic based on what will become obvious gains in productivity. But this will take time, as all cultural changes do. Still, the wait may not be all that long.

Less than ten years ago when two strangers met they would typically ask, "Do you have e-mail?" Today, for everyone from teenagers to great-grandparents, it's "give me your e-mail address" or even "give me your usual e-mail." The equivalent today of the ten-year-old question would be "are you on Twitter?" or "do you have a Facebook account?" Times do change to the point that we even have difficulty remembering how we did things in the very recent past.

The comforting thing about the quaternary revolution is that it won't require armies of evangelists to recruit people to the new culture. Quaternary** habits will be perceived as the most efficient way of achieving both short- term and long-term goals. They will come about imperceptibly, simply because they work. I have no idea who will take the responsibility of updating Wikipedia's entry on the quaternary economy, but I guarantee that it will be done in a very near future.

REFERENCES

Bateson, G. (1968, August). The logical categories of learning and communication (pp. 279–308). Presented at the Conference on World Views sponsored by the National Institute of Mental Health.

Debonneuil, M. (2007). *L'espoir économique. Vers la révolution du quaternaire.* Bourin.

La révolution du quaternaire: www.futuribles.com/TablesRondes/CR20071120_Debonneuil.pdf

Sue, R. (1997). *La richesse des hommes, vers l'économie quaternaire.* Paris: Odile Jacob.

**The idea of a quaternary revolution was born in France in the 1990s, first proposed and described by the sociologist Roger Sue. It has developed recently under the impetus of the Ministry of Economy, largely in relation to the government's concern to understand the mechanisms that will ensure full employment in the future. I know of no other publications in English dealing with the same concepts than those in the References section.

Bobbe Baggio

Bobbe Baggio, Ph.D., is an accomplished author, speaker, and educator. Her specific expertise is in how people learn and how to use technologies to help them learn. Her company, Advantage Learning Technologies, Inc. (ALT), has provided ID services and implemented projects for clients in finance, healthcare, gasses and chemicals, manufacturing, distribution, construction, government, and higher education. A more detailed list of clients can be found on her website at www.bobbebaggio.com. Bobbe provides programs and products so that people who are trying to use technology for teaching and learning can do so effectively. She is currently the director of the graduate program in instructional technology management at La Salle University in Philadelphia, Pennsylvania, and speaks regularly to organizations and companies around the globe. Her latest books include *You Listen with Your Eyes* and *The Pajama Effect*. Bobbe's prior experience includes being a senior scientist, management consultant, director of IT, and director of software development. Her education includes a bachelor's degree from Waynesburg College, an M.A. from West Virginia University, M.S. from Lehigh University, and a Ph.D. from Capella University.

YOU, YOU ONLINE, YOU WHEN NOBODY KNOWS IT'S YOU ONLINE | Bobbe Baggio

The Saturn School in St. Paul, Minnesota, was built as part of the bid to attract General Motors to establish a Saturn factory there. The school was designed to demonstrate advanced practices in teaching and learning. Among the interesting things I witnessed there more than twenty years ago was a system that permitted students to submit questions from their desk keyboards. Questions were posted for all to see and remained there until the submitter felt the question had been sufficiently addressed and withdrew it. When the system allowed questions to be submitted anonymously, participation rose dramatically, with a transforming increase coming from typically shy students. Bobbe shows us that anonymity online can afford us the magic of putting on our invisibility cloak, like Harry Potter, and provide us with opportunities to observe and learn that are not possible in a traditional environment. In the online world, anonymity acts like a veil that permits the redefinition of self. Online identity is a bit paradoxical. On one hand you are free to define yourself without the restrictions of visual cues and social inequalities. On the other hand your interactions with others provide a digital testimony to who you are.

Online learning presents many new opportunities as it morphs traditional face-to-face education into new e-learning environments. An individual's personal and social identity can influence online interactions, but the anonymity of the online world permits the redefinition of self. Online identity is a bit paradoxical. On one hand, you are free to define yourself without the restrictions of visual cues and social inequalities. On the other, your interactions provide a digital testimony to who you are. The online environment offers a chance to observe learning undetected as well as many chances to alter your perspective. I posit that anonymity supports learning through the opportunities it offers for freedom and self-definition.

YOU

Who are you? Your identity, it seems, depends on where you are and who you ask. Your identity can be defined by your relationship with yourself and your relationship with others. You can define your own identity, and others will also define one for you. Most definitions consist of those two parts: personal and social.

Personal identity consists of ways one defines oneself. "I'm short, I'm tall, I'm smart, I'm dumb, I'm shy, I'm talkative, I'm cool, I'm a geek" are all ways individuals differentiate themselves. Other people also label us. Over time, we integrate some of these labels into our personalities. Different experiences one has become integrated also. *Individuation* is what Carl Jung called the development of the self, which is analogous to identity. Individuation includes our do's and our don'ts, our will's and our won'ts, our personal guideposts and defining limits.

The idea of personal identity can also be traced back to work by Milton Erickson. Erickson wrote about the identity crisis and that one's feelings about the self are reflected in our character, goals, and origins. Personal identity, as we said, is an individual's self-appraisal of his or her physical and cognitive abilities, personal traits, motives, and a variety of other attributes. Personal identity affects everything an individual thinks, feels, and does (Jackson, 1968).

Social identity, on the other hand, is derived from membership in a group. Social identity attaches values and emotions to membership in the group. This encompasses connections and role relationships with others, as well as an identity with the collective whole. Social identity includes the expected behaviors, alleged characteristics, and distinguishing features that an individual takes pride in or views as unchangeable but socially consequential as part of membership in a group (Meng, 2005).

Identity has long been seen as integral to learning online. Vygotsky (1962) and Goffman (1959), intermixed with the work of other constructivists, have determined that online identity matters. It follows that learners care about who they are online. They respond to social and external stimuli, creating an online self and sometimes, given the chance, they can and will create multiple online selves. New and better-integrated communication tools provide the context for the emergence of a new identity and, some would

argue, a new type of person who wants to be heard and wants opportunities for self-presentation. New learners fluent in YouTube and Facebook are seeking not only a sense of self but also a sense of integration, not just with what they're learning but also with their co-learners. "To them, facts, explanations, tools, and reasoning are worth learning only in so far as they support their own, personal goals" (Prensky, 2007, p. 64, as quoted in Conrad, 2008, p. 158).

YOU ONLINE | An outcome of our communications online, besides online identities and social and community interactions, is a collective consciousness (Siddiquee & Kagan, 2006). Communication and community are linked, but the two are certainly not the same. It is very possible to communicate without community. The online context serves as a link between cognition and interaction. Online communication is not so much about the delivery of information but about the activation of a relationship in which interrelated conditions support the construction of reality (Riva & Galimberti, 1998).

Most of the literature suggests that online communities and social presence are key elements in establishing online identity. Participation reflects the ability of the participant to express opinions, exert influence, and interact with others. Whatever we say or do is captured in digital form. Our communications and learner engagements develop in a technological context, which influences those interactions.

Our identity is developed through the capacity to act in private. Anonymity, or at least a perceived degree of anonymity, in online learning presents both ethical concerns and learning benefits. How we interact with others is our *social presence.* Social presence theory has been around for nearly three decades, and social presence has been identified as a key element in online learning. The roles we assume are related to a variety of factors. In an online environment, many of the clues to identity and social presence that we take for granted in face-to-face environments are missing.

Knowing the identity of those in the online community is essential to understanding and evaluating their interactions. Identity online can be ambiguous. The conditions can lead to identity deception, but they can also lead to freedom. Online the individual has the opportunity to deindividuate, the psychological state of mind that causes one to be less inhibited and less self-evaluative (Baggio & Beldarrain, 2008), to do things beyond our normal boundaries. We deindividuate for many reasons, including desire for anonymity, loss of a sense of responsibility, arousal, lack of structure, and others.

An alternative explanation of our behavior online is that the social identity of deindividuation effects (SIDE) model put forth by Penz (2007), who believes that the effects of anonymity online are influenced by and subject to our connection to "we." The SIDE model explains behavior in terms of group norms that emerge from interactions in specific contexts and can give way to group conformity.

The online world is composed of information, not of flesh, blood, and bones. One of the basic three-dimensional elements available to us in a face-to-face world is the body. Although the intricacies of the self may change over time, the body provides a stabilizing norm: "One body, one identity" (Donath, 1998, p. 1). Even if we offer pictures or videos online, a sense of ambiguity is attached to them. We disseminate only the information we want known. A person can have as many online identities as he or she has the will and desire to create.

An often-asked question is whether the ability to connect with growing numbers of like-minded people is empowering. Without the restrictions of time and space, the Internet provides a place for the exchange of electronic communications leading to the establishment of a shared "co-presence," commonly called *collective consciousness,* a consensus of our attitudes, beliefs, and shared values that acts as a unifying force.

Howard Rheingold (1993) called online communities places where community happens if enough people carry on enough conversations long enough. Rheingold added that, in order to create community, a certain amount of feeling and relationship had to be established. The defuse nature of online communities makes it difficult to characterize them. Common elements often attributed to community such as "commitment" have a different meaning online. The digital world warrants emphasis on the imagination. Public and private exchanges are mixed. Whether the "I-feeling" or the "we-feeling" is dominant determines the degree of one's conscious connection to the greater whole.

Any interpretation of "You Online" is a bit paradoxical. On one hand, the environment frees us from social influences and inequalities. On the other hand, this may cause us to define ourselves more in terms of our social identities and group affiliations. Your online personality may be made up of your personal identity and multiple social identities you have honed through myriad online interactions. You may see yourself and others in terms of membership in the community. This group identity is applicable to all levels of understanding.

Learner interactions online are changing rapidly. The four traditional modes are learner to learner, learner to content, learner to instructor, and learner to the interface. However, there is an increasing capacity of the semantic web to support interactions between and among humans and/or autonomous agents, and the ability to engage in interactions is expanding. Few subjects are as fueled with emotion and subjective epistemological assumptions as a discussion on learner interactions (Anderson, 2003). The anonymity afforded by the online experience fosters the exploration of a type of interaction often overlooked in learning circles, vicarious interaction.

YOU WHEN NO ONE KNOWS IT'S YOU ONLINE Anonymity online provides us with opportunities to observe and learn that are not possible in a traditional environment. It provides a unique opportunity to engage in unobserved vicarious interaction and to take on a new identity and create new perspectives. There is also an opportunity for deception, which is unethical. Misinformation can be costly. People create false identities form many reasons, but basically because they can. A discussion of the moral and legal aspects of deception is not the purpose of this article. Instead, we focus here on the opportunities for learning when the physical markers of real life are absent.

One of the primary opportunities is to observe others vicariously. Some learners have social and psychological characteristics that inhibit their direct interactions. For them, vicarious interaction is a way to observe and actively process interactions between others and to benefit from a learning experience (Sutton, 2000). Learning in this way is not the same as what has been termed cyber stalking, which may include false accusations, monitoring, making threats, identity theft, and damage to data or equipment, the solicitation of minors for sex, or gathering information. Vicarious interaction is akin to observational learning, which leads to a change in the learner based on the behavior observed. The learner does not have to imitate the behavior; in fact, if the behavior is negative, the learner may learn to avoid it. Vicarious interaction is simply learning without direct interaction.

Vicarious interaction is often the referred to as the "fifth or other" learner interaction. It occurs when a student actively observes and processes both sides of a direct interaction between two other students or between another student and the instructor. But it's more than observation. The observation, processing, and internalization of the actions of another result in empathetic identification with the other's conduct.

Online anonymity also offers us the chance to experience a change in perspective. We can experiment with how it feels to step into someone else's shoes. When no one knows our real identity, we can be a different gender or color or social status. We can change our ethnicity or social boundaries and develop relationships with people we might never meet in a face-to-face environment. Without the cues that stifle our interactions, we can examine our limitations and step beyond the familiar.

The use of aliases can allow us a strong and confident voice. Many learners have found that instant messaging (IM) using aliases hides their social status, which leads to an interesting offspring of the IM process known as "posing," taking on the identity of another. Because they are not physically present, posers have a greater opportunity to monitor the interactions of others. Many young people take pleasure in occasionally posing and see it as play, parody, and performance (Lewis & Fabos, 2005).

Another by-product of psuedonimity is openness. Learners feel more free to express their opinions and are less afraid of being judged. The pressures to adhere to scripts that normally govern behavior diminish. Interactions among cultural groups take place more easily, and social norms and cultural clichés are abandoned. From a constuctivist pedagogy, this type of environment is supportive of learning.

IMPLICATIONS

Online learning environments have been shown to be supportive of learning and excellent venues for teaching and learning. Online environments support a constructivist epistemology. The constructivist approach combines personal mental processes with widely distributed social activities. Through engagement and active learning, these environments support the construction of knowledge. Anonymity can enhance this environment by supporting learner freedom, autonomy, and self-definition.

Freedom. Freedom to construct your own thoughts is at the heart of the constructivist movement. Anonymity brings new freedom for learners who do not want to be categorized or who could be perceived negatively (Lance, 2002). Freedom to explore different perspectives and experiment is essential to constructivist environments. The anonymity in cyberspace supports the freedom to leave one's surroundings, culture, and limitation and wander into another. A sense of discovery is supported by the ability to experiment with one's identity and return home safe and sound. It allows the learner to create new perspectives and be open to new possibilities. Freedom of identity online encourages the acceptance of differences while valuing interactions among community members that contribute to the greater good (Baggio & Beldarrain, 2008).

Research by Chester and Gwynne (1998) on pseudonymity in online learner interactions provides some examples. Many learners expressed that getting to know each other online first was beneficial. One female student wrote in her journal: "I think that we should be grateful for having the opportunity to meet each other online. . . . When you meet someone in real life too many things get in the way for you to be able to talk to someone properly" (Chester & Gwynne, 1998, p. 6). Another learner stated that she was able to give someone a chance to be her friend when she normally would not have because of his physical appearance. Finally, the research showed that learners were less likely to judge on physical characteristics such as gender, age, and race and were more likely to reflect on personality traits. This suggests that the longer we spend online the less important three-dimensional cues will become.

Autonomy. Autonomy is the ability of the learner to self-govern. A constructivist online environment supports active participation and self-direction. This is supported by the ability to control one's identity in the online environment. Learners take responsibility for their learning and manage, analyze, critique, cross-reference, and transform information into valuable knowledge (Huang, 2002). Online learners work collaboratively, sharing information in communities. By self-regulating, they become active participants in their own learning process.

Self-regulated activities online such as reflection, discussion posting, and metacognition help to support learner autonomy. An example can be found in reflection. Several online learners expressed similar thoughts of appreciation, saying that learning online provided time to "share a composed thought or question . . . and be able to reword messages" (Vonderwell, Liang, & Alderman, 2007, p. 318). The ability to revisit their thoughts and reflect is an indication of the determination of learners. Learner-to-learner questions are another indication of autonomy as is the ability of the learner to seek out further assistance.

Self-Definition. Online environments that support virtual world and online games serve as a vivid example for individuals who redefine themselves. They take on a new identity, including a new physical representation, and behave in new ways. Nowhere is this more clear than in virtual worlds where learners chose to customize their own avatars. These avatars are a way of redefining the self. In virtual world and online games millions of people interact with altered self-definitions.

Research conducted by Yee and Bailenson (2007) on self-representation online confirms that the majority of people chose attractive avatars and that those using attractive avatars are more intimate and friendly with strangers. They describe the "Proteus effect" as the reaction we have to our digital representations of self, regardless of how others perceive us. The fact that most people choose to be friendly and redefine the self as attractive gives us a clue to ways to encourage hyper-personal interactions.

CONCLUSION Identity has long been seen as an integral part of learning. It is clear that learners care about who they are online. Even though being online affords us a chance to be "invisible," personal identity, or the way we label ourselves, and social identity, the interpersonal self-concept we derive from membership in a group and our identity with the collective whole, come out in our choices and can be major contributors to the online learning experience. Anonymity provide us with opportunities to observe and learn that are not possible in a traditional environment. The use of aliases and avatars provides us with a chance to experience new perspectives. Anonymity in an online environment can be a catalyst for learners' freedom, autonomy, and self-definition.

REFERENCES

Anderson, T. (2003). Getting the mix right again: An updated and theoretical rationale for interaction. *International Review of Research in Open and Distance Learning, 4*(2).

Baggio, B., & Beldarrain, Y. (2008). Implications of anonymity in cyber education. In R.Z. Zheng & S.P. Ferris (Eds.), *Understanding online instructional modeling: Theories and practices.* New York: Information Science Reference.

Chester, A., & Gwynne, G. (1998). Online teaching: Encouraging collaboration through anonymity. *Journal of Computer Mediated Communications, 4*(2), 1–10.

Conrad, D. (2008). Reflecting on strategies for a new learning culture: Can we do it? *Journal of Distance Education, 22*(3), 157–162.

Donath, J. (1998). Identity and deception in the virtual community. In P. Kollack & M. Smith (Eds.), *Communities in cyberspace.* London, Routledge.

Foster, D. (1996). Community and identity in the electronic village (pp. 23–37). *Internet culture.* New York: Routledge.

Goffman, E. (1959). *The presentation of self in everyday life.* New York: Anchor/Doubleday.

Huang, H. (2002). Toward constructivism for adult learners in online learning environments. *British Journal of Educational Technologies, 33*(1), 27–37.

Jackson, D. (Ed.) (1968b). *Therapy, communication, and change: 2.* Palo Alto: Science and Behavior Books, Inc.

Lance, G.D. (2002). Distance learning and disability: A view from the instructor's side of the virtual lectern. *ITD Journal.*

Lewis, C., & Fabos, B. (2005). Instant messaging, illiteracies, and social identities. *Reading Research Quarterly, 40*(4), 470–501.

Meng, M. (2005). IT design for sustaining virtual communities and identity based approach. Dissertation submitted to the Faculty of the Graduate School of the University of Maryland, College Park.

Penz, E. (2007). Paradoxical effects of the internet from a consumer behavior perspective. *Emerald Business, 3*(4), 364–380.

Rheingold, H. (1993). *The virtual community: Homesteading on the electronic frontier.* Reading, MA: Addison Wesley.

Riva, G., & Galimberti, C. (1998). Computer-mediated communication: Identity and social interaction in an electronic environment. *Genetic, Social and General Psychology Monographs, 124,* 434–464.

Siddiquee, A., & Kagen, C. (2006). The internet, empowerment, and identity: An exploration of participation by refugee women in a community internet project (CIP) in the United Kingdom. *Journal of Community & Applied Social Psychology, 16*(3), 189–206.

Sutton, L.A. (2000, April). Vicarious interactions: A learning theory for computer mediated communications. Presented at the Annual Meeting of the American Educational Research Association, New Orleans, Louisiana.

Vonderwell, S., Liang, X., & Alderman, K. (2007, spring). Asynchronous discussions and assessment in online learning. *Journal of Research on Technology in Education, 39*(3), 309–328. Retrieved June 1, 2009, from Academic Search Premier database.

Vygotsky, F. (1962). Thought and language (E. Hanfmann & G. Vakar, Trans.). Cambridge, MA: MIT Press. (Original work published 1934)

Yee, N., & Bailenson, J. (2007). The Proteus effect: The effect of transformed self-representation on behavior. *Human Communications Research, 33*, 271–290.

Marc Weinstein

Marc Weinstein, Ph.D. (MIT, 1997), is associate professor of human resource development at Florida International University. Marc's research explores the diffusion of organizational innovations in knowledge management, human performance, and occupational safety and health. He has published numerous chapters in books, and his research has appeared in a broad range of peer-reviewed journals, including *International Journal of Human Resource Management, Journal of Management Research, International Journal of Occupational Environmental Health,* and *The Journal of Construction and Engineering Management.* Marc has also been engaged in a number of research-to-practice initiatives sponsored by the National Institute for Occupational Safety and Health and has consulted with numerous organizations, including ABB, Siemens, Lucent Technologies, and the U.S. Department of Labor. He has been a Fulbright scholar and has had previous appointments at Case Western Reserve University and the University of Oregon.

Tonette Rocco

Tonette S. Rocco, Ph.D., is an associate professor at Florida International University in the Adult Education and Human Resource Development Program. She is a Houle Scholar and a 2008 Kauffman Entrepreneurship Professor. Tonette's recent books, *Challenging the Parameters of Adult Education: John Ohliger and the Quest for Social Democracy* (with Andre Grace, Jossey-Bass, 2009; winner of the 2009 University Continuing Education Association Frandson Book Award), *The Handbook of Scholarly Writing and Publishing* (with Tim Hatcher, Jossey-Bass, in press), and a special issue, Sexual Minority Issues in HRD: Raising Awareness (with Julie Gedro and Martin Kormanik), in *Advances in Developing Human Resources.*

She has over 160 publications in journals, books, and proceedings and won the Elwood F. Holton, III Research Excellence Award in 2008 for the article Towards the Employability-Link Model: Current Employment Transition to Future Employment Perspectives, published in *Human Resource Development Review* with Jo Thijssen and Beatrice Van der Heijden.

She is co-editor of *New Horizons in Adult Education and Human Resource Development,* assistant editor of *Human Resource Development Quarterly,* and qualitative methods editor for *Human Resource Development International.* Editorial board memberships include the *Journal of Mixed Methods Research, Adult Education Quarterly, Journal of European and Industrial Training,* and *International Journal of Mixed Methods in Applied Business and Policy Research.* She serves on the American Society for Training and Development Certification Institute board of directors.

Maria Plakhotnik

Maria S. Plakhotnik, Ed.D., is a doctoral candidate in the adult education and human resource development program at Florida International University, USA. Maria received her bachelor's in elementary education in St. Petersburg, Russia, and two master's degrees in TESOL and educational psychology from the University of Northern Iowa. Maria has presented at several international, national, and local conferences and authored and co-authored publications that have appeared in the *Human Resource Development Quarterly, Human Resource Development Review, Adult Education Quarterly, New Horizons in Adult Education and Human Resource Development, New Directions in Adult and Continuing Education,* and *Race, Gender, & Class.* From 2005 through 2009, Maria served as the managing editor of the online peer-reviewed journal, *New Horizons in Adult Education and Human Resource Development.* In 2010, she was awarded Dissertation Year Fellowship at Florida International University.

THE TRANSFORMATION OF THE INFORMATION ECOSYSTEM:

NEW ROLES FOR HUMAN RESOURCE DEVELOPMENT PROFESSIONALS

Marc Weinstein
Tonette Rocco
Maria Plakhotnik

Empowered individuals represent something of a challenge for organizations that were previously able to exert control through the management of information. Advances in Internet and communication technologies have transformed our information ecosystem. Whereas the environment was once characterized by information scarcity, expert-led knowledge creation, and technical limits to networked communication, our new information ecosystem is defined by information munificence, user-created content, and access to open information networks across time and space. How should human resource development (HRD) professionals respond to the new information ecosystem? Can they do better than get out of the way? Authors Rocco, Weinstein, and Plakhotnik thoughtfully consider new opportunities for HRD professionals to foster individual and organizational learning. In this new information ecosystem, HRD professionals have a central role in creation and support of the social and technical organizational infrastructure. The role promotes both formal and informal learning occurring continuously in learning networks that transverse professional, organizational, and national boundaries.

These are exciting and anxious times for professionals who collectively support, create, and deliver training and development in organizations. The pace of innovation in Internet and communications technology is breathtaking, and evidence suggests that the pace of technological innovation is accelerating (Kurzweil, 2005). This has created new options and challenges for training and learning in organizations. Professionals in this field experience this universe of possibilities as a continuous and sometimes bumpy transition to new expectations and new platforms. Even the best among them sometimes confess to certain bewilderment and weariness, a state of eMentia that can sap the desire to learn new technology (Isrealite, 2009). Fortunately, most professionals recover and soon embrace opportunities to incorporate new capabilities that these technologies make possible.

Some, like Jay Cross (2006), believe the most recent developments in Web 2.0 technologies and the advent of the read/write web herald a new era in training and development in organizations when "courses are dead" (p. 39). He argues that "courses are almost always separate from work and that goes against the trend of integrating learning and work" (p. 39). For Cross, the future of learning in organizations for knowledge workers will be through the support of "free-range" informal learning and the development of learning networks. However, free-range learning can be time-consuming and difficult to monitor, and the potential exists to learn "bad" information. Cross (2010) himself more recently concedes on a blog "Optimal learning is a balancing act, not an either/or," prompting a response from another blogger who made the case that a course is sometimes the best place to start when trying to learn about a topic quickly.

While it may be premature to declare the "course is dead," there is little doubt that the advances in Internet and communication technologies have dramatically transformed our information ecosystem (Weinstein, Rocco, & Plakhotnik, in press). In this chapter, we describe this transformation and the possibilities for human resource development (HRD) professionals to further support effective informal learning in organizations. In many instances, the opportunities we identify have long been embraced by companies that recognize the importance of learning and the central role knowledge workers have in contributing to innovation and competitiveness (Davenport, 2005; Stewart, 2001). What is new is the extent to which new knowledge networks can be fostered in this new information ecosystem.

THE TRANSFORMATION OF OUR INFORMATION ECOSYSTEM

Most accounts of the impact of exponential growth in technology begin with some account of Moore's law that anticipates doubling of the number of transistors on a computer chip and the halving of its price every eighteen months. The resiliency of Moore's law over the last fifty years has been an important precondition for advances in educational technology. Modern personal computers have the power of mainframe computers of yesteryear, and miniaturization has enabled the creation of new mobile platforms. Importantly, the exponential growth underpinning Moore's law is not unique to computational power. Rather, exponential growth is an attribute of most technologies; many complementary technologies are currently displaying evidence of exponential growth, including storage capacity, data compression, and display technologies (Kurzweil, 2005).

The law of exponential growth of technological innovation has provided a rough future roadmap for the development of known technologies, allowing us to reasonably anticipate the decreased cost and increased capacity of microprocessors, storage, display, and many other technologies. This has given training and development professionals some guidance about future hardware and software capabilities. However, the law of exponential growth provides less insight about the emergence of the read/write web made possible with Web 2.0 tools. And no technology roadmap could provide a sense of the social dimensions of computing, the desire for individuals to share, interact, and create new content. Even less easily anticipated is the improbable development of user-created content and software tools that rival and exceed products resulting from expert-driven for-profit initiatives.

This ability and desire to access and create information are the drivers of this transformation. Search technology has created the market for information. This, in turn, has spawned a number of private for-profit ventures in providing cost-free access to digitization of our intellectual heritage. An enduring innate desire of humans to share and acquire knowledge has further led to the creation of valuable user-created content, enabled by innovations in software and the rise of blogs, wikis, and other collaborative platforms. Rather than using technology to isolate ourselves, we are using technology to connect and learn from each other. We enjoy searching, sharing, and learning so much that entire business models have been developed around our eagerness to share information and to learn from and about others. While we can always fret that the most frequently used Google search terms reflect our prurient interests and fascination with celebrity, we should also be awed by the desire of so many people and institutions not only to put the information of the world online, but also the alacrity with which they generate and share new knowledge in our newly connected world.

From an environment of relative information scarcity, we now have information munificence. From a period of near reliance on experts, we now have access both to experts and to a large corpus of user-created content. This transformation cannot but have a profound impact on how people learn, what students and workers expect from learning, and the relationship of technology to both. Table 1 compares the traditional information ecosystem to the emergent one discussed here. Until recently, knowledge creation was typically the domain of experts. Access to information was frequently restricted and protected by copyright. Experts and specialists provided quality control and, since most information was in print, error correction was only intermittent, if it occurred at all. The absolute amount of information available to those who had access could be measured in gigabytes and the location of this information was in physical libraries or on isolated information systems. By contrast, our emergent information ecosystem is characterized by both expert- and user-created content. Access to information is open and often governed by Creative Commons (Lessig, 2001) licensing that provided guidelines on how information

could be shared and socially developed. Communication among experts and non-users is networked, error correction is continuous, and xenabytes of information travel the speed of light across networks.

	Traditional	Emergent
Access to information	Restricted	Open
Creators of information	Expert	User created
Intellectual rights	Copyright	Creative Commons
Communication	Uni- or bi-directional	Networked
Quality control	Expert	Crowd
Error correction	Intermittent	Continuous
Quantity	Gigabyte	Xenabyte
Housing of content	Local computer	Cloud

Table 1. Attributes of Traditional and Emergent Information Ecosystem

NEW CONTENT FOR LEARNING

In *The World Is Open*, Bonk (2009) provides a breathless compendium of content available on the World Wide Web. The dynamic nature of the Internet and the nature of user-created content assure that no traditional print publication can keep the pace by which new content is being created. Open access reference and instructional materials are created by experts, such as university professors, scientists, or researchers, and non-experts, anyone interested in submitting a contribution. Table 2 provides a sampling and a snapshot of open source material, available free of cost. In this section, we briefly describe examples of expert- and user-created reference and instructional material.

Stanford Encyclopedia of Philosophy is an example of an open-access expert-led online reference source. The editorial committee of the *Encyclopedia* selects and invites experts in different fields to submit contributions. Subsequently, these contributions are peer reviewed in a process similar to manuscripts submitted to academic journals. A similar website includes *Interdisciplinary Documentation on Religion and Science* that provides a variety of materials whose purpose is to generate a dialogue among researchers, pastors, university professors, and others interested in the connections among religion, philosophy, and science. The website is maintained by several university professors from the Pontifical University of the Holy Cross, Italy, and supported by a Council formed by several experts in the fields of theology, philosophy, and science. *The International Review of Research on Open and Distance Learning* is an open-access peer-reviewed journal related to advances in e-learning.

Wikipedia and its Spanish language sister *Enciclopedia Libre* and Russian language sister *WikiZnanie* are examples of open-access online reference sources that are created by non-experts from all around the world. Any user can register to submit his or her entries and edit other people's entries. Another non-expert created site, *Everything2*, also welcomes submissions from volunteers; however, the submitted entries may be modified or even

removed only by the website editors if the entries have poor quality or contain offensive language. *Managementhelp.org* provides various materials on over 650 topics related to all aspects of management of for-profit and non-profit organizations. The website is managed by Authenticity Consulting, LLC. But all users can contribute. *The NewPR Wiki* represents a collection of information for PR professionals, a tool for collaboration, and networking for PR professionals. Similar resources for marketing professionals are provided on *Marketing.wikia.com.*

Examples of expert-led courses are also available. *MIT OpenCourseWare* is a project of the Massachusetts Institute of Technology that provides educational materials from its undergraduate and graduate courses online. Similar initiatives include *Open Yale Courses* by Yale University and *UC College Prep* by the University of California. Other open-access instructional materials created by experts are not affiliated with one particular university. *VideoLectures.net* represents an online bank of video lectures, workshops, or seminars created by scholars and experts in different fields from different universities. These experts are invited and their videos are screened by the editorial board of the website. *Elearnmag.org* welcomes submissions, such as research articles, best practices, how-to essays, or case studies, related to all aspects of e-learning, including instructional design, online instruction, and corporate training.

As is the case with reference material, expert-generated content is now complemented with user-created courses. *YouTube, TeacherTube,* and *Edublogs.tv* provide opportunities for non-experts to share their instructional materials on a variety of topics with others.

CoolMath.com, maintained by math enthusiasts, provides educational materials to help people of all ages understand mathematics, algebra, and geometry. Salman Khan, an independent educational evangelist, has created over a thousand educational videos available at *khanacademy.com* that cover material ranging from basic arithmetic to advanced topics in physics, engineering, and biology. The popularity of this site attests to the appetite of individuals for informal learning.

Individuals in organizations are not limited to open source, free content. Many professional associations to which employees belong or can join for a fee host portals that allow access to copyrighted material. Additionally, there are numerous wikis and blogs that individuals can access and contribute to. Of course, these supplement traditional proprietary databases that are pressed to demonstrate their value added when faced with competition from open-source material. For quick queries in natural English, Wolfram Research has created the freely available wolframalpha.com that allows users to pose questions on a range of topics. In the next decade, we can anticipate dramatic advances in natural language databases, as demonstrated by IBM's supercomputer Watson that is posed to compete against the best human players in "Jeopardy" (Thompson, 2010). Table 2 shows a list of these and other sites. This is an exciting time for informal learning; the question is how companies can best tap into these important advances as they support informal learning in organizations.

	Reference Material	Instructional Material
Expert-led	• Stanford Encyclopedia of Philosophy • Google Books • Directory of Open Access Journals • Open G-Gate • HINARI • RePEc • SciELO • Interdisciplinary Documentation on Religion and Science • Encyclopedia of Life • h2g2	• MIT OpenCourseWare • Open Yale courses • UC College Prep • Academic Earth • Connexions • FreeVideoLectures.com • VideoLectures.Net • Udemy • ScienceStage.com • ITunesU • ResearchChannel • Stanford Entrepreneurship Corner • Intel® Teach Elements
User-created	• Wikipedia • Infoed • Metaverse • Enciclopedia Libre • Hudong • Baidu Baike • WikiZnanie • Everything2 • Elearnmag.org • The NewPR Wiki • Marketing.wikia.com • Parcepsocialmedia.wikispaces.com • Learning_Organizations_Wiki	• Khan Academy • Miscellaneous YouTube videos • Wikiversity • TeacherTube • Paul's Online Math Notes • Edublogs.tv • Edutopia • CoolMath.com • Theprpractitioner.com • Publicrelationsblogger.com • Leadership-skills-training-develop.blogspot.com

Table 2. Examples of Open-Access Learning-Relevant Content

NEW ROLES FOR HRD PROFESSIONALS IN THE NEW INFORMATION ECOLOGY

For a number of years, leading academics and practitioners have noted the central role of HRD in contributing to innovation and competitive advantage in organizations. In this view, the task of the HRD professional is to "provide learning and career development activities, performance improvement and management initiatives, organization development interventions, and insights through which organizational effectiveness is enhanced" (Gilley, Eggland, & Gilley, 2002, p. 2). In addition to needs assessment and the design and delivery of training, HRD professionals are engaged in a wide range of initiatives to promote informal learning through crafting mentorships and other on-the-job learning activities. Organizations that understand the important role of informal learning in organizations have already begun to allow and encourage employees to use the World Wide Web to learn and to build learning networks.

In Table 3 we map some of the roles and responsibilities of HRD professionals in promoting learning among knowledge workers in the transformed information ecosystem. In some areas these roles vary depending on whether the learners are new or experienced employees (Mosher, 2009). New employees are likely to be the key beneficiaries of traditional courses. For these employees, informal learning can be haphazard and at times inefficient. Experienced employees not only have a clearer idea of the information they need, but are also more likely to be able to tap into networks of experts both inside and outside the company. A second dimension we distinguish is between knowledge that everyone in the organization needs to know and the specific needs of individual employees.

The role that is most familiar to many HRD professionals is related to the shared learning needs of the employees in the organization. Where the needs are specific to the organization, HRD professionals will blend the best of traditional and distant learning in formulating training solutions. Additionally, these professionals will continue to assess critically the quality of off-the-shelf solutions and determine whether purchasing new products or developing them in-house is the best option. In either case, we are likely to see a continued devolvement of responsibility for technical mastery in the implementation and use of learning management systems (LMS). Although the initial installation of an LMS may be the responsibility of the technical specialist, the management of the system has and will continue to devolve to learning professionals. Also important here will be the support HRD professionals provide to subject-matter experts as they develop courses for both new and experienced employees.

New opportunities for HRD professionals exist in addressing individual learning needs in the transformed information ecosystem. At the strategic level, HRD professionals should be engaged in corporate policies that create an environment in which individuals are empowered to take control of their personal learning needs. On a technical level, corporate firewalls and filters may need to be altered. On a policy level, some accommodation will have to be made between the need for operational efficiency and the need for individuals to learn on a just-in-time basis. HRD professionals can consult with experienced employees and subject-matter experts regarding the value of providing financial support to employees who can benefit from access to content only available from member-only content portals. They should provide input as well into decisions for company support for individual and group subscriptions to copyrighted material.

they have learned with other workers. The main point here is that HRD professionals can enhance self-directed employees' navigation of the information ecosystem in a variety of ways not delivered as courses. These roles are outlined in Table 3.

	New Employees	Experienced Employees
Shared learning needs	Master of learning management system Instructional design support for SMEs Strategic consultation on outsourced solutions Partner in corporate compliance	
		Consultant on the development and purchase of courses for expert learners
Individual learning needs	Master of collaborative tools Net librarian Master masher Architect of learning landscapes	

Table 3. The Role of HRD Professionals in the Transformed Information Ecosystem

In addition to the facilitation of traditional mentoring relationships, learning professionals must foster norms that promote learning networks that include both novice and experts in the organization and those individuals outside the organization. Finally, in collaboration with subject-matter experts, learning professionals will play the role of net librarians and master mashers, as they facilitate both novice and expert navigation of the rich content available on the World Wide Web. e-Learning professionals can capture new learning and assist the organization with knowledge creation by maintaining blogs, wikis, and using other resources to capture and share what

CONCLUSION Although self-directed, informal learning has always occurred at work, the transformation of our information ecosystem has opened up new possibilities. As new employees enter the workforce, they will be acculturated to information grazing and learning. Experienced employees recognize that they are the masters of their own learning needs, and they are likely to be the best ones to know how and where to access new information. Courses will remain an important part of employee training and development, but formal courses are likely to ebb as individuals seek to learn on a just-in-time basis. HRD professionals have an important role in supporting this transition and can proactively contribute to and support company policies that encourage the development of an environment in which continuous access, development, and distribution of new information are the norm. One challenge will be how to measure the value of informal learning in organizations, but this is unlikely to deter the most ambitious companies as they seek new ways to support individual learning in their organizations.

REFERENCES

Bonk, C. (2009). *The world is open: How web technology is revolutionizing education.* San Francisco: Jossey-Bass.

Cross, J. (2006). *Informal learning: Rediscovering the natural pathways that inspire innovation and performance.* San Francisco: Pfeiffer.

Cross, J. (2010). Response to *"Learning networking, PHP, and SQL".* Blog message posted May 25, 2010, on http://alearning.wordpress.com/2010/05/24/learning-networking-php-and-sql/

Davenport, T. (2005). *Think for a living: How to get better performance and results from knowledge workers.* Cambridge, MA: Harvard Business School Press.

Gilley, J., Eggland, S.A., & Gilley, A.M. (2002). *Principles of human resource development* (2nd ed.). Cambridge, MA: Perseus.

Israelite, L. (2009). Age-related e-mentia. In M. Allen (Ed.), *Michael Allen's 2009 e-learning annual* (pp. 1–10). San Francisco: Pfeiffer.

Kurzweil, R. (2005). *The singularity is near: When humans transcend biology.* New York: Viking.

Lessig, L. (2001). *The future of ideas: The fate of the commons in a connected world.* New York: Random House.

Mosher, B. (2009). *Performance support: Delivering on the real JIT promise.* In M. Allen (Ed.), *Michael Allen's 2009 e-learning annual* (pp. 101–110). San Francisco: Pfeiffer.

Stewart, T. (2001). *The wealth of knowledge: Intellectual capital in the twenty-first century organization.* New York: Currency.

Thompson, C. (2010, June 14). What is IBM's Watson. *The New York Times.* Retrieved June 17, 2010, from www.nytimes.com/2010/06/20/magazine/20Computer-t.html?src=me&ref=homepage\

Weinstein, M., Rocco, T.S., & Plakhotnik, M.S. (in press). Web 2.0 and the actualization of the ideals of adult education. In V.C.X. Wang (Ed.), *Encyclopedia of information communication technologies and adult education.* Hershey, PA: IGI Global.

Corinne Miller

Corinne Miller, MS, is founder and principal consultant at Innovating Results! where she consults, trains, and coaches on virtual communication, managing a virtual workforce, virtual teaming, and applying innovation practices to everyday problem solving.

By leveraging a 25+ year career in leadership positions at companies such as Motorola, Rockwell International, Northrop, and TRW—across engineering, learning and development, business operations, and innovation platforms—she delivers an unparalleled service to both large and mid-size corporations.

As an early adopter of telecommuting and virtual teaming, Corinne has over 20 years of experience in virtually managing both domestic and global organizations in a variety of functions.

Always the innovator, Corinne was instrumental in creating and delivering a number of high-tech products throughout her engineering career. She also broke new ground applying innovation to business operations and learning and development as the director of Motorola University.

Corinne holds a BS, mathematics and computer science from the University of Illinois and an MS, communication, from Northwestern University. Her publications can be found at innovatingresults.com and managingvirtualworkforce.com.

E-LEARNING INNOVATION: | Corinne Miller
USING PAST E-LESSONS TO SHAPE
THE FUTURE OF LEARNING

We're at an interesting juncture in the e-learning field today, pinned between practices born out of an environment very different from today's and the needs of a very different tomorrow. Author Corinne Miller draws on her considerable experience in deploying strategic corporate training solutions to ponder what e-learning innovations will deliver on tomorrow's needs. By examining the past four decades of e-learning innovations, Corinne garners three specific "e-drivers" and twelve "e-lessons" that can be applied starting today to prepare for the learning innovations we will need in order to succeed tomorrow. Will we have 20/20 e-vision? And who is "we"? She cautions, "Don't leave it to the e-learning companies alone. It will take innovative 21st century collaboration among the consumers of learning, the producers of learning, and thought leaders in research."

WHY? Why did *they* innovate the e-learning tools and practices used today? How can we take those "e-lessons" and use them to create the future of e-learning . . . or perhaps I should just say learning? We need some provocative discussion around the future of learning, and through the lens of innovation, I'd like to jump-start that here. The "we" I refer to includes senior executives of the e-learning ecosystem. That means businesses that consume e-learning (talent executives), businesses that produce e-learning solutions, and research entities that focus on better ways to educate through the use of technology. Will we have 20/20 e-vision?

Join me now on a brief journey to understand how innovation happens, because there are indeed patterns, regardless of industry; then we will take what we learn to look back at the history of e-learning innovation to identify the specific conditions that drove disruptive e-learning innovations. With those e-drivers in hand, as well as some e-lessons learned along the way, I'll suggest actions that can be taken today to best position us for the future, and I'll take a stab at what that future might look like.

AN E-LEARNING INNOVATION LENS The term Web 2.0 is widely used, but if you were to ask twenty people what it means, you might hear twenty different answers. Same with e-learning. Same with innovation. For purposes of this article, I will use the term e-learning, a word that entered the language in 1997, as the overarching term for all computer-enabled learning, regardless of whether delivered on a mainframe, a PC, or a mobile device. When using the term innovation, I'll draw from the definitions that Harvard professor Clayton Christensen (1997, 2003, 2008) used in his books *Innovator's Dilemma, Innovation's Solution,* and *Disrupting Class,* as well as my more than thirty years of professional experience in innovation, technology, communication, quality, management, and learning and development.

Innovation is the process by which new or novel ideas are put into practice to bring customer value. Innovations can be products, services, or methods such as business models (think Dell) or market approaches (think Nokia in India). It's really that simple.

Innovation and invention are frequently confused. *Invention* is a new or novel idea that has not been put into practice to bring customer value. The U.S. Patent Office knows all too well how many millions of inventions they have patented that consumers never see! Customer value is defined from the corporation's perspective: cheaper, faster, better ways to get the job done. We'll assume the job brings shareholder, customer, and owner value.

When we think *innovation*, we of think of revolutionary innovation—the "big bang" stuff, a new or novel approach that does not disrupt a market. Automobiles, telephones, and television are examples of innovations that started as revolutionary. They were at a luxury price point, only becoming disruptive when their costs came down. When adopted into practice by the middle class, automobiles then disrupted horse-drawn carriages. Telephones then disrupted telegraphs. Television then disrupted radio. Sound e-familiar?

Revolutionary innovations have relatively minor initial impact on changing how a large mass of people work, live, or play, but disruptive innovations do. *Disruptive innovation* is an innovation that, due to affordability, attracts non-consumers or certain lower-need customers of an existing market because the product , service, or method is viewed as

good enough, despite possibly being of less quality or performance than what the one that is disrupted. Think of digital photography. At first, cheap digital cameras produced images that were not nearly as good as those produced by film, but good enough for certain consumers. Did you buy one? Eventually, a whole new business ecosystem grew around digital photography, including online ordering, electronic albums, photo editors, and even digital video.

Christensen has identified the basic pattern and some of the pitfalls that companies fall into when they fail to recognize and appropriately leverage a disruptive innovation. Again thinking of the photography industry, where's Polaroid? Buy any film lately? What disruptive e-learning innovations come to mind? Take Christensen's concepts to the e-learning ecosystem level, that is, the businesses that utilize e-learning for their talent, the e-learning companies that produce professional e-learning solutions, the companies that provide web-based collaboration solutions, meeting or training platforms, and universities who research technology-enabled learning. At this time, when technology is taking yet another leap with Web 2.0, technology-enabled student-centric learning is a focus at universities, a new generation of workers who learn collaboratively is upon us, and business is speeding up. If we don't take a step back and take an aerial, ecosystem-level view, we might fall prey to the pitfalls of disruptive innovation. Then everyone will suffer—most importantly, the workers we need to keep America globally competitive.

So let's take a look back at e-learning's innovation history from two angles—professionally delivered e-learning solutions and authoring tools. What was revolutionary? What was disruptive? What were the e-drivers of the disruptive innovation? and What e-lessons we can take away?

To jump-start us, e-lesson 0: forget what your teachers said—write in this book! As you read below, circle what you disagree with, check what you agree with, write examples of innovations I missed, note questions you have, and annotate where more information is needed. At the end, I'll let you know how we can collaborate. Let's start the discussion now!

THE INNOVATION OF E-LEARNING: THREE E-DRIVERS

Like many innovations of the past, e-learning started out as an invention when it was created in universities as early as the late 1950s. It became disruptive in the university setting when it was used for distance learning, but it remained a revolutionary innovation in corporations until it became disruptive. I suggest the three primary drivers for that disruption were the *speed at which new knowledge and skills were needed* to get the job done, the average workers' *access* to the e-learning platform, and the corporation's view of the *cost/benefit* of the e-learning. These three drivers determined whether the e-learning solution had customer value, that is, Was it cheaper/faster/better? Do you remember when these three drivers came together for the perfect storm? It was when the average worker had a PC—thirty years after the invention that ran on mainframe computers. It's hard to remember a time when the speed of technology was that slow. Do you think that will happen again anytime soon?

The three drivers came together periodically throughout e-learning innovation history, sometimes one more gusty than the others. Some originated from the learning industry and some did not. Recalling the e-lessons from these times can help us understand where we are today in the next innovation cycle.

1960 to Mid-1970s

➢ e-Learning was a revolutionary innovation.
➢ e-Learning was rarely used in the corporate world.
➢ Authoring tools were a revolutionary innovation.
➢ Formal and informal training were on the job.

While universities were exploring the use of computers for education as early as the late 1950s with tools such as PLATO, neither e-learning nor the PLATO development language took major hold in corporations during the pre-1970 period.

The nature of work during this time was industrial and highly procedural because products were concrete. Products had multi-year cycles, which made for a much slower pace than we know today with multi-month cycles. Companies sought greater efficiency by bringing varying portions of the supply chain together under a centralized pyramidal management structure, which made for simple and obvious business ecosystems. This meant workers could mainly rely on known local resources to get the job done. Work processes were slow to change and workers spent most of their careers at the same company, so institutional knowledge was readily available.

The knowledge and skills needed to do the job didn't change often. Workers learned from each other via on-the-job training.

Face-to-face interaction was the "training platform." In the rare cases when technical professionals had access to mainframe computers as part of the job or were provided access for certifications and retraining, computers as well as a development language were used.

There was barely a breeze, let alone a perfect storm, for disruptive e-learning innovation during this period. None of the e-learning innovation drivers had much gust behind them. e-Learning was a revolutionary innovation, but not a disruptive one quite yet. Here are some e-learning innovation e-lessons that we can take away from this period.

> *e-Lesson 1:* An e-learning innovation for one population (universities) doesn't necessarily mean it's an innovation for another (corporations).

> *e-Lesson 2:* When a revolutionary e-learning innovation happens, initial uptake is by workers who use the enabling technology or are provided access to it as part of their jobs.

Mid-1970s to Mid-1980s

> e-Learning sustaining innovations.
> e-Learning uptake increases among knowledge workers.
> Classroom and most e-learning was off the job.

Due to a desire for more advanced products, coupled with technology advancements such as minicomputers and rudimentary personal computers, a continuing increase in technical jobs meant a shift to more and

more knowledge work. A drive for efficiency through automation (beyond manufacturing) was on the rise and so e-learning became a new target. Why? On-the-job training and classrooms used people resources, and they were expensive.

During this period, e-learning continued to incrementally improve along its original trajectory as a result of increased computing power, software, and the more sophisticated use of video. The term "authoring tool" is believed to have been originated in 1979. Still somewhat difficult to use, PLATO-based authoring tools were mostly employed by larger corporations whose savings due to the large number of trainees offset the cost of the authoring tools and the highly skilled staff necessary to use them.

> *e-Lesson 3:* Just like other aspects of a corporation's operations, as training costs increase, training is a target for cost savings. This drive for cost reduction provides fertile ground for a low-cost disruptive innovation to occur.

> *e-Lesson 4:* Sustaining e-learning innovations are largely enabled by incremental software and hardware technology advances.

Mid-1980s to Mid-1990s

> e-Learning disrupts classroom training when workers get access: PCs!
> Classroom and most e-learning was off the job.

Society's drive for a better life, coupled with the advancements in technology, continued to drive the increase of knowledge workers. Job complexity increased, and business eco-systems became more distributed. Jobs continued to become less procedural and more dynamic, requiring more creativity and more complex decision making. All of this led to an increase in the need for new knowledge and skills.

As workers gained access to PCs, e-learning moved from a rarely used, revolutionary innovation to a disruptive innovation, displacing classroom and the past film-based and slideshow training solutions. Using the mediums of the day, floppy disks and CDs, e-learning solutions could couple the quality of video and the learning power that interactive software provided. Workers were able to utilize the e-learning at a convenient time, starting a shift of power to the user.

During this period, easier-to-use authoring tools such as Course of Action that later became Authorware hit the market. Although easy to use, these tools were still costly, and they were mainly used in larger corporations that could realize a cost savings from their in-house implementation.

> *e-Lesson 5:* e-Learning innovation becomes disruptive when the average worker has access to the delivery platform.

Mid-1990s to Mid-2000s

> Web-based e-learning further disrupts classroom training and CD-based e-learning when workers gain access to the Internet.
> Power shifts toward the worker.
> Workers author and deliver their own e-learning.
> Workers use technology for informal learning.
> Some formal e-learning is on the job, but most is still off the job.

With the emergence of the Internet and thanks to Moore's Law, knowledge work increased again and became more complex. Business ecosystems became more distributed, and workers became more physically distributed. Did you ever try to write a job description, only to find that it was difficult to capture the dynamic nature of the job; and then within months it needed to change again?

The Internet was a huge business disruptor, forming a symbiotic relationship with the mass communication requirements to operate in a distributed business ecosystem. The speed of business increased dramatically, driving further complexity for the knowledge worker. Workers struggled with the speed required to acquire new knowledge and skills to do their jobs. Because of this, e-learning increased in popularity. Now with the Internet there was an ability to reach more workers faster and more cheaply. Workers' needs drove an increase in all types of e-learning, including more professionally generated solutions, creation of e-learning libraries for purchase, and more authoring tools.

Professional e-learning solutions appeared costly to some corporations, so they reserved these solutions for needs highly critical to business success, such as call center training and product training.

A way to meet the speed requirements for new knowledge and skills while keeping costs under wraps, instant access to the basic skill needs of the day drove the creation of canned e-learning libraries. While fast and easy to access, they appealed to the more procedural aspects of knowledge work such as commodity tools training. Later, they began to include more complex subjects such as creativity, leadership, and decision making, but because the e-learning courses were generic in nature and the workers' work so dynamic, many workers didn't feel they could make the leap to the context of their jobs. In time, such offerings were coupled with other learning media that brought more context.

A greater variety of authoring tools became available, some with more features than others, some targeted for more technical applications than others, and some more costly than others. This greater cost spread enabled more corporations to realize a return on investment, but still, with the need to have skilled in-house personnel to manage and operate the tools, there wasn't widespread adoption.

Until . . . PowerPoint—the e-learning authoring disruptive innovation. Yes, PowerPoint, a tool that came out of a different industry. Workers had access to it, it was an already sunk cost, it was cheap, workers knew how to use it; and with the need for speed of knowledge, you've got all three e-drivers. This was a volcanic disruption, especially when PowerPoint was married with a virtual meeting tool. Yes, the e-learning produced was rudimentary in the eyes of a learning professional, and in some cases poor, but it was found to be good enough by the worker. It took some time for the cost-conscious to realize that bad PowerPoint equaled bad e-learning. And bad e-learning that appeared cheap at the onset turned out to be very expensive in the end when learning objectives were not met. This pushed the demand for better e-learning.

With technology now accelerating the use of informal learning, the discussion of formal versus informal learning rose to the forefront. And with technologically generated informal learning came physical assets that could be captured, organized, and made available to others. Now learning professionals started thinking hard about what to do with all of this. Due to technology, formal e-learning and informal learning were starting to converge. The platforms on which workers worked and workers learned were starting to converge. It is like the 1960s all over again—working and learning on the same platform—just that the platform is a different one today. What can we learn from the past to shape the future?

➤ *e-Lesson 6:* Remember e-Lessons 3 and 5. Disruptive e-learning innovation is when cost is low, need is high, and workers have access. Further, and very importantly, the innovation can originate from any industry, that is,, PowerPoint and web meeting tools did not come from the training and development industry.

➤ *e-Lesson 7:* The worker is in control. With technology at their fingertips, they will do what it takes to get the job done via their own innovative mindset, combining and enhancing tools they already have available or can access quickly and inexpensively. Watch out for open-source products!

➤ *e-Lesson 8:* Sometimes when a new technology emerges, e-learning has to take a temporary step back before it can go forward. (For example, low bandwidth Internet inhibited rich video previously available on e-learning CDs.)

➤ *e-Lesson 9:* Humans have an insatiable need to move up the human value chain, leaving more and more to technology or less expensive means. We will always need specialists. But professional e-learning providers must move up the value chain as the workers gain more authoring and delivery power.

Today

➢ Workers use technology for most of their informal learning.

➢ Workers use technology for more of their formal learning.

➢ Workers author better e-learning through smarter tools and hybrid solutions.

➢ More power shifts to the worker.

Fast forward to today, when variance, change, and speed abound. The desire for advanced products, services, methods, and approaches—now coupled with technology advancements in computers, portable devices, and mobile devices—is accelerating knowledge work to warp speeds. Corporations now produce hard and soft products as well as services. Multi-year cycles are in the minority, and multi-month or even multi-day cycles dominate.

Workers can be anywhere in the world and have varying relationships to the company. They might be full-time, part-time, tele-working, exercising flex-hours, or working as full-time or part-time contractors or consultants. Workers are more transient than in the past due to a host of reasons, including companies' reduced commitment to the employee's personal fulfillment and job security. Because many corporations have sought to undo their tightly integrated enterprises due to the increased cost of specialization and the decreased cost of communication, others are introduced into the process of creating and delivering a product or service from potentially anywhere on the planet. Key suppliers, outsourcing partners, newly merged or acquired organizations, academic partners, customers or potential customers, standards or compliance bodies could be anywhere. Big, medium, or small business partners who may be partners in one relationship are competitors in another.

Because technology is ubiquitous and wireless Internet access is nearly everywhere, the tools to perform the job are no longer restricted to the physical workplace, and workers' locations and the times to perform the job are no longer restricted to 9 to 5.

This is a highly variant, fast-changing, complex environment in which almost every line is blurring. Add the recent economic conditions, and doing the job has reached greater heights of complexity than ever before. Getting the job done now requires making sense of a large volume of information that floods workers daily. Interactions not just across internal workers but across the global business ecosystem are sometimes required for even the most basic tasks.

With the speed of change, workers must constantly stay abreast with their subject matter, which is often melding and reforming across multiple fields. In such a distributed and interconnected business ecosystem, determining what information workers need and where to find it can be paralyzing. Deadlines continue to change. Workers are being asked to do more with less, but the reality is often less with less.

This environment is compelling businesses to scout for cheaper/faster/better solutions to survive. Again, workers are turning to technology to speed their acquisition of knowledge and skills. Why not? It's what they use to do their jobs. It's available and handy. It's easy to use. It's always connected.

Workers are also more demanding that training delivers results. Having had the taste of authoring their own e-learning, workers aren't willing to give up the power. What can they do? Hybrid solutions are emerging. This is where professionals provide tools with improved instructional design built in, templates, and training for workers to use or else workers create much of their own e-learning content and drop in complex components that are created by professionals.

As far as informal learning, many workers, especially Gen Xers and Gen Y/Millenials, continue to increase the use of technology for informal learning. They are using Web 2.0 tools outside of the corporate setting and want to use these tools for their jobs. However, the need for protecting corporate assets presents issues for some Web 2.0 tools. It's about protection, and ownership is the ultimate form of protection in this scenario. That's why wiki, blog, and collaboration software are attractive. Corporations can create their own behind their firewall, rather than use Open Source versions like Facebook. Some companies have been able to shift off the full ownership paradigm into the protection paradigm, finding ways to protect their assets and interests without full ownership through the savvy use of information technology methods and tools. A 2009 survey indicated a problem, however: 71 percent of IT departments have blocked social networking tools (ZdNet.com, TechRepublic). Clearly, there is still a strong resistance.

The problem is the distributed business ecosystem. It takes a village these days to design, develop, test and deliver a product or service. It takes a village to market it. It takes a village to sell it. It takes a village to service it. Wikis that those in the village with appropriate need can utilize via savvy IT access and protection mechanisms are in common practice today. Blogs haven't really gotten much traction because we're not quite sure where the productivity needle settles in that space.

The biggest hurdle is Facebook. Duplicating a Facebook-type mechanism is costly and fatalistic. And companies that try to "cram" it into their existing product lines may be falling into one of the pitfalls of disruptive innovation, what Christensen would call *cramming*. This is where a company seeks to sustain a current product line trajectory by integrating or force-fitting the new technology. When this happens, it generally drives the complexity and costs sky high. What collaboration tool does this remind you of?

Here's an example to get your juices flowing. Christensen cites the example of how Merrill Lynch failed at transitioning to online brokering and Charles Schwab succeeded. Schwab created a new business and eventually faded out the old broker-centric version. Merrill, on the other hand, tried to integrate online brokering into the existing broker-based business and its supporting systems. The way brokers earned their money just didn't fit. "An organization simply cannot disrupt itself" (Christensen, 2008, p. 102).

> ➤ *e-Lesson 10:* When workers become dissatisfied with the results of their e-learning authoring, they seek smarter authoring tools and only look to professionals to provide the complex components they cannot produce, at least with the technology they have

at the moment. It can all change tomorrow.

- ➤ *e-Lesson 11:* e-Learning products or services that cram overshoot the market.
- ➤ *e-Lesson 12:* Innovation requires adoption into practice. Corporations care deeply about protecting assets and branding. Any e-learning tools and methods thought to violate that protection will not be adopted.

TOMORROW: IT'S MELDING TIME

At the speed of business today, tomorrow is truly just a day away. 2020 will come quickly. Remember 2000? It doesn't seem that long ago. No one really knows what tomorrow will bring, but for the sake of further stimulating the discussion, I'll put forward a few of my ideas that were influenced by the technology and job predictions of some futurists. In many cases, I think what is old will become new again.

1. Work will become indistinguishable from learning, because informal and much of formal learning will use the same medium, technology, which is the same medium that workers use to get their work done. Consider what futurist Ray Kurzweil (2005) says, "Technology is evolving so quickly that in the near future humans and computers will, in effect, meld to create a hybrid biomechanical life form that will extend our capacities unimaginably."

2. People will still want physical spaces to come together, but it will be more dialectic in nature, like ancient Greece. We will still possess the human desire to physically connect and the need to remove ourselves from the day-to-day activities to reflect and build new knowledge, skills, and alliances.

3. The IT protection code will be cracked for the use of Open Source tools like Facebook, Twitter, and others to follow. Everyone in a company's business ecosystem is in Facebook. Like a constellation of stars in the sky, lines connect the stars. Workers are dots dynamically connected based on the company, the project, etc. Each constellation has certain IT privileges. As people move about from project to project, company to company, the dots reconnect and their IT privileges are adjusted accordingly. They use the features of Facebook, which get better and better to meet the needs. Wikis, blogs, documents, whatever the relevant assets, they are linked in as needed.

4. Professionals will continue to advance their value proposition in providing services and products that workers cannot do on their own in a timely or costly fashion. This will be especially true as traditional jobs, "regular activities performed in exchange for payment," disappear and their need for traditional e-learning solutions do too. Smart authoring tools will continue to advance. They'll allow the ability to mix and match and meld all the various learning options, sources, and connections into an integrative personal/student-centric learning environment. These tools will be disruptive, starting out simple and low cost. Over time they will hook workers, and this will create a demand to buy premium services and options. Think the best of Open Source with new spins on it we haven't thought of yet.

5. The corporate learning function will be re-invented because the lines between learning, communication, and work will approach homogenization, producing "hyper-jobs." Hyper-jobs help humans focus on and leverage their "aliveness." Since learning through use of your own learning style is an intrinsic motivator, I suggest that learning directly attribute to people's feeling of aliveness and this will propel productivity in and of itself. (The World Future Society [WFS] suggests hyper-jobs in aliveness will occur in the future.) Characteristics of hyper-jobs include discovery, creativity, implementation, influence, and physical action skills. These characteristics will be powered by basic mental skills, symbolic thinking, and responsibility.

Instead of "learning and development," we might have "learning and communication." Instead of a provider of training, the function will shift to expert enabler and connector. An enabler provides the environment by which the learner can have access to learn, such as the ability for user-generated content and social networking. A connector is skilled in the art of finding the knowledge and skills the worker needs. Similar to finding a needle in a haystack, considering the plethora of information available, the connector can quickly point learners to those solutions through a number of mechanisms.

Perhaps what is called a learning professional in 2010 might still be called one or, because of various melding factors, such people might be called quality or communication professionals. Or perhaps a term might arise for those who are assisting workers directly on a day-to-day basis. These professionals may be called professional work coaches or even professional concierges (similar to the Apple store concierge who learns what your needs are and then points you to the right Apple products and services). These professionals might be entirely embedded in the core business, having a skill set across learning, communication, and the specific business area, and be considered line workers. Some might be employees and some might be free agents as Daniel Pink (2001) describes in his book *Free Agent Nation*. These types of workers, free agents who work for themselves and travel between jobs in the business ecosystem, will be very valuable to understanding how learning enablers and connectors can improve business results. Those at the more strategic level might be continually collaborating with a diverse innovation-style team to find new and improved solutions.

Can you imagine it? No more discrete computers, just devices integrated as part of the job. Working is learning. Learning makes people feel alive. Productivity skyrockets from the pure intrinsic motivation of it all. Humans do what humans do best. Where are George and Judy Jetson?

A BRIDGE TO TOMORROW: WHAT CAN WE DO TODAY?

I hope you have written in this book. I bet you had a lot of insightful thoughts and deep questions. Perhaps you were making your own observations as well while you took our quick journey through the past.

Here are some of my observations:

Informal and Formal Learning. We started out with both face-to-face, people-to-people communication—the same method for both formal and informal learning—and it was on the job and no one differentiated between the two. Then they started to diverge as communication technologies came on the scene. Only after the communication technologies became such an integral part of the work did informal and formal learning largely converge into one again. Should it just be learning now? Are we inhibiting ourselves from moving into a new paradigm by using terms and mental models of the current paradigm?

e-Learning and Learning. We started out calling it learning. Then technology enabled new ways to learn so we called that e-learning (along with twenty-two other terms that evolved over time, including e-learning 2.0). Now that technology is so ubiquitous, is saying e-learning like saying motor car? Should we drop the "e" and the resist the urge for "m" and "t" and whatever. Should it just be learning now? Are we inhibiting ourselves from moving into a new paradigm by using terms and mental models of the current paradigm? What other terms are we using today that we should drop or change to help us think outside the current paradigm?

Workers Have and Want the Power. Three e-learning authoring tiers have emerged. I liken them to art (see Figure 1). The top-most tier is like a custom work of art. This would be custom professional e-learning for large populations of procedurally oriented jobs or complex applications that are critical to the success of the business. This is a blank canvas totally designed by specialists in the field.

The next tier is like a semi-custom work of art—the artist provided you a template and the worker painted it with his or her own colors. This would be worker-generated e-learning using smart authoring tools and/or including embedded custom objects provided by professionals. The tools guide the worker to include good e-learning design and practices, but the worker still has some control. If the e-learning is synchronous, the quality of this tier is highly dependent on the skill of the deliverer.

The lowest tier is also a blank canvas, but workers are on their own and the quality is highly dependent on personal, learning, design, and delivery skills. This is the worker, PowerPoint, and a web meeting/training tool.

Research Bodies Are Studying Technology-Enabled Learning to Meet Different Learning Styles. Using technology for student-centric learning research is continuing in universities, focused on enabling each student to learn using his or her own learning styles versus the one-size-fits-all approach of a traditional human teacher/student approach. Clayton Christensen (2008) forecasts that "80 percent of [university] courses taken in 2024 will have been taught online in a student-centric way" (p. 102).

There's So Much in the Bag of Tricks Now. Thirty years ago, there weren't many different technology-based learning

options to chose from. Today, there are so many that people are becoming increasingly confused about what to use when. Good news. This is a ripe condition for innovation in which approaches and tools can be mixed, matched, and melded.

Cracking the Code Versus Cramming.
Companies are cracking the IT protection code on informal learning/ collaboration tools such as Facebook. Many companies are using Twitter. Corporations are resisting high-priced collaboration tools.

Now, what actions might we take?

1. *Build an Alliance.* An industry alliance of business users and the talent thought-leaders from their companies, companies that provide e-learning solutions, and universities or research bodies with technology-based learning research should be formed to paint the strategy forward. It will take a special type of collaboration, because there won't be thirty years for technology in corporations to catch up like it did from the invention of e-learning in universities to the disruptive innovation in corporations spawned by PCs. It will take collaboration and the sharing of data and information for the better good. With some high-level direction, everyone will save time in moving America forward. Who should lead this alliance? Well, if the worker/user has the power, should the talent organization from a corporation step up? Should an e-learning solution provider lead? Keep in mind your suggestion for who should lead as you read on. (I don't think academia should lead because

academics are too far removed from the corporate applications, and their financial business model may cast intentions counter to corporations.)

2. *Forecast and Work Fast.* Because businesses aren't going to make major investments in tools exclusively for learning for the average worker, we have to forecast what technology will be adopted into everyday work and when, so that we can be ready with great new learning solutions when workers gain access to the platforms. We also need to keep our fingers on the pulse of what type of jobs and learner behaviors are evolving. This will take foresight, which, according to the World Future Society, is a specific skill that futurists use involving scanning, trend analysis, trend monitoring, trend projection, scenario deployment and analysis, and polling. We will need to hone our foresight skills because there won't be thirty years this time. Based on Moore's Law, the past rate of technology substitution, and futurists' technology predictions, how long do you think we will have?

3. *Help People Learn.* Let's help the new technology platforms be adopted. Let's help IT, legal, and management and wherever else misunderstandings, confusion, resistance, or a desire to explore exists, learn what they need to learn in order to move forward. This might take IT innovation, so let's enable the learning needed for those innovations to happen.

4. *Be Prepared to Blow Up the Current Paradigm.* Prepare mentally and financially. Those who paint the future strategy must have an intense openness to the probability of blowing up our current paradigms

and reinventing them. Remember what Christensen says: "An organization can't disrupt itself."

5. *Use Innovation.* We should be guided by innovation processes and methodologies to optimize our path forward. A great thinking tool might be a tree. Not the graphical kind, but the nature kind. Imagine a wall poster–sized tree with branches and leaves and writing all along it that describes the e-learning innovation journey from its invention to today, including pitfalls and e-lessons. Could the alliance, as described in number 1 above, draw the next-most upper portion of the tree? What would be in the sky?

WHAT DO YOU THINK? We've just taken a quick glimpse of the e-learning innovations of the past, suggested some actions we might take today, and presented some thoughts about what tomorrow might look like through the lens of innovation. I hope you have lots written in your book, because my purpose for writing this was to stimulate provocative discussion about what we can do today to shape the learning of tomorrow. And at the speed of business today, tomorrow truly is just a day away. Will we have 2020 e-vision? Join the discussion on Twitter using #futureofe (stands for "future of e-learning").

REFERENCES

Christensen, C. (1997). *The innovator's dilemma: When new technologies cause great firms to fail.* Cambridge, MA: Harvard Business School Press.

Christensen, C., & Horn, M. (2008). *Disrupting class: How disruptive innovation will change the way the world learns.* New York: McGraw-Hill.

Christensen, C., & Raynor, M.E. (2003). *The innovator's solution: Creating and sustaining successful growth.* Cambridge, MA: Harvard Business School Press.

Dignan, L., Diaz, S., & Steinert-Threlkeld, T. (2009, July 22). Survey: 71% of IT departments block users from social networking. *Between the Lines.* ZdNet.com,.

Kurzweil, R. (2005, November). The ideas interview. www.guardian.co.uk.

Moore, G. (2003, February). No exponential is forever: But "forever" can be delayed. *Solid-State Circuits Conference: Digest of technical papers.* New York: Institute of Electrical and Electronic Engineers.

Pink, D.H. (2001). *Free agent nation.* New York: Warner Business.

World Future Society (WFS). (2009). *Special report on jobs. Future careers: The high-potential jobs of tomorrow.* Bethesda, MD: WFS.

Phil Cowcill

Phil Cowcill started his multimedia development career in 1984 when chosen as a team member to develop Canada's first Level III Interactive Videodisc. He worked as a videographer, computer programmer, and graphic designer on the Goldcoin project.

In 1995, Canadore College hired Phil as the coordinator of the post-graduate Interactive Multimedia program. Students learned how to develop using Flash, Director, and Authorware. In 2004, Thomson publishing released Phil's first academic book, *Application Development with Dreamweaver MX Using ASP.NET.* Over the years, he has also developed and released a number of very successful training CD-ROMs. Two of the titles sold include the *Interactive Driver* and the *100 Authorware Tutorials.*

Phil actively builds online e-learning courses and learning activities for a variety of companies throughout the world and serves as an e-learning consultant. He is also a regular speaker at a number of multimedia, education, and e-learning conferences.

On top of coordinating the Interactive Multimedia program, he also coordinates the Advertising Creative Media and the Journalism Print and Broadcast programs at Canadore College. Phil enjoys the challenge of using technology effectively to meet the students' learning requirements.

E-LEARNING FOR THE NET GENERATION | Phil Cowcill

Generation Y, sometimes called the Net Generation, are arguably the most influential cohort in business today. Using technology, they have changed the world. This includes how business is conducted, how they consume media, and how they can best be educated. This article provides some background on the Net Generation and some insight into their world. After helping us get to know the Net Generation better, the author reviews several ways they prefer to learn. Phil believes that building e-learning courses that fit the learning style of the Net Generation will improve their retention and increase your chances of developing and implementing a successful course.

Generation Y is one of the most influential groups in today's society, most likely because they are one of the largest cohorts and also because of their rapid adoption and use of technology. This group, for the most part, has grown up with access to the Internet and is therefore also known as the Net Gen or "Digital Natives." Parents of Digital Natives are often seen as "Digital Immigrants." Net Gen parents did not grow up with computers, cell phones, PDAs, or the Internet. They more or less immigrated into the digital world.

As you will read later in this article, the Net Gen thinks, works, plays, and acts differently from previous generations. A lack of understanding of the Net Gen can lead to conflicts and general stereotypical classification. I hope to provide some helpful insights into the typical Net Gen person.

WHAT ARE THE GENERATIONS?

Specific years for generation characterizations vary among observers. It is possible that you may be considered a Gen X in one study and a Baby Boomer in another. The chart in Figure 1 indicates the generation definitions I have used for this chapter and the size of each group.

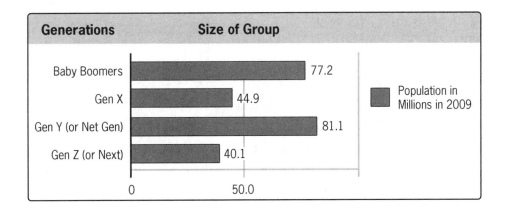

Figure 1. Generational Distribution

Generation	Birth Year	Age in 2011
Baby Boomers	1946–1964	47 to 65
Generation X	1965–1976	35 to 46
Generation Y (AKA: Net Gen)	1977–1997	14 to 34
Generation Z (AKA: Millennium or Gen Next)	1998–2018 (approximately)	0 to 13

Table 1. Breakdown of Generations by Year of Birth

Gen Y (or Net Gen) is currently the largest group. Table 1 shows the years of birth for each generation and what their ages will be by the end of 2011.

Demographers are discussing whether Gen Z or the Millennium Generation may be subdivided because of 9/11. The events on that tragic day have changed how we move and operate in our day-to-day lives. At the time of this writing, it is too soon to determine whether this group will be divided into pre- and post-9/11.

OVERVIEW OF THE NET GEN'S CHARACTERISTICS

One word of caution—the characteristics of Net Gen described here people are only a general overview of an entire generation. Not all people fit into categories. For example, the Net Gen person is typically comfortable with technology. However, some people in this generation are still intimidated by the technology and slow to adapt and use newer technology. This variation is often very evident in the classroom. So please keep in mind that these are general characteristics and often only a majority of the Net Gen would fall into one of these categories.

Try the following quiz to see how well you understand the Net Gen.

1. The Net Gen is not as smart as the previous generation. (True or False)
2. The Net Gen watches less TV than the previous generation. (True or False)
3. The Net Gen spends more time playing computer games than surfing the web. (True or False)
4. The Net Gen thinks differently than the previous generation. (True or False)
5. The Net Gen can truly multitask. (True or False)

OK, let's see how well you did.

1. *The Net Gen is not as smart as the previous generation.* This is **false**. The statistics for recording IQ levels have been on the rise by an average of 3 points per decade. Also, the College Board Advanced Placement exams have doubled in number of people taking and passing the exams. This indicates a rise in intelligence, as the exams have been in place for a long period of time (Viadero, 2002).

2. *The Net Gen watches less TV than the previous generation.* This is **true**. According to Nielsen's meters in 2008, they don't watch nearly as much TV. They tend to use the TV as background while searching online or texting others. However, they do watch TV at their convenience. This could be through the use of a digital video recorder (DVR, sometimes called a PVR) or through a network's website. Third-party sites such as Hulu.com provide access to recently run network shows shortly after they have premiered. Basically, prime time TV is replaced with "my time" TV.

3. *The Net Gen spends more time playing computer games than surfing the web.* This is **false**. By the time a person reaches the age of twenty, he or she would spend an average of 20,000 hours surfing the web and about 10,000 hours playing games. The games may be on the computer or a mobile device such as PSP, iPod, iPhone, Pocket PC, or a tablet, but they still spend more time surfing. For example, think about the number of hours spent watching videos from sites like YouTube or Blip.TV (Tapscott, 2008).

4. *The Net Gen thinks differently than the previous generation.* This is **true**. The Net Gen person actually has the ability to notice things more quickly than previous generations could. Net Gen-ers are able to skip from one thought to another faster than previous generations. It's as if their brains are "hyper-wired," which allows them to jump to other thoughts quickly (Twenge, Konrath, Foster, Campbell, & Bushman, 2008).

5. *The Net Gen can truly multitask.* This is **false**. Although many people may think the Net Gens are multitasking, they are actually "task swapping"—which they do faster than previous generations did. It is possible that the Net Gen person is working on homework with the TV playing music in the background and texting friends at the same time. However, only one task will occupy the person's full attention (Tapscott, 2008).

So how did you do? Most people don't get all the answers right. I hope that you will have a much better picture of this generation by the end of this article.

NET GEN CHARACTERISTICS

As you are aware, technology has changed our world and new applications are changing the way we live, learn, and play. Conflicts often arise when these new methods and ideals collide with more traditional methods of conducting business. To help provide some insights to how Net Gen responds, this section will cover some of their expectations about work and school based on their digital experience.

Characteristic 1: Customize.
When the Internet started gaining popularity in the early to mid-1990s, a majority of the sites were static. The content was stored in the web page and looked the same for all users. It couldn't be customized. Today, a majority of the sites are dynamic. Many allow users to

customize the site to their preference. So it is possible for two people to load the same page but see different content.

iGoogle is an example of a site that allows you to customize the content. Figure 2 shows an example of a way you can customize it. Figure 3 shows the same site with a different look.

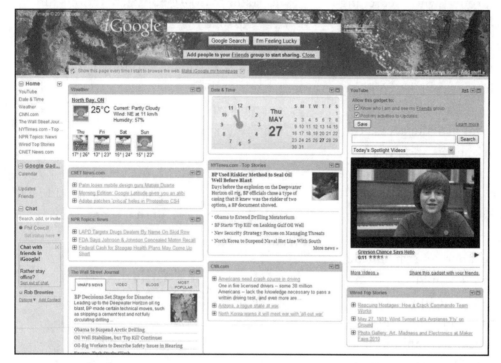

Figure 2. A Version of iGoogle

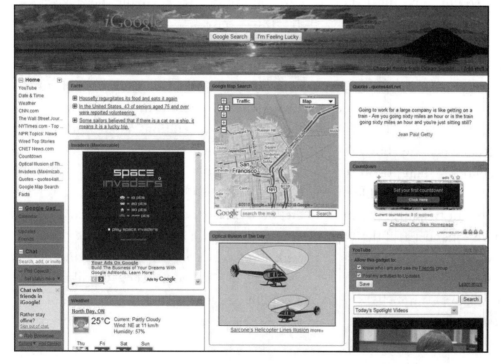

Figure 3. An Alternate Version of iGoogle

Characteristic 2: Information Push.

Over the Internet, people can either pull information down or receive information pushed to them. For example, when you visit Facebook and look at your friend's status, you are pulling information down. On the other hand, Facebook has an iPod app that allows you to receive status updates. These status updates can also be sent to your mobile phone. When the information comes to you without any action on your part, this is a push. The fact that many of these social network sites offer a push service indicates that the Net Generation often prefer select information to be pushed to them.

Push technology is not exclusive to mobile technology. Information can be pushed to a laptop or a desktop. An application like TweetDeck can run on a traditional computer. Updates from Twitter can then automatically appear in a small window as they arrive.

Characteristic 3: Integrity.

For the most part, the Net Generation insists on companies being honest and up-front. And for the most part, businesses operate with a sense of integrity that Net Gens can relate to and desire. If there is a perceived deception in a communication from a company, word will spread via a variety of social networks, which are far more powerful than any broadcast message. Net Gens will believe advice from a friend before they believe a message from a company. For example, Blockbuster started a new and exciting campaign in 2005 about no longer having any "late fees." Consumers didn't realize that seven days past the due date, the customer's credit card would be charged the purchase price of the item rented. If the product were brought back late, the consumer was then charged with a "restocking fee." While Blockbuster reported that only 4 percent of their customers were charged the restocking fee, it was a significant number of people in the eyes of the Net Gen. The outcry over the misleading communication led to a number of lawsuits. In the end, forty-seven states filed complaints against Blockbuster. Eventually, Blockbuster conceded and made several changes. They improved their in-store communications about their policy. They started printing the policy on the receipt and refunded the restocking fee. Blockbuster also had to refund the states that sued over $640,000 in court fees. In all, it's estimated that the misleading message cost Blockbuster over $1M. Since the backlash, Blockbuster has changed its policy and communicates more clearly about its fees (www.msnbc.msn.com/id/7327309).

Net Gen insistence on honesty applies to educational institutions as well. Potential students can look up information about schools on social network sites. What can be worrisome to institution is that they have little to no control over what is on these sites. It's not only about the school itself, but the professors in the school. If you go through the site www.ratemyprofessors.com/, you should be able to find your old institution and maybe even a former professor. Take a look to see what people are saying. If you are a professor, you definitely should go to this site and see what has been said about you. There are options for a professor's rebuttal and some even have damaging comments flagged or removed.

Characteristic 4: Any Time—Anywhere.

The Net Gen is used to getting a response immediately. If they are having a sleepless night and decide to work on an assignment, they want to be able to access that assignment immediately. Similarly, if there is a problem with a service in their homes, they want to be able to call a person at any point and receive immediate service. Another example is how software is now purchased compared to the early to mid-2000s. You can purchase your software directly online from vendors such as Microsoft or Adobe. After the purchase, you are given the option of having the product mailed to you or just downloading it to save a bit and also have the software immediately. If a company selling software only ships the software on a medium like CD-ROM or DVD, the company is actually in danger of losing business audience. Waiting for a disc to arrive does not fit the any time—anywhere mantra of the Net Gen.

Characteristic 5: Collaboration.

Again, not all Net Gens like to work together, although most do enjoy collaborating. Collaboration doesn't always involve technology. Now schools and libraries, for example, often offer areas that better facilitate group work. Technology has provided new ways of allowing people to get together and has removed geography as a barrier. Collaboration can be a good and enjoyable experience and raise the competence level of the participants. Later in this article is a list of some simple collaboration activities and their results.

Characteristic 6: Play. In the
early to mid-1990s, it was common for IT departments to remove the default games

that came with an operating system. They didn't want employees playing games during work periods. Today, some IT departments block some of the social network sites. They feel there is no need to visit social network sites during work hours. However, blocking access to social network sites can actually be detrimental to the company, as many companies now use social media networks to communicate with potential customers in ways that can't be matched by traditional media.

The average Net Gen needs to play and socialize. His or her brain is hyper-wired and likes to switch between tasks very quickly. The visit to a social network site is now the equivalent of a previous generation meeting around the water cooler. Playing the occasional game is a good way to use a different part of the brain and allows for creative thinking. Play is now part of the Net Gen life and they feel it is important that they not be cut off from that life while at work.

Characteristic 7: Need for Speed.

In the mid-1990s, the standard for loading a web page was six seconds and no more than twelve seconds. The most popular search engine then would normally load within that range. A majority of people accessing the Internet at home had a dial-up modem with 56,000 kilobits per second (56Kbps). People became impatient and wouldn't wait for the page to load if it took longer than twelve seconds, but today's Net Gen surfer craves even more speed. Waiting six to twelve seconds is unheard of. If a page doesn't come up right away, users may click on the link again, then double-click, and eventually leave.

They also expect the computer to deliver the content with "professional execution," running fast and smoothly.

OVERVIEW OF THE CURRENT EDUCATION SYSTEM

The current education system is gradually evolving, but not as quickly as the Net Gen (and now the Gen Z) cohorts have changed. Let's consider the characteristics that describe the Net Gen:

- ➢ Like to *customize*
- ➢ Expect information to be *pushed* to them
- ➢ Want *integrity* from companies
- ➢ Want to connect *any time—anywhere*
- ➢ Like *collaboration* activities
- ➢ Like to *play*—it's part of their lives
- ➢ Require *speed*

The current education system has difficulty accommodating these expectations. The term "sage on the stage" often reflects more of what happens in our institutions. For the most part, the education system is entrenched in an Industrial Age style of education. The teacher broadcasts the information at specific times, and the students receive the information. There is no opportunity for students to customize. If students are sick or miss a class or an appointment, there is very little recourse for them to view the missing lesson. Also, in a broadcast style of teaching, it is difficult to receive instant feedback. Shy students are often reluctant to raise their hands if they don't understand something. So these students are being left behind.

One-third of the high school students don't graduate (Barton, 2005). College and universi-ty professors complain that some of their students' reading, writing, and problem-solving abilities are rather low. The students entering colleges and universities are the ones who were successful in completing high school. What does that say about the one-third of the student population who didn't graduate high school?

TEACHING THE NEW WAY

With one-third of the students entering high school dropping out or failing, a change is needed. Thankfully, we see some evidence of a shift in education for the better. For example, math and reading skills of fourth and eighth graders have improved from the previous generation. While twelfth grade reading and math skills have stayed the same, the better-taught students will be moving up through the system. Many bachelor of education programs are educating their students to facilitate learning in their classrooms that is better suited for the Net Gen. Most of these new faculty members will start teaching in some of the lower grades

In the remainder of this article, I will briefly review a few techniques to improve the education of the Net Generation.

Online Collaboration.

Generally, Net Gen students like to work together. Collaboration can be facilitated in a traditional classroom as well as externally. Here is an example one professor used in his advanced photography class. Keeping in mind Bloom's Taxonomy, he wanted his students to apply skills in the top domain, *evaluation*, so he set up a document on Google Docs (http://docs.google.com) and inserted several images from the class. He then sent an invitation to all the students to sign in and edit the document. The students were to join a team of four by typing their names into the blank spaces for the team boxes. Then each team would evaluate the picture and make suggestions on how to improve it. After the exercise, the class was brought back together and asked what they learned.

The entire class loved the exercise both because they were using some new technology and because they were collaborating. They also found the suggestions helped them re-think what to do when shooting pictures. Students who missed class did the same exercise later from home and offered their thoughts on the pictures.

Distributive Cognition. Researchers

at MIT coined the phrase "distributive cognition," which basically means that the intelligence of the group is better than that of any individual in that group. It follows that allowing a group to share knowledge will make everyone in the group more intelligent.

Technology can provide the means of employing distributive cognition. For example, during a class, participants can be encouraged to use a service such as Twitter to write comments about the class. Within the tweets, users can insert hash tags that are unique to that session. For example, while speaking at the Innovation Days conference, I asked participants to tweet and insert the hash tag #can2010. Then I used TweetDeck to filter and display all the tweets that had #can2010. This technique can be used to ask participants for advice, opinions, or help without disrupting the flow of class. It also allows the facilita-

tor to go over the tweets afterward and follow up with anyone who had questions. Information sharing helps raise the intelligence of the group as well as keeping participants engaged.

Test, Then Talk. Traditional classroom

instruction is usually composed of lectures followed by a test to see whether learners have retained, or at least understood, the lesson. Basically, instructors talk and then test. Imagine how a person who is familiar with this content will feel. Bored! How much different it would be if this teaching strategy were flipped backward. What if students were tested on their knowledge and then told how they did. This would give students instant feedback on how they were doing. Students who were familiar with the content could move through it much more quickly. This would prevent them from being bored and possibly dropping out. Students who wanted more information would be able to replay the scenario and receive information or guidance as they needed it. To help facilitate this type of learning, it would be advantageous to have some interactive support built into a training package in the form of reference notes or short audio/video clips from a mentor.

One of the characteristics of the Net Gen is that they like to play. By the age of twenty, they may have logged 10,000 hours of game playing. A number of games incorporate a discovery method. People who play games are used to looking around and discovering things within their environment. The "test and tell" method would allow them to discover the content and make it more relevant. *Each time you teach someone something, you have removed the element of discovery.*

CONCLUSION This article only touches on the many learning activities that are more suited for the Net Generation. It is paramount to recognize the characteristics of the Net Gen and factor them into our instructional practices. This influential cohort will be bringing their characteristics and expectations into schools and their places of work, determining the effectiveness of our approaches in significant ways.

REFERENCES

Barton, P. (2005b). *One-third of a nation: Rising dropout rates and declining opportunities.* Princeton, NJ: Educational Testing Service.

The Nielsen Company. (2008). *Americans watching more TV than ever; web and mobile video up too.* www.blog.nielsen.com/nielsenwire/online_mobile/americans-watching-more-tv-than-ever/.

Tapscott, D. (2008). *Grown up digital.* New York: McGraw-Hill.

Twenge, J., Konrath, S., Foster, J., Campbell, W.K., & Bushman, B. (2008). *Egos inflating over time: A cross-temporal meta-analysis of the narcissistic personality inventory, Journal of Personality,* 879(94).

Viadero, D. (2002, January 23). Nature x nurture = Startling jump in IQs. *Education Week, 21*(19).

Cheryl Johnson

Cheryl Johnson is a performance solutions specialist with RWL Tech Inc. She has more than fifteen years of experience in learning, development, and performance. With her pioneering attitude, she has made strong contributions in the areas of learning, with emphasis on behavioral change. She has been recognized for innovating and building programs from scratch and pioneering the use of technology in education. She has also been recognized for her dedication to developing learning solutions that drive performance at work and in one's personal life. Working with a partner she assisted in the instructional design strategy for a powerful interactive patented online training solution for voice recognition technology before online learning was deemed to be an effective learning solution. (See demo at www.readwritetechnology. com/cms/landing/voicewindows.) She currently develops training programs for companies of all sizes as well as for government entities.

A VIABLE WORKPLACE LEARNING STRATEGY IN CHOATIC TIMES

Cheryl Johnson

Learning is a process, not an event. Training and development have evolved rapidly over the last decade. New technologies have emerged. New methodologies to develop training using those technologies have been introduced, and a new generation of learners is flooding the market. As if instructional design didn't present sufficient challenges, Cheryl Johnson identifies the chaos that often exists within corporations, especially with respect to their training and performance efforts. She asks, "How do all these factors affect our ability as instructional systems designers to create quality learning experiences that motivate, inspire, and, most importantly, change behavior in the audience you serve?" This article explores these changing dynamics. Training specialists who keep abreast of these changes, in addition to researching and validating the results, will be well positioned to "reinvent the learning process" and provide transformative learning experiences to their clients.

Formal education has been conducted for generations—from Plato and Socrates sitting at the feet of the best scholars of their day to 18th-century one-room schoolhouses with a variety of students from various backgrounds and ages grouped together to learn. For the most part, formal education is characterized by a "push" philosophy, rather than a seek-and-find concept. Teachers were revered as the ones with the knowledge, and students were to "pay attention" so as to absorb and (hopefully) retain what their instructors offered.

➢ *Enter* a new generation of learners who don't always "pay attention" or respect the wisdom of the ages. They challenge, they seek, and they are learning to "find knowledge" rather than absorb it from the experts and retain it for future use.

➢ *Enter* a new dimension in business. Competition for talent is stiff. Competition for customers is even stiffer. Maintaining a loyal customer base is challenging as new competitors emerge and offer better service with faster turnaround at lower costs.

➢ *Enter* a new dimension in learning and technology, including wikis, blogs, social media, coaching, mentors, virtual learning, webinars, experiential learning, and electronic performance support systems, online learning, simulations, serious gaming, and others.

How can you stay competitive and ensure your employees have the information they need in this rapidly evolving environment?

Let's indulge in an analysis of change management and discover how this concept can work for you in the chaotic learning environment.

CHAOS THEORY IN THE WORKPLACE

Managing change has always been an issue for organizations, but it's especially true at this time when the changes in learners, businesses, and technology have converged to create chaos.

➤ *Definition of change management:* Using processes to ensure that changes are visible, tracked, and monitored in order to ensure a desired outcome. Often, change management practitioners also attempt to deal with resistance and discomfort experienced by people throughout the process.

➤ *Definition of chaos theory:* Chaos theory studies the behavior of dynamic systems that are highly sensitive. These systems are deterministic, meaning that their future behavior is determined by their initial conditions, and they are not predictable. The author believes that modern business fits the definition of a deterministic system that can be studied using chaos theory.

Using chaos theory as a primary model for change management may be too esoteric for management to buy into in many cases. Chaos is not easy to grasp, especially compared to many "safer" models. But putting a modified version in place will not only produce stable and predictable change, but also bring out the creative and innovative ideas that keep your business ahead of its competition.

"Although chaos eventually gives way to self-organization, how can we control the duration, intensity, and shape of its outcome? It seems that punctuating equilibrium and instilling disorder in an organization is risky business. Throwing an organization off balance could possibly send it in a downward spiral toward dissemination by ultimately compromising the structural integrity (the identity) of the system to the point of no return. The only way to reap the benefits of chaos theory in organizational

development while maintaining a sense of security is to adjust the organization toward a state of existence which lies on the edge of chaos."
(*Chaos Theory in Organizational Development,* 2010, para. 7)

"Living on the edge of chaos" is typically not recommended. But for a moment let's explore the positive outcomes of just such a condition. When you live on the edge you are forced to find new ways to compete, ideas that may not have come forth otherwise. Southwest Airlines was for years a good example of a company that thought "out of the box" to stay competitive in a highly competitive and often down market. Think for a moment about all of the dot.com companies that forced us into a new way of thinking and a new way of doing. At the time it seemed technology was evolving faster than we could keep up. Some things worked, some did not. Some companies emerged and expanded rapidly, only to find they could not manage chaos well and they failed. Other companies embraced and found a way to harness chaos, using it to build dynasties that still exist today.

We can all remember when there was chaos in our companies. For example, chaos is almost guaranteed after implementing of any new type of learning solution. If your organization has recently undergone such an implementation, you may be able to relate. How can you take your organization, which has just emerged from a period of perceived chaos, forward in order to satisfy stakeholder initiatives, attract and retain talent, and improve performance goals? It all begins with an evaluation of your current training process.

Steps include:

1. Define training triggers.
2. Evaluate where you are now.
3. Use performance-driven strategies that promote your organizational goals.
4. Adapt and change as the needs of your employees and customers evolve.
5. Evaluate again!

DEFINE TRAINING TRIGGERS

What "triggers" at your organization determine whether you provide training and what types of training? Triggers are the catalysts that take your training program in the direction that your organization needs to go. They are vital for aligning your objectives with organization strategy. If you do not identify the correct triggers, then any learning you do provide is likely to be a "nice to have" as opposed to a "need to have." It may hit the target, but chances are greater that it won't. Why should your organization fund a program that is not in line with its long-term goals and vision?

Possible triggers include:

➢ Customer complaints
➢ Need for productivity improvement
➢ Desire to be a leader in the industry
➢ Morale issues among employees
➢ New technology or processes
➢ Compliance requirements

EVALUATE WHERE YOU ARE

Evaluation is the primary key in creating a successful program, whatever methodology you use. If you don't evaluate, you do not know where you have come from or how you arrived at the point where you are; thus, you typically will have the same issues moving forward that you encountered previously. Evaluation allows one to develop an effective strategy moving forward, based on past experience, whether that experience is good or bad.

The steps for implementing any new process seem very basic: evaluate, adapt, focus on goals, grow, and evaluate again. But implementation can be challenging. Outcomes are difficult to measure. Evaluation is time-consuming. The outcomes may not directly contribute to bottom-line results. In fact, the process takes time away from other, more pressing activities. But successful growth and change are always contingent on some form of evaluation. Would a farmer plant his crop in a field where he had not evaluated the composition or quality of the soil? It would take years of trial and error to acquire the information necessary to grow a plentiful crop. Whereas if the farmer simply took the time to analyze the soil, he would increase the odds of a successful crop with minimal delay.

We need to evaluate our organizations in the same way.

➢ Who are our customers?
➢ What are their needs and wants?
➢ What is the makeup of our employee base?
➢ What are their needs, but more important, what do they need and want to remain loyal?
➢ How do we build on our employees' current skill sets to maintain our competitiveness in the future?

Once we develop learning programs, it is critical that we evaluate them also. We must develop ways to measure their ROI and the degree of performance improvement that results from them in order to build a strong case for our organizations to invest in our new learning programs.

Sometimes we don't stop to evaluate because we don't really want to know the answers, which may require us to change the program. Change can be painful, pulling us out of our comfortable work environment and challenging us to rise to a new level. We could have to do things differently, learn new skills, or change buying habits. We are comfortable now, so why take the risk of finding out we need to change?

USE PERFORMANCE-DRIVEN STRATEGIES

Even more difficult than performing evaluations is taking the time to be sure that your training strategies are performance-driven. As we said earlier, the status quo is comforting. The current strategy is working—or seems to be. Your company hasn't been nudged out of the market yet. Your employees seem content with the learning experiences you have provided. Things are going OK. Organizational goals are being met, although not exceeded. But ask yourself:

- ➢ Will what we are doing now still be effective in two to three years?
- ➢ What are the trends in the industry?
- ➢ Do these trends fit into our business model?
- ➢ What can we gain from following the new trends? Or are these just passing fads?
- ➢ What do we stand to lose if we don't find out what our competitors are doing?

- ➢ What measurable outcomes are others obtaining from embracing these trends?
- ➢ How can new trends improve employee performance or help us gain competitor advantage?

Performance-driven learning strategies can be challenging to define and very complex to implement. Begin by evaluating your learners. Learning must be a priority, not just a one-time event. It means creating a learning culture in which whatever employees need to do their jobs better is available to them. However, it is more than making courses available. It means a strategy whereby information is easily accessible and employees are rewarded for improving skills they bring to the job.

There are many types of learning, many types of learners, and many learning styles. It can be challenging to create learning events that cater to the needs of all of these. In addition, certain topics lend themselves better to particular instructional strategies. So let's find a way to get our minds around these challenges.

There are basically three competencies we need our employees to have:

- ➢ *Cognitive:* mental skills (knowledge)
- ➢ *Affective:* growth in feelings or emotional areas (attitude)
- ➢ *Psychomotor:* manual or physical (skills)

Visual, auditory, and kinesthetic are the most widely known learning styles. A little less well known are Kolb's types:

- ➢ *Pragmatic*—prefer concrete information, like to experience, feeling
- ➢ *Theorists*—prefer abstract information, like to conceptualize, thinking
- ➢ *Reflectors*—prefer to observe and watch

➤ *Activists*—prefer to experiment, be active, doing
(Kolb, 1984)

Others ways of looking at learning were laid out by Gardner in his theory of multiple intelligences (Gardner, 1999). Some of the multiple intelligences are:

➤ *Logical (mathematical)*—prefer to use logic, reasoning, and systems

➤ *Social (interpersonal)*—prefer to learn in groups or with other people

➤ *Solitary (intrapersonal)*—prefer to work alone and use self-study

With all the possible dimensions of learning and learner preferences, training must meet many needs and come in many forms. Clearly, using only one form of delivery could limit who can benefit. Truly innovative instructional design must take all possibilities into account.

ADAPT AND CHANGE

Much is to be said for doing things the way they have been done, especially if what you have done in the past has brought success. But a better strategy is to hold onto what works, while keeping an eye on future changes that may affect your business. Study the possible impact and research the pros and cons of implementing new strategies. Why did a competitor go in a new direction? How did they implement changes? Glean lessons from others' experience and ask why they have been successful. Relate what you learn to your current situation and calculate whether taking a risk will help you maintain a competitive edge. Based on what you find, implement new learning strategies and programs to achieve desired results.

EVALUTE AGAIN

Evaluating is a continuous cycle. You must evaluate and change over and over and over again to continue to obtain your desired results. New benchmarks must be set and measured against to keep your organization competitive in these chaotic times. You may want to try a blended approach to learning to take advantage of all the aspects mentioned above.

A BLENDED APPROACH TO LEARNING

You can develop a blended approach to meet the needs of people with various learning styles. You can find a balance between formal and "just-in-time" approaches to learning. A blended approach takes into account the fact that the new generation does not look to formal or traditional models, but wants to learn from peers. Allow learners to practice in an environment in which they feel comfortable making mistakes and trying new things.

To accommodate differences among learners, use many different types of technology and delivery mechanisms that will empower your talent and take your organization to new heights.

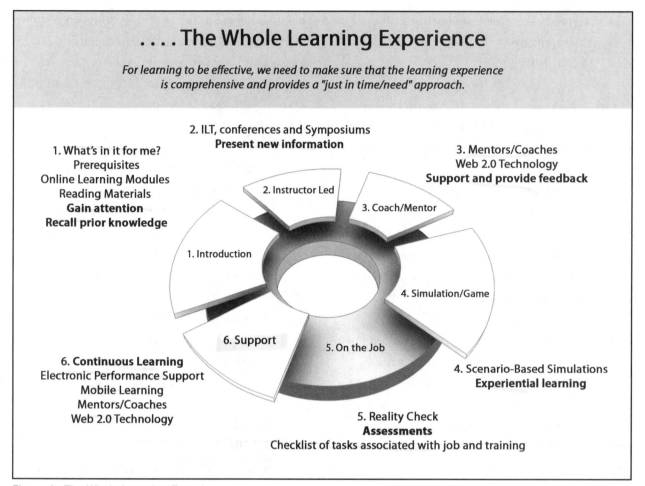

Figure 1. The Whole Learning Experience

Performance-Driven Methods.

Be sure that any learning experience you provide meets the needs of employees. Figure 1 introduces a model of a blended whole learning experience, described below.

1. Introduction: What's in It for Me?

When new topics are being introduced, a formal introduction helps learners get a broad-based, high-level view of the material and goals of the learning. This is an ideal platform for simple, cost-effective e-learning modules created with the more popular content authoring tools such as ToolBook, Captivate, Articulate, and Lectora. In this

stage we gain learners' attention, help them recall what they already know, and give them a reason to participate in the learning experience.

2. Instructor-Led Seminars and Conferences: Present New Information

When information is new and the learner needs to acquire a great deal of knowledge in a short period of time, an instructor-led approach builds a bridge to the new information by connecting the learner with trainers and subject-matter experts who can fill in the gaps, answer questions, and engage in meaningful discussions. It is also a good time to introduce an action learning project. Instructor-led sessions can be live or conducted via interactive webinar. You can introduce action learning projects at any point. Although Action Learning is a form of experiential learning, this is a good stage for setting up a project and addressing any questions or concerns that may arise about the concept. (See Number 5 in the Whole Learning Experience)

3. Use Coaches and Mentors: Support and Provide Feedback

Coaching and mentoring can be implemented at any stage of the process, but these are crucial elements for the new generation of learners. It is also a good idea to introduce social learning environments in which learners can support one another. In the Web 2.0 environment peers can connect with more experienced colleagues who can help them learn the ropes and locate resources quickly. Coaching and mentoring also foster a sense of community and encourage team building. Wikis, blogs, discussion boards, social applications, and virtual worlds are just some examples of technology you can use that support this delivery method.

4. Simulations and Games: Experiential Learning

Experiential learning can come in several forms. An online simulated event can be used that depicts real-life scenarios learners may encounter on their jobs or it can be a structured "on the job" learning experience or simply a series of tasks the learner must complete. Experiential learning is typified by what most term "learning in a safe environment," where the cost of making

mistakes is not high and learners can experiment and try things they might not be in a position to try in their current positions. Learning is achieved through reflection on a representation of an everyday experience.

Another method that enables learners to practice the knowledge and skills during the learning process is that of Action Learning. Action Learning is a form of experiential learning that allows the participant to solve real world problems within the context of the learning experience.

> ➤ *Action Learning:* A powerful form of problem solving combined with intentional learning in order to bring about change in individuals and the organization (Revans, 1998).

5. On-the-Job: Job Aids and Assessments

Just-in-time learning delivers training to workers when and where they need it. Rather than sitting through hours of traditional classroom training, users can tap into web-based tutorials, interactive CD-ROMs, and job aid provide just the information workers need to solve problems, perform specific tasks, or quickly update their skills. In addition, books, videos, presentations, wikis, and blogs can be sources of real time, recently updated information.

All of these methods, when properly employed, can support all the learning styles your learners may employ. Performance support systems are utilized by many types of organizations to track training that workers have accessed.

6. Support: Continuous Learning

Powerful technology is available to support all your learning methods and to help you track results. Any great learning environment uses a blended strategy that employs many of the methods listed above to derive optimal results. The key to success is identifying key triggers, evaluating the situation, creating performance-driven training methods with key benchmarks in line with business objectives, tracking results, adapting and changing as required, and evaluating the results again using performance technology— leading to a continuous learning process in your organization.

CONCLUSION When an organization learns to manage the boundaries of change taking place in the environment and uses technological means to keep pace while training employees to deal with rapidly changing information and methods of operating, change does not have to be painful or costly. Change is what will keep your organization on top. If you don't keep pace, you will be outpaced.

REFERENCES

Chaos. (2010, July 8). Definition retrieved from http://en.wikipedia.org/wiki/Chaos.

Chaos theory in organizational development. (2010, June 20). Retrieved May 23, 2010, from http://en.wikipedia.org/wiki/Chaos_theory_in_organizational_development.

Gardner, H. (1999). *Intelligence reframed: Multiple intelligences for the 21st century.* New York: Perseus.

Kolb, D. (1984). *Experiential learning: Experience as the source of learning and development.* Upper Saddle River, NJ: Prentice Hall.

Marquardt, M.J. (2004). Harnessing the power of action learning. *T&D, 58*(6), 26–32.

Revans, R.W. (1998). *ABCs of action learning.* London: Lemos and Crane.

Szabo, F. (2008, June 8). Presentation at Global Forum on Action Learning, Seoul, South Korea.

Leslie Kirshaw

Leslie Kirshaw is an internationally acclaimed thought leader, speaker, writer, and consultant in the progressive area of mobile learning. Leslie is co-founder of WebAdvantage, a mobile learning consulting company. Prior to WebAdvantage, Leslie was a founding member and vice president of OutlookSoft Corporation, where her development of OutlookSoft University was a significant contributing factor in the success and rapid growth of OutlookSoft from start-up to more than seven hundred customers and more than eighty thousand users worldwide prior to an acquisition by SAP.

She is the co-author of *eLearning, mLearning, and sLearning.* Leslie is a prior winner of the Centra Worldwide eLearning Excellence Award and has won APEX awards for publication excellence eight consecutive years, most recently for video iPod training. She also is a regular speaker at international training seminars and is a Brandon Hall Excellence in Learning Awards Judge. Leslie is a graduate of the University of Western Ontario.

FROM E-LEARNING TO M-LEARNING:
GOING MOBILE NOW!

Leslie Kirshaw

The explosion of the mobile device market and learner expectations for relevant just-in-time content is rapidly changing learning dynamics. The proliferation of mobile devices provides an opportunity to deliver mobile learning components that support and complement traditional e-learning content in response to business issues and opportunities. Mobile technology provides a powerful platform for interactive learning via live collaboration applications, such as WebEx, and peer-to-peer (P2P) video chat. From asynchronous and synchronous training to paperless mobile manuals, training professionals around the world are rapidly repurposing their training content to meet the changing needs of their users. Author Leslie Kirshaw examines how dynamic and interactive mobile learning components can be incorporated into a successful blended learning strategy.

CHANGING LEARNING DYNAMICS

In this challenging global economy, there is an increased urgency to inform, prepare, and inspire learners to achieve desired business performance. Over the past decade, we have witnessed the migration from traditional classroom learning to the adoption and proliferation of e-learning solutions for training.

Now m-learning is the new catch phrase. The key difference between "e-learning" and "m-learning" is providing learning content via a mobile device in lieu of e-learning's traditional computer and fixed location constraints. The spectrum from classroom through m-learning is shown in Figure 1.

As learning professionals, our own challenge is to identify business objectives and equip learners with the tools needed for desired business results. In an overall blended learning strategy, the ability to provide information any time, anywhere is perhaps m-learning's most valuable asset. Mobile delivery provides many unique opportunities for learners to access relevant content regardless of their location.

In simple terms, mobile learning is e-learning delivered via a mobile device. Our mobile devices are evolving into platforms for learning, collaboration, and performance support. Many of the early adopters of e-learning are

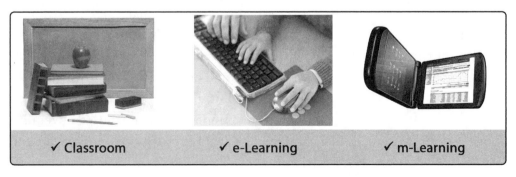

✓ Classroom ✓ e-Learning ✓ m-Learning

Figure 1. The Key Is Matching the Delivery Method with Learners' Needs

leading the mobile learning revolution. Interestingly, about a decade ago Cisco Systems CEO John Chambers made the following bold statement at the COMDEX '99 conference: "The next big killer application for the Internet is going to be education. Education over the Internet is going to be so big it is going to make email look like a rounding error." Cisco, now a leader in *mobile learning*, recently unveiled The Cisco Mobility Solutions for the 21st Century University. Unlike the gradual migration from classroom training to e-learning, a "perfect storm" of the proliferation of mobile devices, the need for just-in-time learning for an evolving workforce has the potential to drive mobile delivery adoption rates.

FACTORS SUPPORTING M-LEARNING | The business need to deliver just-in-time, relevant, planned, learning experiences requires the exploration of a new blended learning methodology. Several factors are driving the interest in m-learning as a solution:

Evolution in Learner Expectations and Experience

➤ Generation X, whose members grew up with personal computers, video games, cable TV, and the Internet, currently accounts for 33 percent of the U.S. labor force, with fifty million employees. This group is poised to move into positions of leadership and authority (Murphy, 2007).

Developments in Mobile Technology

➤ The latest forecast from the analysts at Gartner shows that mobile phones are set to overtake PCs as the most common web-browsing device by 2013 (Hartley, 2010).

➤ *Digital Trends* predicts that "Global sales of e-readers are expected to reach 11.4 million units by the end of the year, a significant increase from the 3.82 million units worldwide in 2009" (Fleming, 2010).

➤ The proliferation of web conferencing and business collaboration platforms, such as WebEx and SharePoint, that are readily accessible via Apple mobile devices.

Business Requirements

➤ The business need to provide learners with just-in-time, task-specific information to achieve desired business results

➤ The need to reduce costs and time associated with training

As with any change in learning strategy, several factors have to be addressed before jumping to embrace the new technology, such as learning culture, current training methodology, corporate technology standards, and the overall prevailing corporate culture. Some training experts argue that mobile learning has limited value and that broader pedagogical implications must be considered before investing time or money in an m-learning initiative. But, for many organizations, the addition of mobile elements into an overall blended learning strategy can provide a tactical approach to the strategic support of business performance.

THE EVOLUTION OF A NEW LEARNING PARADIGM

Learning dynamics are changing. Gone are the days when the traditional classroom model dominated the overall learning experience. For many training initiatives, the introduction of Internet-accessible mobile devices will provide a flexible delivery alternative to the standard e-learning requirement of desktop computers and Internet access.

At present, not everyone agrees that delivering content via a mobile device can provide a meaningful learning experience. In fact, most mobile content, by its nature, will not provide learners with the valuable hands-on, real-world practical experience required to accomplish many learning objectives. Even e-learning's devoted advocates who have struggled through online "Death-by-PowerPoint" courses might find it difficult to appreciate the potential of m-learning.

As with any effective learning endeavor, content is paramount, and the packaging and delivery are secondary. Mobile delivery of content provides a unique opportunity to meet the needs of motivated learners. M-learning supports business performance by permitting easy access to relevant information any time, anywhere. Mobile delivery of content is not a replacement for traditional learning. Its value lies in the ability to provide cost-effective access to content when and where it is needed.

MOBILE LEARNING COMPONENTS: From Synchronous Mobile WebEx Classes to the Mobile Manual.

The key to m-learning is *learning*, so a basic understanding of potential opportunities as well as challenges and limitations of the medium is critical. A common misconception about m-learning is that there is no value in converting conventional training content into something that will be accessed via a mobile device. The key difference between today's mobile technology and e-learning is the ability to package and distribute a broad range of learning content any time, anywhere. A typical e-learning solution might consist of synchronous and asynchronous classes, training materials, and evaluation and knowledge assessments; mobile delivery can *also* provide the same components, but with the added benefit of matching the mode of delivery to the learner's needs. As with any training technology, we must consider learning dynamics when developing content for the mobile age.

Mobile Learning Already in Use.

The ability to deliver relevant information any time, anywhere can limit the spread of misinformation and, over time, it can play a significant role in improving corporate productivity and performance. Many organizations are unaware that they are already providing important m-learning content to their employees.

Simple examples of m-learning include:

➤ A corporate meeting that is delivered via a conference call or pod-cast that can either be attended live or listened to via a mobile phone

➤ A corporate policy manual that is available in an e-book format that an employee can use to quickly look up a sick day policy from a mobile phone while home in bed

Development and Deployment Considerations.

As with any new training initiative, we must give careful consideration to content, development, and deployment of the m-learning. Some key factors include:

➤ Prevailing corporate culture

➤ Existing corporate standards for mobile devices

➤ Learning methodology, including content development, authoring and publishing, delivery, tracking and user support

➤ Ability to integrate key components with a learning management system

➤ Corporate performance expectations and success measurements

m-Learning Formats.

Depending on the prevailing corporate culture and the nature of the content, a variety of formats may be considered for a comprehensive m-learning strategy, including the following:

Mobile Communication

Organizations are already using a variety of cost-effective ways to reach their workforce, to defray corporate communication costs, and to modernize the overall corporate communication process. While audio content won't necessarily replace live presentations, it does provide the opportunity for employees to access information that would otherwise not be available.

Examples:

➤ Instant communication of key messages delivered via IM

➤ Communication via live and recorded pod-casts

➤ Live meetings via mobile web conferencing

Mobile Classroom

The mobile classroom provides a unique opportunity to incorporate case studies or scenario-based learning methodologies that "speak" directly to the learner via the learner's headset. Many organizations have well-designed asynchronous e-learning content that can be cost-effectively repackaged for mobile delivery.

Examples:

➤ Synchronous mobile web conferencing, typically used for sales, product, on-boarding, mandatory compliance, and system training

➤ Asynchronous content, typically used for sales, product, on-boarding, mandatory compliance, and system training

➤ Mobile application certification training programs

➤ Surveys

➤ Just-in-time learning

➤ Evaluation and knowledge assessments

Mobile Documents

The proliferation of Open Source e-book conversion programs and mobile e-book viewers has enabled existing manuals and documents to be repurposed as e-books. The process of converting a Microsoft Word file into a mobile e-book format is almost as easy as converting it into a PDF file.

Examples:

➢ Corporate manuals
➢ Product manuals
➢ Training manuals
➢ Corporate and policy forms
➢ On-the-job aids
➢ Mobile access to business collaboration platforms

Mobile Social Networking

Several low-cost methods are available for capturing, recording, and sharing knowledge with peers. A mobile-accessible corporate knowledge center with a wiki can be used for disseminating information while providing just-in-time access to mentors.

Examples:

➢ Mentoring
➢ Wiki
➢ Contact mentor/help line via text messaging
➢ Mobile access to business collaboration platforms

As with any new learning initiative, success is driven by the quality and usability of the content, not the delivery platform. Although there are many opportunities to incorporate m-learning components into a blended learning strategy, carefully consider cultural and change management factors. Many of the same challenges apply to m-learning as to e-learning, such as content security and copyright issues, multiple standards and devices, user support, and the need to track the return on investment of the learning experience.

In the end, the key will be both the quality of the content and the ability to package it to provide learners with just-in-time knowledge and skills to improve productivity.

RIGHT HERE, RIGHT NOW Many organizations understand the business need for just-in-time training and on-the-job support via mobile delivery. Many early adopters have encountered their own unique opportunities and challenges while implementing m-learning. Clark Quinn, an expert in computer-based education, predicted that one day mobile learning would provide learning that is independent of time and place and capable of providing a comprehensive learning experience (Quinn, quoted in Valdes & Valdes-Corbeil, 2007).

Successful m-Learning Implementations.

Many organizations have successfully incorporated mobile learning initiatives. From the U.S. government to comprehensive blended learning certification programs, the following examples provide insight into the endless possibilities of mobile learning.

Hilton's Homewood Suites

Hilton's Homewood Suites needed a way to provide timely, consistent, and cost-effective employee training for more than two hundred properties in the United States and Canada. In 2007, Homewood Suites launched a new mobile training initiative by outfitting all properties with video iPods loaded with its new mobile training program.

The pre-loaded play lists contain a variety of two-minute training modules that are used for standardized on-the-job training for thousands of employees throughout North America. Due to the flexibility of the video iPod platform, Homewood Suites can quickly and easily provide updates to all locations. With this m-learning initiative, Homewood Suites provides their franchisees with a fee-based video iPod training product to facilitate standardized, scalable and cost effective training. In 2008, Homewood Suites received a J.D. Power Associates Award for "Highest Guest Satisfaction Among Extended Stay Hotel Chains" (Hilton press release, 2008; PRWeb, 2007).

OutlookSoft Corporation

In 2005, OutlookSoft, a business process management software company, had a business need to scale their comprehensive e-learning-based employee and partner certification training program for worldwide expansion. Due to time zone considerations and the inability of implementation consultants to attend scheduled training, the company developed and packaged a blended learning offering that combined video iPod-based learning modules with the corresponding training application and hands-on workshop files. Upon completion of the training, certification candidates were given access to an LMS and provided with a realistic client case study assignment to simulate a real-life implementation. Learners then delivered a live presentation of their completed applications and underwent an online product knowledge assessment prior to certification. The scalability and success of this program was a significant contributing

factor in the rapid company growth from start-up to more than seven hundred customers and more than eighty thousand users worldwide prior to its acquisition by SAP.

Tagetik Software

Italian-based Tagetik Software offers a comprehensive blended m-learning kit for their employees, clients, and partners. The kit includes modular play list–based recorded training presentations and demonstrations, an e-book manual, and training application for hands-on workshops.

Deloitte

A division of Deloitte wanted to find a way to equip users with relevant and timely on-the-job support to supplement the company's existing training initiative. In 2009, they launched a comprehensive mobile-enabled knowledge center. Users were given the option of customizing their learning experience by selecting either e-learning or mobile learning–based classes. In addition, all knowledge center content, including social collaboration and support, was made available via an iPhone application or traditional PC.

Jason Jennings, MLB Pitcher

Pitcher Jason Jennings, the 2002 National League Rookie of the Year, uses a video iPod before and during games to view video of opposing teams' batters. This just-in-time training provides him with the ability to develop a real-time pitching strategy (Associated Press, 2006).

U.S. Military

The U.S. military had a need to train culturally appropriate behavior, scenario-specific phrases, and cross-cultural communication just-in-time to deployed personnel in Iraq, Afghanistan, and Sudan. They implemented an effective soldier friend video iPod–based modular training program that includes culture specific video, audio, graphics, and text (VCom3D, Inc., 2010).

Canine Training Behavior Services

Canine Training Behavior Services is a leading provider of American Kennel Club training classes. They needed a scalable training support tool to augment their traditional live AKC Good Citizen Dog Certification training class. They determined that the ideal platform was a mobile learning iTunes application. The mobile training application provides a comprehensive learning experience to help prepare a dog for the AKC Certification test. The application includes training strategy, step-by-step videos, and a dog command counter to track the number of times a command has been completed.

Each of these organizations/individuals successfully incorporated mobile components as a tactical strategy to provide relevant just-in-time learning to support their unique performance requirements.

CONCLUSION

A comprehensive mobile learning strategy can have a positive influence on business performance. Just like any other learning delivery method, the phrase "garbage in, garbage out" applies. Inevitably some organizations will make the mistake of simply porting over content from already dreadful e-learning sessions that will neither engage nor motivate any learner. Many will fail. The organizations that understand the need and uses for mobility and can successfully integrate mobile delivery into an overall blended learning strategy will create a competitive advantage. Just imagine the inherent advantage for a sales organization if provided with a mobile version of a new corporate pitch or product demonstration video that can be accessed while working out at the gym or sitting on a plane. As part of an integrated strategy, mobile learning can enhance the effectiveness of both teaching and learning. As with all learning, the key is to stay focused on the learners' requirements without becoming distracted by the technology.

REFERENCES

Associated Press. (2006, June). Rockies using video iPods to study swings, hitters. *ESPN Sports.* http://sports.espn.go.com/mlb/news/story?id=2486924

Chambers, J. (1999). Presentation at COMDEX '99. Computer Dealers' Exhibition, Las Vegas, Nevada.

Fleming, R. (2010, April 26). Nook outsells Kindle in March, e-reader sales expected to hit 11 million. *Digital Trends.* www.digitaltrends.com/mobile/nook-outsells-kindle-in-march-e-reader-sales-expected-to-hit-11-million/

Hartley, A. (2010, January 16). Phones to be world's most popular web browsers by 2013. www.TechRadar.com/news/phone-and-communications/mobile-phones/phones-to-overtake-pcs-as-most-popular-web-browsers-664093?src=rss&attr=all#ixzz0pd7gyD9g

Hilton press release. (2008, July 29). Homewood Suites by Hilton receives highest ranking for sixth time in J.D. Power Associates awards. www.homewoodfranchise.com/marketing/two_highest_ranking_jdpower_awards_08_dt.asp

Murphy, S.A. (2007). *Leading a multigenerational workforce* (p. 8). Washington, DC: AARP. http://assets.aarp.org/www.aarp.org_/articles/money/employers/leading_multigenerational_workforce.pdf

PRWeb. (2007, August 29). Homewood Suites by Hilton rolls out iPod mobile training. www.prweb.com/releases/2007/08/prweb549438.htm

Valdes, J.R., & Valdes-Corbeil, M.E. (2007, November 2). Are you ready for mobile learning? *Educause Quarterly.* http://net.educause.edu/ir/library/pdf/eqm0726.pdf

VCom3D, Inc. (2010). Vcommunicator® Mobile. www.vcom3d.com/index.php?id=vc_mobile_lc

David Metcalf

David Metcalf, Ph.D., is a senior researcher at the University of Central Florida's Institute for Simulation and Training. David explores leading-edge innovations in learning. Specific areas of focus include learning business strategy, performance measurement, operational excellence, outsourcing, blended learning, games/sims, and mobile learning.

David was formerly the chief learning technologist at RWD Technologies. He joined RWD with the sale of his NASA Kennedy Space Center laboratory spin-off company, Merri-mac. Prior to spin-off, he was the lead multimedia designer at NASA KSC.

David is the author of several recent works, including *Blended eLearning: Integrating Knowledge, Performance Support, and Online Learning* and "Operational Excellence" in Elliott Masie's book, *mLearning: Mobile Learning and Performance.* For a full vitae, visit www.davidmetcalf.com

Nabeel Ahmad

Nabeel Ahmad, Ed.D., leads IBM's mobile learning initiative, exploring strategic and practical ways IBM employees can extend their learning via mobile devices. He recently completed his doctorate at Columbia University, focusing on how mobile devices can be used in the workplace for performance support. Nabeel co-teaches the nation's first mobile phone learning class at Columbia and has authored and presented on many mobile learning topics.

Nabeel is also an alumnus of Carnegie Mellon University and the University of Oklahoma. He has been spotted in Central Park multiple times during work hours. You know you'd do the same thing. Stay mobile.

MOBILE DEVICES FOR LEARNING:
A CONVERSATION

David Metcalf
Nabeel Ahmad

Mobile devices are quickly becoming ubiquitous technology and are increasingly being used for educational purposes. As alluded to in the preceding article by Leslie Kirshaw, there are strongly differing opinions regarding the utility of mobile devices in a learning context. Here, authors Metcalf and Ahmad provide a hearty debate about how to approach mobile learning, where it fits in the learning landscape, and what devices and access points enable mobile learning. Drs. Metcalf and Ahmad, both known for their research and work in the mobile learning field, have an exchange on important decision-making aspects.

Mobile learning, or m-learning, is a fast-emerging field and has been an outgrowth of e-learning, but there are many unique characteristics of it that warrant our attention. The authors discuss four topics of interest where we think there are some guiding principles, but also room for debate:

1. Is m-learning an extension of e-learning or a new way of looking at learning?
2. Is m-learning an extension of formal learning or more like performance support?
3. Are smart phones better to deliver m-learning than feature phones, which provide much broader access?
4. Which is better: web-based mobile applications or platform-based applications?

1. IS M-LEARNING AN EXTENSION OF E-LEARNING OR A NEW WAY OF LOOKING AT LEARNING?

Nabeel Ahmad (NA): Think back to when traditional classroom-based learning began to transform into e-learning. It started with porting traditional paper-based courses onto a computer, for instance, making electronic PDFs of course documents. Many considered that to be e-learning, but we quickly found that not only was that not e-learning, but it was not the best way to leverage the technology. But that's where we start out from a historical perspective.

Let's translate it now into m-learning, originating in the past decade and gaining steam in the past five or seven years. We see almost the same trend happening. With e-learning modules, there is an understanding that you can just take e-learning courses and port them over to a mobile device and call it m-learning. Often, porting content and doing nothing else may not be the most effective way to expand learning onto a mobile device.

To Port or Not to Port. David Metcalf (DM): We've seen some very successful ports of e-learning content to mobile platforms, as in the case of Merrill Lynch's compliance training for their Go Learn Initiative. We've also seen that many people have not really thought through the particular learning theories or learning models that they will use and why they are using mobile. Sometimes, with a primarily mobile audience, you will find a better fit to use m-learning rather than e-learning, but not always. It is not exclusive, meaning that you either go with m-learning or with e-learning. It is very possible and likely that you could extend your e-learning into m-learning. However, ensure you are looking at the right learning outcomes and doing a proper front-end or job-task analysis to see that mobile is the right fit. Once you do that, you might also find that you have other potential delivery mechanism besides what looks like the mobile web. That is where you start to extend into the real possibilities of m-learning with messaging, podcasts, and performance support. These all extend e-learning, but perhaps in new ways that you wouldn't expect.

Context. NA: It is very important to understand the context of the user, especially with m-learning. With e-learning, the users' environment is constant. They're in a fixed place such as their office or home, so the context of use is independent of the environment. With m-learning, context is important. How long do you use your mobile device at a given time? Probably no more than fifteen minutes. Why? Because your environment changes quickly. Compare that to the average time you use a desktop computer and you start to see the difference. So understanding the context is an important way to design and develop m-learning concepts.

A Tool in Your Tool Belt. NA: The mobile device is often one of multiple devices

a user has. As David mentioned before with Merrill Lynch and other large corporations, users often do not possess just one mobile device. They have other tools, whether a laptop, desktop computer, tablet computer, etc. So you do not have to push all the content to a mobile device only. A mobile device is just one tool in a user's tool belt. Focus on the learning theories and goals that you want to accomplish.

Learning First, Delivery Modality Second. DM: Often, the best learning initiatives look at the learning first and the delivery modality second. If you design learning assets well, you can often develop once and deliver on many different platforms, whether an e-learning context, a simulation context, or a mobile context that might even have multiple formats and versions based on different audiences and contexts in mobile. So it doesn't have to be just one or the other, and it doesn't even have to be defined by these two modes of delivery or interaction. That is where the power of a sound learning design comes into play.

NA: It is critical to first understand the process you are trying to improve. Too often, people take the opposite approach, saying, "Mobile devices are very popular and we want to use them for learning." So they try to fit a process to a technology, as opposed to fitting a technology to a process. If you design m-learning, don't look at the device first. Look at the process you are trying to improve, and then decide what mobile device or other type of technology will help to facilitate that process.

2. IS M-LEARNING AN EXTENSION OF FORMAL LEARNING OR MORE LIKE PERFORMANCE SUPPORT?

m-Learning can do either. There are good examples of it extending formal learning, but also many short bursts of learning look more like performance support or informal learning. The way you interact drives that as much as what you're trying to teach and how you're trying to teach it. So it is one of the things that we should focus on when we start to look at this topic of formal learning versus performance support, or formal versus informal.

Formal Learning.

NA: Where it makes sense to do so in the proper user context, you can effectively use formal learning. Formal learning, in many contexts, should be easily measurable. Even on the mobile device, you have quality metrics that can help inform future decisions.

DM: Similarly, thinking about m-learning in terms of just formal learning puts it into a very small box, which might look much like the traditional "page turner" types of e-learning courses we already have ported to a very small screen. This really creates a very limited view of what m-learning is capable of.

Performance Support.

For informal learning, there is performance support, or just-in-time information, how you can find information when you aren't necessarily learning something new. Performance support references something that you already knew by allowing quick access to information. Whenever you board an airplane, you see the pilot going through a checklist. Pilots use checklists to ensure they cover all the different items before they can taxi on the runway and take off. Of course, the pilots aren't learning all of that information for the first time, but they also aren't required to memorize it all. So that is why learners need something like this checklist or performance support piece, where they can access information to help them do their jobs better, and a mobile device is an optimal tool for this purpose.

DM: Some of the new features and capabilities of mobile extend performance support so that it becomes just-in-time information at your fingertips. For instance, pressing a button on your phone to activate a voice search makes it much easier to access information while on the go. Your typing is minimal and you can easily find a wide variety of information. The same is true for visual search technologies, where you just point and shoot at a particular object and it gives you relevant information. It might be taking a photo of a product, a barcode or serial number on a particular device, or gaining access to the whole web of information on that particular topic with just the press of a button or two. This capability has changed the dynamic of how quickly you can obtain information about something you are curious about or need to know at that moment, in a way that meets the context of your learning. When driving, you obviously want to keep your eyes on the road, but you can still access information through voice. If in a crowded subway, it might be too noisy for that, so you can text in and find the information. If in a highly visual place, like a factory, and certain parts need to be scanned, it may be quickest to just point and shoot the camera at a particular object. All these are examples of extended performance support that would be difficult to provide on a computer or in a formal learning setting, but that are simple on a mobile device. We need to think about these when we look at the true power of m-learning.

Goal Time Versus Tool Time.

NA: The best technology and performance support tools lie where the tool and interface are transparent to the task at hand. The idea is for you to devote nearly 100 percent of your time to achieving goals and nearly 0 percent of it understanding the tools needed to achieve those goals. Instead of trying to understand how to scan a barcode or use audio search on your mobile device, focus on how that task aids in reaching your goals. If we can have that be transparent to the task, then the better we can perform our job. Our efficiency and productivity increase.

3. ARE SMART PHONES BETTER TO DELIVER M-LEARNING THAN FEATURE PHONES, WHICH PROVIDE MUCH BROADER ACCESS?

Are smart phones or feature phones the best way to deliver m-learning? Let's explore what tools enable some of these new features.

Blurring Landscape.
The choice of smart phones versus feature phones is a very timely issue that is going to become increasingly irrelevant as we approach 2015. Most phones will start to have some of the features that are now only available in smart phones, such as video, location-based GPS services, and some of the rich media and mobile application capabilities.

Smart Phones.
NA: Think about the last ten times you have seen a mobile phone in the media. Chances are high that you see smart phones, which are function-rich phones that allow you do things such as check your email, consult a calendar, use instant messaging, or browse the web. Smart phones are able to deliver a rich user experience and advanced capabilities, which is why you see them in the mainstream media. We are starting to realize that we can do more things on our phones; of course, many of these features are just task-based, but think about it from a learning perspective. One advantage of smart phones is the ability to deliver rich media, whether audio, video, or graphics. Video is a powerful medium to learn in new and more dynamic ways than traditional text-based learning allows. For instance, if you are attending a meeting with a difficult client, you can watch a video on your smart phone that models certain behaviors and informs the way you can handle this situation.

DM: There is a lot of power to be unlocked in the whole area of m-learning because of those features. The ability to have podcasts on mobile phones, video, and dynamic features that engage the learner with different sensory inputs is an important way to further learner engagement. It also involves them in the activity, especially if you are using elements of story that drive engagement.

Feature Phones.
NA: Often there is confusion about what a feature phone actually is. Put simply, if you have a smart phone, the feature phone is what you threw out when upgrading. Feature phones do two things just

as well as a smart phone. The first is voice calling, which is a very powerful medium that can be used in a variety of learning scenarios. The second is the use of Short Message Service (SMS), commonly known as text messaging. The capabilities are vast and it is important to understand that, while most of the world now owns mobile phones, most are feature phones.

DM: Thinking broadly about designing a suite of mobile solutions for use by the widest possible audience is important. It requires thinking about smart phone decisions very carefully and having a backup plan for how to also build something close in functionality for those with feature phones. For instance, when an m-learning application runs well on a smart phone, with full audio, video, converted slideshows, and graphics available, you should ensure it works across several different smart phones. Also have a version that is only slightly degraded from the smart phone quality that is available for feature phones. For instance, implement a series of text messages or emails that can be sent to those feature phones containing the same information in text that was in video. Or put the audio track in a podcast-like system that you can listen to over a standard audio channel, often called interactive voice response technology (IVR). So you could dial a number and listen to the same audio that you would hear if you had full podcasting capabilities on your mobile device.

These are some things you can do to extend the learning to the widest possible distribution across the broadest capability set of devices. Make sure you are meeting at least some of the learning needs of those who don't have access to smart phones. In most environments, device ownership is heterogeneous

and you don't know what devices people have—and what they have rapidly changes. With weekly major phone announcements and a plethora of mobile phones available, the testing needed to release anything following these guiding principles would be astronomical. Let's avoid that, while still giving the best user experience regardless of platform.

SMS. **NA:** There are many examples in the m-health space that speak to this. UNICEF created RapidSMS, which allows health workers to input and receive individual health information in remote villages using a feature phone. The data help health care workers determine what type of medicine to give to certain individuals. This simple solution is used to save lives through proper knowledge via text message. Not only do you learn new information, but in this case you also improve health and social well-being. And you begin to see how basic programs using the standard phones, which in many places throughout the world just cost a few dollars and many people own them, can have a significant impact. It is interesting that you rarely hear about these success stories in the news.

DM: Instead of using iTunes or a dedicated podcasting, data-driven channel, you can use standard voice technology. In Haiti, for example, a system is in place that allows a learner to send one text message with a particular code in it, receive a phone call to his or her phone, and play back a recorded lecture or particular information in Creole. This solution is device-agnostic and extends the learning to the lowest common denominator of phones, particularly in needy areas where it can be quite useful. In the developed world, too, many examples exist using smart phone and feature phone capabilities. Using text messages to pay a parking meter, to reserve a seat in a movie theatre, or to book tickets for airfare are all things they can do now in Sweden. They enhance performance and productivity, but are sometimes overlooked. There is much room for innovation and creative use in those areas. In a recent e-Learning Guild report, more than seven hundred companies indicated text messaging and email were top considerations for m-learning (e-Learning Guild, 2010). Blending these messaging techniques with other modes of learning delivery to meet underlying learning and performance objectives could help put learning first. We should be creating learning theory mashups (LTMs) and then applying the right technology mashups for engaging delivery. This is not just a trend that we are promoting, but rather, it is something that you will see across a wide variety of organizations, from corporate to non-profit sectors.

4. WHICH IS BETTER: WEB-BASED MOBILE APPLICATIONS OR PLATFORM-BASED APPLICATIONS?

How do you build apps that work across different platforms? How can you get the best experience with the broadest utility? Web-based mobile or platform-based applications are your choices. Web apps allow you to access content over the mobile Internet, independent of device. Platform apps are device-specific and installed on your device (think iPhone apps). Let's see whether there are ways to bridge the gap and identify benefits in each area.

Web Apps. NA: If you want the widest audience, then a web-based mobile application, or web app, tends to work out very well. Why? Because no matter the type of mobile device you own, the website will look more or less the same. More importantly, all of your users with mobile web capability can access the content. In the next two or three years, even when you read this book, the mobile web will gain steam as the technology and infrastructure are built out to handle more capability for accessing web apps. You use the Internet. You understand the browser experience. The mobile web browser may vary slightly, but it is similar. Rogers' Diffusion of Innovations theory (Rogers, 1995) talks about compatibility, whereby if you can make the interface similar to a user's prior knowledge, it helps in comprehension and learning experiences. Because you are familiar with using the Internet, you understand that links look certain ways and have certain characteristics, and the layout of a web page is more or less the same. Having that context and prior knowledge when looking at a mobile web page lets you clearly and quickly understand what you are looking at it. Here, context matters more than content.

DM: It is because of your familiarity with the Internet and the web browser that this becomes pretty easy to access. There are some encouraging signs for web apps and ubiquity. Web apps are generally a bit slower than platform apps, and sometimes it is harder to access the other device capabilities, such as GPS, camera, or voice recording features. The bad news is that this slowness limits the integration of web apps. The good news is the extensibility across platforms, the ability to have users subscribe to services, and the similarity to what you might have on a standard desktop web browser. This also goes for security and other business applications that you are familiar with for Internet-based applications. Recently, Sergey Brin, co-founder of Google, stated that web apps would catch up and converge with native apps in the next few years as HTML 5 becomes widely available and as phones become more powerful (Google I/O Conference, 2010).

Platform Apps. One key feature of platform-based applications is speed and ability to access the core device features. This is important, especially as you try to do two-way video or audio interactions or try to access location-based features for contextual learning.

NA: Getting back to the rich user experience, web apps have the compatibility factor. Sometimes, you may not want that, instead opting to create and define your own user experience. Platform apps give you more control over how the application operates. With platform apps you access resources offline. If you are in a subway or plane where you don't have a signal, platform apps allow use the same as if you had a signal. With web apps, your usage stops the moment you lose the signal. So you must ask how much you value whether users have offline access. While there are advantages and disadvantages on each side, understanding the context of your learning goals will guide your decision.

CLOSURE   **NA:** In the next few years, the way people use mobile devices will change and inform best practices for developing learning. If you are contemplating entering the m-learning arena, doing something is likely better than doing nothing at all. Our recommendation is to go with one or the other of the four methods in each case, as opposed to going with none of them. Organizations, schools, and companies receive constant feedback from employees and students wanting access to information on a mobile device. It is time to take that next step and enable them with the information they desire. Sitting on the sidelines and doing nothing may not be the best option, as opposed to doing something and seeing what happens.

DM: m-Learning is coming, either through the front door or the back door. Identify a pilot whereby you can test an m-learning program and have some control over the future of how this is rolled out. See what works and create a plan you can be part of. See how you can extend your e-learning to m-learning and, beyond m-learning, to the new ways in which knowledge, performance, and learning can be used across a wide variety of delivery mechanisms, including mobile.

REFERENCES

Brin, S. (2010, May 19). Keynote speech at Google I/O Conference, San Francisco, California.

Getting started with e-learning: Mobile learning (mLearning). (2010). Santa Rosa, CA: eLearning Guild.

Rogers, E. (1995). *Diffusion of innovation* (4th ed.). New York: The Free Press.

Susan Smith Nash

Susan Smith Nash, Ph.D., is currently director of education and professional development for the American Association of Petroleum Geologists (AAPG) in Tulsa, Oklahoma. She was associate dean for graduate programs at Excelsior College (Albany, New York). Previous to that, she was online courses manager, Institute for Exploration and Development Geosciences, and director of curriculum development for the College of Liberal Studies, University of Oklahoma, Norman, where she developed an online degree program curriculum for online courses at The University of Oklahoma. She also developed an interface for courses as well as administrative and procedural support, support programmers, protocol and training manuals, and marketing approaches. She obtained her Ph.D. and M.A. in English as well as a B.S. in geology from the University of Oklahoma. Susan blogs at E-Learning Queen (www.elearningqueen.com) and E-Learners (www.elearner.com) and has written articles and chapters on avant-garde poetics, contemporary culture, and e-learning for numerous publications, including *Talisman, Press1, International Journal of Learning Objects, GHR, World Literature,* and *Gargoyle.* Her latest books include *Moodle 1.9 Teaching Techniques* (Packt Publishing, 2010), *e-Learners Survival Guide* (Texture Press, 2009), and *Klub Dobrih Dejanj* (2008).

MOBILE LEARNING
IN EDUCATION | Susan Smith Nash

With every advance in technology, there are new possibilities to explore. Some aren't apparent, while others fall short of our hopes and others raise previous efforts to greater levels of value. In this very informative article, Susan Nash provides an overview of the current state of mobile learning in education and describes its various forms and uses, the places and circumstances where and when mobile learning is most effective, and new trends and directions. The author covers how mobile learning delivers the content, devices, and applications that are best suited for it. In addition, two case studies are presented: one on how stand-alone mobile learning objects were incorporated into different solutions and one on the specific steps involved in making a webinar more accessible to a wide, globally distributed audience.

Mobile learning can be found in almost all learning environments, including colleges and the workplace. Further, mobile learning is prominent in both formal and informal education. Communications technology is rapidly expanding and evolving, and while mobile learning could in theory be a term used to refer to any kind of portable instructional material, it more accurately denotes delivery through portable devices, which include mp3 players, video players, smart phones, and e-book readers.

Blending old and new technologies can be an effective approach to developing mobile teaching, training, and learning programs. Utilizing both mobile and desktop-based e-learning, for example, helps instructors accommodate learner differences. The key is to align instructional strategies with learning goals, while accommodating the learners' individual situations and the learning environment.

Sound instructional design must be adhered to in the case of mobile learning, even more than in e-learning that uses a very circumscribed learning management system, because there are numerous distractions in mobile learning that the typical LMS such as Blackboard manages to mitigate. In e-learning, once a person enters the portal, he or she is essentially in a locked-away world of a single class with a single set of peers. But mobile learning is much more porous. When social networks are employed, along with projects that require collecting and posting data from the field, the situation can spin out of control and the content can be obscured by the distracters.

Specifically, the following situations are typically encountered when developing mobile learning for educational programs:

1. *Mobile devices with almost no connectivity.* The primary challenge consists of delivering the content and engaging students in conditions of extremely limited connectivity. Handheld devices and portable media devices can be used to provide e-book content, lesson plans, and audio lectures by the subject-matter experts and to review materials.

2. *Mobile devices in remote locations with limited connectivity.* The primary challenge is handling the limited connectivity, complicated when books and materials are expensive. iPods can be used to provide instructional podcasts (videos and audio), interactive grammar activities, instructions for activities, and guides for collaborative/peer activities.

3. *Mobile devices used for content and interaction.* Here, text messaging, Skype, and web-conferencing software can used for synchronous elements. Email and blogs can be used for asynchronous interaction. A major challenge can be meeting the needs for portability while keeping the ability to communicate synchronously; that is, people need their phones for other purposes. Mobile devices can be used to download and store instructional content (e-book, video podcasts, lesson plans, audio lectures) and also to provide interactivity and share timely information (field information from markets, photos, etc.).

EVOLVING DEFINITIONS OF MOBILE LEARNING

Definitions of mobile learning vary depending on how closely mobile learning is tied to the general category of e-learning. In general, researchers either emphasize the technology used or the informal nature of the learning experience. For example, some researchers look at mobile learning in a general sense and see it as a measurable change in behavior resulting from the application of an "anytime, anywhere" mobile technology. Other authors look at the environment of learning and focus on the fact that the learner is in an informal learning environment and not in a regular, more formal learning environment (home, workplace, educational institution).

Differentiation between e-learning and mobile learning can also become clearer when looking at the nature of the instructional materials and how they are to be used within the educational context. Because of the small size of the device, slow speeds, and limited memory, mobile learning has tended to focus on the delivery of small learning objects, including text, images, audio, animations, and video. Even with more robust networks, better connectivity and more complex mobile applications, mobile applications are limited by size. As a result, any blogging or posts have been in the realm of micro-blogging. Similarly, assessments and interactive quizzes have been small.

Many authors see the future of mobile learning as tied closely to the further evolution of social networks and the comfort that learners have in sharing information via RSS feeds, "tweets," or graphics and media-rich sites. The use of social networks in mobile is limited, however, by concerns for privacy and the fear of having too many distractions for students to effectively achieve learning outcomes.

For many learners, mobile devices and expanded connectivity have been vital in creating spontaneous, pervasive, and ubiquitous learning environments. It is useful to keep in mind that in some countries, m-learning is more of a necessity than a luxury due to the abundance of cell phones and the limited number of households with high-speed Internet connections. Further, learners who are accustomed to using mobile phones for a wide variety of applications tend to feel comfortable with the medium.

MOBILE LEARNING APPLICATIONS | Mobile learning applications typically consist of a series of stand-alone learning objects that are then placed within a content management system and ultimately, in the case of a college course that accommodates mobile learning, in a learning management system. The downloadable files generally have a few things in common; namely, they are optimized in size for easy download and they work well on the small size of most handheld devices such as smart phones. Tablets, with their larger screens, are an anomaly.

➤ *Text.* Text is often made available via pdf files, which can be downloaded to most players.

➤ *Graphics.* Maps, diagrams, images, and other illustrative graphics are favorites. To be effective, it must be possible to scale them and to zoom in.

➤ *Videos.* Videos should be optimized for quick download. Video snippets of under four minutes are the most portable.

➤ *Presentations.* Presentation software should be saved as a pdf, which facilitates the download process and makes it possible to use the same utilities and plug-ins to view the presentation in many different perspectives.

➤ *Digital flashcards.* Several software companies have made mobile-friendly digital flashcards, which help with low-level Bloom's taxonomy activities, such as recognition and identification. The screenshot in Figure 1 is from the online interface used to create the text for the digital flashcards for that will work well on handhelds.

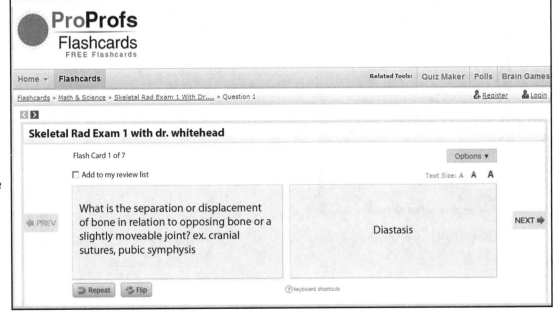

Figure 1. Digital Flashcard for Handheld's Online Interface Screenshot. Courtesy of Batia Infotech

Other examples of mobile-friendly e-learning applications include vocabulary builders and quizzes. Figure 2 is a screenshot of Quiz-Buddy, which uses an online interface to create quizzes that can be used for both laptops and handhelds.

In addition, a few products have specialized in handheld solutions. OutStart (formerly known as Hot Lava) provides solutions that are both static and streaming. Their solution allows what is known as a mobile-cast, which is a mobile-friendly webcast. In addition, they offer a fairly robust mobile learning solution that involves mobile-casts as well as static content that can easily be downloaded to a handheld, including BlackBerry. Figure 3 is an example of a BlackBerry-friendly learning application that demonstrates the characteristics of crude oil.

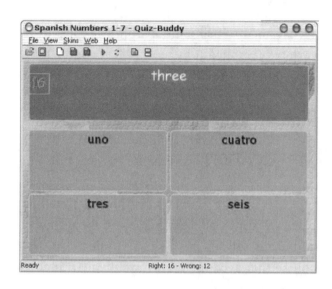

Figure 2. Quiz-Buddy Screenshot.
Courtesy of Batia Infotech

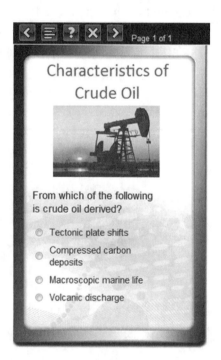

Figure 3. BlackBerry-Friendly Learning Application.
Courtesy of OutStart, Inc.
Source: http://hdwap.com/demo1/s.html?p=pass&c=13248&r=DefaultRole&g=1&n=y

USING MOBILE LEARNING TO ENHANCE CONNECTEDNESS AND REHUMANIZE THE E-LEARNING SPACE

Although e-learning is convenient, it can also lead to a sense of disconnectedness and isolation. One of the most challenging aspects of developing an effective online learning program is finding a way to help students feel engaged with both the material and with their fellow learners. Discussion boards, announcements, and e-mail have helped students feel they are part of a learning community.

Learning communities can be created more quickly and effectively with mobile learning. Here are a few ways mobile learning can serve an important function, even when user access is limited:

> *Instant broadcast text messages (tweets, etc.):* Even though users with limited access will not receive the information until they're back in range, allowing the sponsoring organization, instructors,

and students the ability to be in touch with each other helps assuage the "ambiguity anxiety" that often arises in distance education.

➤ *Impromptu instructor videos:* One of the best ways to re-humanize the e-learning space and help learners feel as though they have a connection with their instruction is to make it easy for instructors to record and upload spontaneous, informal videos. One of the most convenient approaches is to upload to YouTube and then to send the link. One can also share videos in social network or resource sharing sites such as Flickr.

➤ *User-generated video introductions:* Students can record videos using their smart phones and then post them. If they aren't able to record a video, they can post a text introduction along with a photograph of themselves (and perhaps a pet or something that reflects their jobs).

➤ *Resource sharing:* Knowing that others are struggling can be reassuring in a way. One way to keep the mutual struggle positive is to encourage students to share links, information, and library resources that relate to the course/tasks at hand.

➤ *Study buddy program:* Because communicating with mobile devices is easy and convenient, it can be easy to develop a system of "study buddies." Students can be required to contact their study buddies and to review activities and share drafts of papers, portfolios, and presentations.

MOBILE LEARNING FOR THERAPEUTIC WRITING | Case Study: "The Heart Journal" Therapeutic Writing (Memoirs).

"The Heart Journal" is an object-oriented approach to mobile learning that consists of a series of videos which are grouped by individual one- to three-minute video snippet, rather than one long video lecture. The individual objects were created with ease of download and accessibility of paramount importance. An example of one of the video snippets can be found at http://video.google.com/videoplay?docid=3341921571546859985&hl=en.

"The Heart Journal" is a creative writing/creative self-expression course, which focuses on the writing of memoirs and autobiography for self-discovery. The need for the journal was predicated on the notion that "we've lost touch with our own hearts" and that writing gives one the opportunity to reconnect one's mind and spirit. It was developed in 2008 by Susan Smith Nash. It has been offered free as stand-alone video Open Courseware since 2008. In 2009 and 2010, individual snippets were incorporated into online courses offered at the University of Oklahoma.

The videos are spontaneous, informal mini-lectures by the author of the materials, and they were done with inexpensive digital camera equipment. When they were processed, they were optimized for ease of download on mobile devices.

The fact that the videos exist as stand-alone objects makes is possible to use them as a repository of learning objects that can be used within a formal class, and also in informal learning. The instructor can pick and choose among the videos, which are hosted by Google Video. The plan is to also host them on YouTube some time in the future. The students could also pick and choose from links/embedded videos provided by the professor, from an index to all the individual videos.

The process for using the stand-alone objects and social networking for flexible mobile learning follows:

- ➢ Instructor selects a video
- ➢ Emails the video or embeds it in a blog, Facebook, or learning management system post (shown in Figure 4)
- ➢ Student watches video and writes a creative journal entry in response to the instructions/guidance in the video
- ➢ Student posts the journal he/she has written on a blog (which can be private)
- ➢ Members of the course read the journal that has been posted on a blog
- ➢ Peer responses are posted on the blog
- ➢ The student has a chance to review student comments

- ➢ Revisions posted
- ➢ Instructor reviews/makes comments (via email)

It is useful to note that the stand-alone components do not have to be used in conjunction with social networking and an instructor. The stand-alones can be used as self-study modules, and the entire Heart Journal series of videos could be considered Open Courseware.

Self-study can be as simple as accessing the index page that contains links to all the Heart Journal video snippets (www.beyondutopia.net/heartjournal—essentially a site map), and picking and choosing which ones are most appealing.

As Open Courseware, the course is very appealing because it holds out the promise of a writing-as-therapy approach that could is effective in establishing emotional connections and bringing about emotional healing. To enhance the Open Courseware aspect, one could go through and add a link to a website

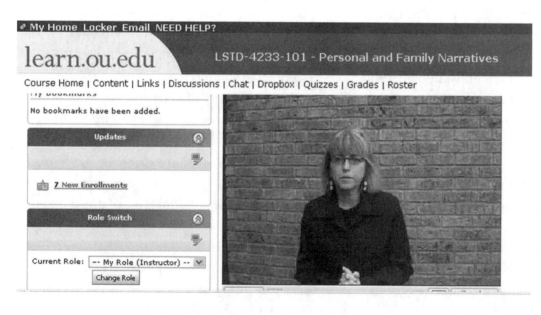

Figure 4. Heart Journal Snippet Embedded in Personal and Family Narratives
Source: Online course offered by the University of Oklahoma through the College of Liberal Studies, summer 2010

Figure 5. Heart Journal Video Snippets Used as Stand-Alone Learning Objects, Ideal for Self-Guided Self-Study

or blog that provides text-based instructions and perhaps links to examples of writing that follows the design proposed in the video, as shown in Figure 5.

INFORMAL LEARNING AND MOBILE LEARNING

Because mobile learning is so convenient and flexible, it's a key element in informal learning. For example, suppose you're an urgent care entrepreneur thinking about opening a series of urgent care clinics in primarily Hispanic neighborhoods. You'd like to learn the basics of conversational Spanish as well as basic medical Spanish. You don't have time to attend a course at the local community college, so you've decided to purchase a CD-ROM from a popular language learning series. You can listen to conversations while you commute to work. You can use the interactive activities in the evenings while you're relaxing.

Here are some of the most common elements of mobile learning used in informal learning settings.

- Interactive CD-ROMs
- e-Books
- Audio files: lectures, books on tape, conversations
- Virtual worlds and simulations: Islands in Second Life, simulations that you do on your own time that relate to your personal interests
- "Serious games," which incorporate scenarios, role playing, or quizzes
- Social networks: sharing links and information
- Wikis: sharing and building knowledge in areas of interest
- User-generated content: graphics, reports, videos, wiki entries
- Live polls, questionnaires, user reactions (tweets, posts, etc.)

Advantages of mobile learning in informal learning include:

- Can align to your interests and/or specific purposes
- Highly situated learning, which is to say that it relates to a specific interest and set of learning goals

➢ Ties to prior learning and prior knowledge and thus can employ connectivist cognitive learning strategies

➢ User-generated content can be highly engaging and entertaining

➢ Can be very motivating to pinpoint areas of interest

➢ Content and method of interaction (social networks, etc.) can be entertaining and motivating

Disadvantages of mobile learning in informal learning include:

➢ Learning goals not always clearly defined

➢ Difficult to determine what has been learned

➢ Instructional materials can be user-generated and thus of highly variable quality and reliability

➢ Assessment is not systematic

➢ Learner can become lost in information overload

➢ Learner can be distracted by unrelated social network "noise"

FORMAL LEARNING AND MOBILE LEARNING

Mobile learning is highly effective in formal learning settings when solid instructional design has been followed and when the content delivered by mobile learning is available in a number of different formats and forms in conjunction with learning outcomes.

Here are the most common and widely employed elements of mobile learning in formal settings:

➢ Quizzes and practice tests / assessment

➢ Audio files: lectures, reviews, debates, news reports, books on tape

➢ e-Books: primarily pdf format, but also html and Kindle

➢ Video: presentations, informational clips, recorded events, movies, documentaries

➢ Graphics: charts, maps, photos

➢ Textbook-generated content (less user-generated content, except in the case of collaborations, portfolios, discussions)

➢ Interactive learning objects: Flashcards, learning games, vocabulary reviews

➢ Message board and light discussion board

Applications of Mobile Learning in Formal Learning Settings include:

Workforce Training and Professional Development: Mobile learning is often used with a workforce that is highly mobile or geographically distributed. The individuals may be in different departments, and they may have different backgrounds and specialties. What they have in common is the need to gain knowledge and/or skills in specific content areas. The employees often need to demonstrate competency in order to be in compliance with legal requirements. Thus, the employer must retain accurate records of outcome assessments. Key elements in mobile learning solutions for workforce training and professional development include the following:

➢ Clearly defined learning goals/objectives

➢ Instructional materials that tie to goals and objectives

➢ Content available in multiple formats to accommodate multiple learning styles

➢ Procedure for administering assessments and recording and archiving records

➢ Practice exams or quizzes

Mobile Learning and College/University

Courses: Elements of mobile learning can be found in almost all e-learning courses in the sense that much of the course content can be downloaded to portable devices and accessed in an "any time/any place" modality. These elements include:

➢ Clearly defined learning goals and objectives

➢ Clear sequence of instructional elements and activities

➢ Mobile elements that tie closely to learning objectives

➢ Consistent availability of mobile elements

➢ Content available in multiple formats to accommodate multiple learning styles

➢ Procedure for administering assessments and recording and archiving records

➢ Practice exams or quizzes

Mobile Learning and Certification

Programs: Certification programs differ from college degree programs and workforce/ professional development in that, while they involve multiple courses and a series of assessments, they are often clearly tied to a professional career or goal. They may involve an internship, practicum, or preceptorship.

For that reason, the elements in a mobile learning course in this case would be a bit unique. It is important to have a clear se-quence of courses and to make sure that each course and each learning module ties to a specific learning objective. When possible, prior knowledge should be incorporated and used as a foundational building block. Situated learning—putting the learning modules within their own specific time, place, and context—can help as well.

Case Study: AAPG: Science and Technology Professional Development with Mobile

Learning. The American Association of Petroleum Geologists (AAPG), a global not-for-profit professional association of geoscientists with a member base of more than 36,000 worldwide, identified the need to provide high-quality education in a cost-effective, convenient manner in a way that would be accessible to its membership around the world. AAPG has a ninety-five-year history of providing high-quality education to its members in order to help them stay up-to-date with the science of petroleum geology.

In the summer of 2009, webinars were pro-posed as a medium-cost, easy-to-implement solution. However, the fact that many com-panies offered webinars as thinly veiled sales pitches made the AAPG a bit nervous, par-ticularly because they intended to charge a fee in order to recover direct costs. So the con-cept of an "e-symposium" was born. The value proposition had to do with the fact that, in addition to the synchronous webinar element, learners would have access to an archived version (asynchronous) of the webinar, which could be streamed, but not downloaded, plus additional instructional materials, which in-cluded articles, presentations, audio files, and an assessment section for continuing education units (CEUs) and professional development hours. The AAPG decided to make the webinar component even more mobile-friendly by decoupling the graphics from the audio in the webinar and offering the mp3 and a pdf of the presentation as stand-alone downloads.

In the spring of 2010, the downloadable mp3s and mobile-friendly presentations were made available, in addition to the articles, streamable video, and assessment questions. Benefits of downloadable components were:

➢ Ability to play and replay on demand
➢ Ability to download and replay if the synchronous part was missed
➢ Small file size, assuring quick download, easy portability and transfer
➢ Designed for clarity of presentation (because of the need for readability on a small screen)
➢ Accommodates multiple learning styles—auditory, visual, and kinesthetic
➢ Encourages situated learning— reviewing the materials while on the road or in the field in the same circumstances as those described in the webinar. For example, a webinar on the Marcellus shale could be downloaded to an iTouch and then listened to/viewed in the field while viewing a Marcellus shale outcrop.

The elements of e-learning that could be downloaded to smart phones and other handheld digital devices included:

➢ Technical articles (in pdf format)
➢ Presentations (in pdf format)
➢ Audio recording of the webinar (mp3 format)

All files were optimized to assure an efficient download and to accommodate individuals who had to download in locations with limited bandwidth and slow connection speeds.

CONCLUSION

The future of mobile learning in education is bright as it becomes increasingly apparent that effective programs can be designed for a range of learning settings, from mobile learning-enhanced programs to 100 percent mobile learning. Informal learning using mobile learning will continue to skyrocket as content and applications are available for widely used portable devices (mp3 players, smart phones). Formal learning using mobile devices will also boom as mobile learning is demonstrated to be highly effective in helping students achieve learning outcomes.

Tony Bingham

Tony Bingham serves as president and CEO of the American Society for Training and Development (ASTD), the world's largest professional association dedicated to the training and development field. ASTD is at the forefront of trends in learning and workforce development.

With broad-based business, financial, operational, and technical management expertise, Tony joined ASTD in 2001 as the chief operating officer/chief information officer. He became president and CEO in February 2004.

Tony is the co-author of the book, *The New Social Learning,* published in 2010. Through stories and case studies, he and Marcia Conner offer compelling evidence for the training profession on how to transform learning using social media. Tony's 2007 book, *Presenting Learning,* was co-authored by Tony Jeary. It was written to help learning professionals articulate the business case for learning more persuasively, position themselves as strategic partners, and communicate a compelling story about the impact of learning on business results.

Together with the board of directors and supported by a staff of one hundred and a wide volunteer network, Tony is focused on helping members: lead talent management in their organizations, build their business skills, understand the impact of social media on informal learning, close skills gaps, and connect their work to the strategic priorities of business.

THE POWER OF COLLABORATIVE LEARNING:
TRANSFORMING YOUR ORGANIZATION THROUGH SOCIAL MEDIA

Tony Bingham

People are demanding it, the technology is enabling it, and the economy is supporting it. What is it? Informal learning! Social media are radically transforming learning within organizations, and the use of collaborative tools will continue to grow as the Millennial generation surges into the workforce. This cohort of workers, who have grown up learning and working with social media, will drive the adoption of these tools. But it's not just the Millennials who see the value. As Tony Bingham, a uniquely positioned and informed leader, is able to see, we've never had the opportunity to broaden our impact as we do today through support of informal learning. Three research studies from the American Society for Training and Development (ASTD) note that large majorities of workplace learning professionals say that: (1) informal learning enhances employee performance; (2) in the next three years there will be wider adoption of Web 2.0 technologies in the learning function; and (3) regardless of generation, workers across the board believe that their organizations should be using social media more. This convergence of people, technology, and economic drivers gives the learning profession an unprecedented opportunity to be a paradigm shifter and in the process position our organizations and ourselves for future success.

Social media are radically transforming learning within organizations, helping to connect people with the right information, at the right time, in the right way. Beyond the hype, buzzwords, and entertainment value of reconnecting with old friends, people in organizations across the globe are using social media to collaborate and to learn. Emerging technologies enable a new kind of knowledge-building ecosystem with people at its core.

Classic business models presumed that relevant information was created and shared either through management or training. But classic isn't enough: there's too much to know and make sense of, too little time to gain perspective, and information changes too fast to dispense. A virtual water cooler becomes a gathering place to share ideas and ask questions beyond the limits of formal organizations, company meetings, or classrooms.

Our inherent drive to learn together can be facilitated through emerging technologies that extend, widen, and deepen our reach. More so than any other technology, social media allow us to embrace the needs of changing workplace demographics and allow people of all ages to learn in ways that are comfortable and convenient for them.

Today, networks of knowledgeable people, working across time and space, can make informed decisions and solve complex problems in ways they didn't dream of years ago. By bringing together people who share interests, no matter their location or time zone, social media have the potential to transform the workplace into an environment in which learning is as natural as it is powerful.

Looking at all of the learning that happens in organizations, the majority is informal. It typically takes place without an instructor and is in the hands of the employee in terms of breadth, depth, and timing. Employees want to learn on-demand and access information and experts when they need to use a variety of tools to do so. Informal learning helps employees stay knowledgeable and productive in a very dynamic work environment.

NET GENS To really understand the power of informal learning, we have to learn more about a key driver for it: the Millennial generation, born between 1977 and 1997 (per Don Tapscott). The themes in one of Don Tapscott's books, *Grown Up Digital* (2008), helps us to better understand the drivers for informal learning.

Tapscott refers to the Millennials or Gen Ys as the Net Generation or "Net Gens" based on their defining characteristic: the network. In his book, he explains that technology is like air to them. That's a critical point when looking at how this generation works, learns, collaborates, and lives.

The Net Gens are the largest generation ever to join the workforce. We are already seeing their impact in the workplace. According to the U.S. Bureau of Labor Statistics, the size of the workforce in the United States in 2014 will be roughly 162 million. Estimates suggest that the Net Gens will potentially make up a whopping 47 percent of the workforce in 2014!

We're all aware of the stereotypes of this generation: they can't make a decision, don't want to "pay their dues," ignore hours and dress codes, need constant feedback, their parents are involved in everything, and so on.

But in his book, Tapscott notes, "The evidence is strong that they are the smartest generation ever. Raw IQ scores are climbing by three points a decade since World War II, and they have been increasing across racial, income, and regional boundaries." He continues, "This generation thinks it's cool to be smart, and they see themselves as an essential part of the world's future success. When he asked his global sample of thousands of Net Gens, "Which would you rather be: smart or good looking?" seven out of ten chose having smarts.

Tapscott also writes, "In this war for talent, employers are going to have to understand the key Net Gen norms if they want to hire them, and keep them. They want the freedom to work when and where they want, and the freedom to enjoy work and family life."

He discusses other expectations of this generation:

➢ They want customization—this is what they're used to.
➢ They want to be managed as individuals, not as a big group. This means individualized learning-and-development opportunities, project-based role descriptions, lots of feedback on their performance, and open and regular dialogues with their managers.
➢ Integrity and transparency are essential to this generation. This is how their virtual communities operate.
➢ Collaboration: they are not turned on by climbing the corporate ladder. They demand challenging work and want to achieve with other people. This is how they get things done.
➢ Entertainment: they want work to be fun, and they see work and fun as the same thing.

Tapscott lays down the gauntlet: "The bottom line is this: if you understand the Net Generation, you will understand the future. You will also understand how our institutions and society need to change today." That is very compelling.

Not surprisingly, ASTD's research study on The Rise of Social Media found that Millennials were the largest consumers of social media for work and personal use. (See Figure 1.) More than 50 percent of Millennials—higher than Baby Boomers and Gen X'ers combined—said that social media tools help them get more work done, get better work done, learn more in less time, and learn truly useful things. Collaboration is how they get things done.

GETTING DEEPER INTO INFORMAL LEARNING

How much informal learning is taking place in organizations, and are we tapping its real potential? ASTD and i4cp conducted research on informal learning to answer that question in the report, Tapping the Potential of Informal Learning. To start, we wanted to know how much informal learning was actually occurring in organizations.

➢ 98 percent of the respondents saw that it was occurring to some extent, 34 percent said to a high extent, and 2 percent said that it wasn't occurring at all.

➢ More than 56 percent expect it to increase over the next three years.

➢ 98 percent of those surveyed say that informal learning enhances employee performance, and 39 percent of respondents said it is enhancing employee performance to a high extent.

Figure 1. Rise of Social Media   Source: ASTD research report, The Rise of Social Media: Enhancing Collaboration and Productivity Across Generations.

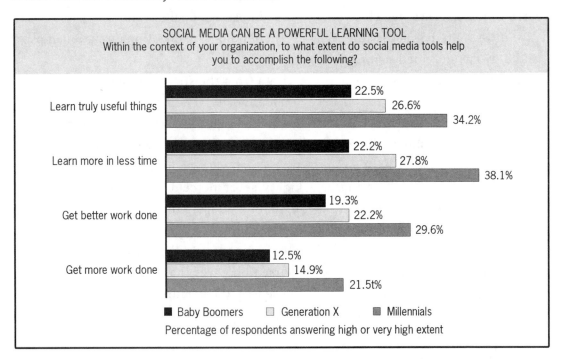

SOCIAL MEDIA CAN BE A POWERFUL LEARNING TOOL
Within the context of your organization, to what extent do social media tools help you to accomplish the following?

Learn truly useful things: Baby Boomers 22.5%, Generation X 26.6%, Millennials 34.2%
Learn more in less time: Baby Boomers 22.2%, Generation X 27.8%, Millennials 38.1%
Get better work done: Baby Boomers 19.3%, Generation X 22.2%, Millennials 29.6%
Get more work done: Baby Boomers 12.5%, Generation X 14.9%, Millennials 21.5t%

■ Baby Boomers   □ Generation X   ■ Millennials
Percentage of respondents answering high or very high extent

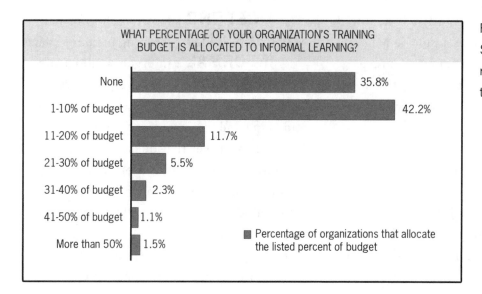

Figure 2. Informal Learning Source: ASTD research report, Tapping the Potential of Informal Learning.

When we asked what percentage of the training budget is allocated to informal learning, 36 percent dedicate no money to informal learning and 78 percent dedicate 10 percent or less of the training budget to it. (See Figure 2.)

This statistic is frightening because between 70 and 90 percent of learning occurring in organizations is informal, yet most of the money is allocated to formal learning. This ratio must change if we are to be successful in the future, and it means that the learning profession has a great opportunity to make an impact with informal learning.

IMPACT OF WEB 2.0

In partnership with i4cp, ASTD produced a Web 2.0 study, Transforming Learning with Web 2.0 Technologies, sponsored by Booz Allen Hamilton. The purpose of the study was to determine how, why, to what degree, and with what success organizations are using Web 2.0 technologies in learning functions. Reasons for adopting Web 2.0 include:

- ➢ Improving knowledge sharing
- ➢ Fostering learning
- ➢ Providing more informal learning opportunities
- ➢ Improving communication
- ➢ Finding resources more easily
- ➢ Boosting collaboration
- ➢ Building organizational relationships

Data from the study revealed that only a small minority of companies are using Web 2.0 technologies in learning. This is not the first study to find that Web 2.0 technologies are not yet widely adopted in organizations. Eighty-seven percent of respondents predicted that, during the next three years, their organizations were more likely to use Web 2.0 technologies in the learning function. Of course, there was that 2 percent who expected to use less. (See Figure 3.)

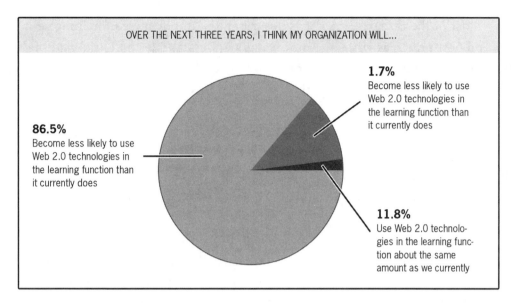

OVER THE NEXT THREE YEARS, I THINK MY ORGANIZATION WILL...

1.7%
Become less likely to use Web 2.0 technologies in the learning function than it currently does

86.5%
Become less likely to use Web 2.0 technologies in the learning function than it currently does

11.8%
Use Web 2.0 technologies in the learning function about the same amount as we currently

Figure 3. Web 2.0
Source: ASTD research report, Transforming Learning with Web 2.0 Technologies.

When examining the effectiveness of Web 2.0, 95 percent of those surveyed indicated that the technology is effective, although the highest marks for it are not that high. This appears to be a reflection of not knowing how to use the technologies and the associated fear of them.

The Net Gens are driving informal learning, which, as we've seen through the research, does not have the financial commitment or the appropriate involvement of the learning organization yet.

There has been an enormous increase in people who want to share their expertise, their opinions, and their time through Web 2.0 collaborative technologies, and these technologies are being adopted by society on a global scale as well as by our individual learning organizations. The use of collaborative technologies also has a huge impact on orga-

nizations' ability to recruit and retain talent. It's important to remember that, while much of the focus of this article has been on the Net Gens, social learning can benefit the entire organization, especially newcomers.

Ultimately, we must adapt the learning environment to ensure it supports all generations in the workforce if we want to recruit, engage, retain, and develop employees. One way to adapt the learning environment is to employ the tools and technologies with which they're most comfortable and apply them to their collaborative styles. And social media are at the top of the list.

Our job, our focus, and our creative energy must include learning all we can about and employing informal learning. As training professionals, it is our job to facilitate all of the learning occurring within the organization, not just the formal learning.

BEST PRACTICES IN SOCIAL LEARNING

Most of the research on best practices with informal and social learning suggests that organizations:

➤ Start slowly
➤ Find an executive sponsor
➤ Identify a department or area that is highly interested in it—participation is key
➤ Partner with IT, particularly compliance, if you're in a highly regulated industry
➤ Use the low-cost software tools available today
➤ Govern lightly

ASTD's research report on The Rise of Social Media indicates that companies that encourage the use of social media tools—and put the proper guidelines in place—can expect to see more effective learning. And, regardless of generation, workers across the board believe that their organizations should be using social media more.

Chris Brogan, a highly read and respected blogger and author, wrote an excellent book for getting started with social media, *Social Media 101*, an excellence resource for understanding and applying social media in an organization. Brogan talks about many of the tools available and his ideas for engaging any organization in social media. If you're relatively new to social media, this is a must read to help you navigate the many options.

What is more challenging, but just as important for success, is engaging senior leadership in social media and learning. Everyone we have spoken with regarding social learning has described the importance of helping senior leaders understand its potential and the power of having them use it personally within their organizations.

HOW CAN WE PUT INFORMAL LEARNING INTO ACTION?

David Shoemaker from eCornell spoke at the ASTD 2008 International Conference and Exposition. In his session, "Formal vs. Informal Learning: Is the Course Dead?" he provided some steps for facilitating informal learning:

➤ Take advantage of Web 2.0 technologies—wikis, blogs, and social networking tools to create and nurture ongoing communities of practice.
➤ Create formal coaching and mentoring relationships. Think of the model in teaching hospitals—a group of interns is assigned to a senior doctor; they accompany him or her on daily rounds, during which the doctor may employ a Socratic method to test and teach the students.
➤ Provide dedicated time for informal learning on the job.
➤ Create places and spaces for workers to congregate, collaborate, and learn from each other. These could range from breakout rooms and common areas to creating an open office environment.

In addition, organizations should create systems so that the information shared in these informal settings is captured, as well as ensure that the proper reasonable governance is in place.

In her report, Get Serious About Informal Learning, Claire Schooley from Forrester Research adds:

➢ Examine how you conduct employee training. Take stock of your present training and determine the components that lend themselves to more informal approaches. Provide the tools and resources for learners to find content easily.

➢ Collaborate with business units to develop the most effective learning strategies. This applies to both formal and informal learning.

➢ Use employee performance results as a measure of successful learning experiences. Learning management system vendors have assessment questionnaires to survey the employees' managers regularly after the course to determine the impact on employee performance.

➢ Keep track of how people rate informal and formal content. These ratings will help employees find the best content and help you to weed out the poor content and identify where additional formal or informal learning development is required.

Much of this comes down to how all of us in the training field position social learning within our organizations. It is critical to demonstrate clearly how it's going to further the organization's goals and strategies, and in many cases, this isn't a traditional return-on-investment calculation. It requires alignment to what's important to the organization, and often that includes:

➢ Retaining institutional knowledge
➢ Driving innovation and creativity
➢ Attracting people to your organization
➢ Connecting dispersed employees
➢ Solving complex problems collaboratively
➢ Providing an integrated and holistic approach to people development

This is the learning profession's opportunity to be a game-changer—a paradigm shifter—and in the process position our organizations and ourselves well for future success. Web 2.0 technologies and the Net Gens will catalyze us to drive informal learning: the most elusive, yet the most prevalent and potentially the most important learning occurring in our organizations now and for years to come. It's clear that social learning is critical to being able to attract, engage, collaborate with, and retain talent. And, just as importantly, it encourages us to create the structures that support accessing and retaining the information shared for learning.

In the learning profession, we've never before had the opportunity to broaden our impact as we do today through informal learning. People are demanding it, the technology is enabling it, and the economy is supporting it.

If you're new to social media and social learning, you're not alone: while only 24 percent of respondents in ASTD's research said their informal learning at work included social media, more than 80 percent said social media would be an important part of learning within the next three years.

If you're a veteran in social learning, please share what you know with your colleagues and peers in the training field. ASTD and other organizations can help you on the journey. All that you need is the courage to begin. It might be as simple as noticing where social learning is already working in your organization and asking what you can do to improve on it.

Start from where you are. Do what you can. Ask for help. Enjoy the ride. And share your thoughts and knowledge with others.

REFERENCES

ASTD. (2008). *Tapping the potential of informal learning.* Alexandria, VA: Author.

ASTD. (2009). *Transforming learning with Web 2.0 technologies.* Alexandria, VA: Author.

ASTD. (2010). *The five of social media: Enhancing collaboration and productivity across generations.* Alexandria, VA: Author.

Frank Nguyen

Frank Nguyen, Ph.D., has managed the development and deployment of learning strategies and technologies for various Fortune 500 companies, including American Express, Intel, and MicroAge. He earned his master's and doctorate degrees in educational technology at Arizona State University and was an assistant professor at San Diego State University. Frank has written various articles, books, and chapters on e-learning, instructional design, and performance support. He has served on a number of committees within the learning community, including the Adobe eLearning Advisory Board, ASTD, *British Journal of Educational Technology,* eLearning Guild, and ISPI.

E-LEARNING ISN'T EVERYTHING:
ADAPTING INSTRUCTIONAL DESIGN TO A WEB 2.0 WORLD

Frank Nguyen

Much has changed since the birth of instructional design, including the advent of e-learning, the emergence of Web 2.0 technologies, and the shift away from learning confined to the four walls of a classroom. Despite the evolution of learning technology, the basic principles and practices used to design learning fifty years ago are the same as those used today. The author identifies three ways in which e-learning designers must adapt their designs for learning experiences rather than learning events.

THE GAME HAS CHANGED

Much has changed in the world since those dark, early days of e-learning. The number of people plugged into the Internet worldwide has quintupled from 360 million in 2000 to almost two billion just ten years later (Internet World Stats, 2010). While screeching dial-up modems were common at the start of the decade, more than 300 million households worldwide now have broadband access (Internet World Stats, 2010).

More importantly, whereas previous web technologies (now dubbed Web 1.0) limited content contribution to those with the tools, skills, and infrastructure to publish content, the advent of Web 2.0 technologies has opened content creation and contribution to the masses. Anyone can share his or her stream of conscious thoughts on a blog, catch up with old friends on Facebook, document everything he or she knows about the Byzantine empire on Wikipedia, or publish a video of a baby named Charlie biting his brother's finger on YouTube. This paradigm change has pushed the growth of the web exponentially.

In 1998, there were just shy of three million web pages worldwide, compared to estimates of around fifteen billion in 2010 (Internet World Stats, 2010).

None of this is really surprising. There has been much discussion over the past several years about the advent of informal learning, mobile learning, microlearning, m-learning, learning ecosystems, performance ecosystems, Learning 2.0, eLearning 2.0, e-learning 2.0, workflow learning, immersive learning, and *insert new trendy catch phrase here* learning. Which of these are legitimate trends, passing fads, or harsh realities is a matter of personal opinion, conjecture, and time.

What is clear, however, is that the environment has irrevocably changed. Training is no longer the only shop in town for trusted information (let's face it; we haven't been for a long time). Learning can and will take place beyond the classroom or office cube. Learners no longer see learning as a one-way street. They can and will share what they know with others. e-Learning and how we approach the design of learning in general must adapt as well. e-Learning wasn't everything when we started and it still isn't today.

ADAPTING INSTRUCTIONAL DESIGN 1: BUILD LEARNING EXPERIENCES AND NOT JUST EVENTS

In the aftermath of World War II, the United States military realized that it had to find a better way to consistently and rapidly train vast numbers of new soldiers who had to quickly learn how to navigate ships, fire artillery, drive tanks, and fly planes. It also had to find a way to mobilize a civilian workforce that was asked to build the ship hulls, mortar shells, tank chasses, and airplane fuselages used by soldiers during the war.

In 1949, the U.S. Air Force recruited a young professor from Connecticut College, Robert Gagne, to run its Perceptual and Motor Skills Laboratory—with the goal of finding better methods of developing future generations of pilots. That young professor spent the next ten years developing an approach that formed the foundations of instructional systems design. In 1965, he published a book, *Conditions of Learning*, that outlined a specific sequence of events that must occur to support optimal learning. You will probably know this framework as Gagne's Nine Events of Instruction, shown in Figure 1.

The instructional design constructs that Robert Gagne gave us worked back then, and they still do today. But the post-WWII world that Gagne faced was obviously very different. The cutting-edge multimedia of the day were filmstrips. The first electronic computer, the ENIAC, was finished just three years prior to Gagne starting his work for the Department of Defense. The closest thing to instant messaging at the time was the teletypewriter. As a result, the nine events that

	Event
1	Gain attention
2	Inform learners of objectives
3	Stimulate recall of prior learning
4	Present the content
5	Provide learning guidance
6	Elicit performance
7	Provide feedback
8	Assess performance
9	Enhance retention and transfer to the job

Figure 1. Gagne's Nine Events of Instruction (Gagne, 1985)

Gagne referred to occur squarely within a briefing room full of young and brash fighter pilots, a group of welders assembled on the docks of a shipyard, and the four walls of a class of elementary school students. Gagne's Nine Events of Instruction focus on learning events that occur in a certain place, at a certain time.

Over the past decade, e-learning has made significant progress in breaking down the time and geographic constraints of such learning events. Learners no longer have to sign up for a class, schedule time away from their jobs, and travel to another site just to attend training. They can log on to a learning management system twenty-four hours a day, seven days a week to take a web-based training course. They can sign up for a scheduled virtual classroom session or even watch a recording afterward from the comfort of their offices.

But from an instructional design standpoint, we still focus much of our instructional design energies on isolated learning events. We expect learning to occur within a certain period of time, even though we may be more flexible about when that time is and where it takes place. We make sure that each web-based training course gains the learners' attention with a whiz-bang Flash animation or motivational video from the CEO. We give them a summary of what the objectives are. The learners still have to read walls of words or listen to audio narration. We give them practice activities to elicit performance. We give them feedback and test to make sure they have mastered the instructional objectives.

Gagne's Nine Events of Instruction were focused on the design of singular learning events in a world of filmstrips, the ENIAC, and teletypewriters. In a world of YouTube, iPhones, and IM, we are still designing singular learning events.

As an e-learning industry, we have to expand the scope of what we design from simple *learning events* to more comprehensive *learning experiences.* As shown in Figure 2, what Gagne gave us is still relevant and useful, but we must take advantage of the fact that learning does not only occur in a certain place, at a certain time. It will occur before formal training and well afterward. If we let learning outside of the event happen informally or in a haphazard way, it will probably still happen. However, it will be inefficient, painful, and costly for our respective organizations.

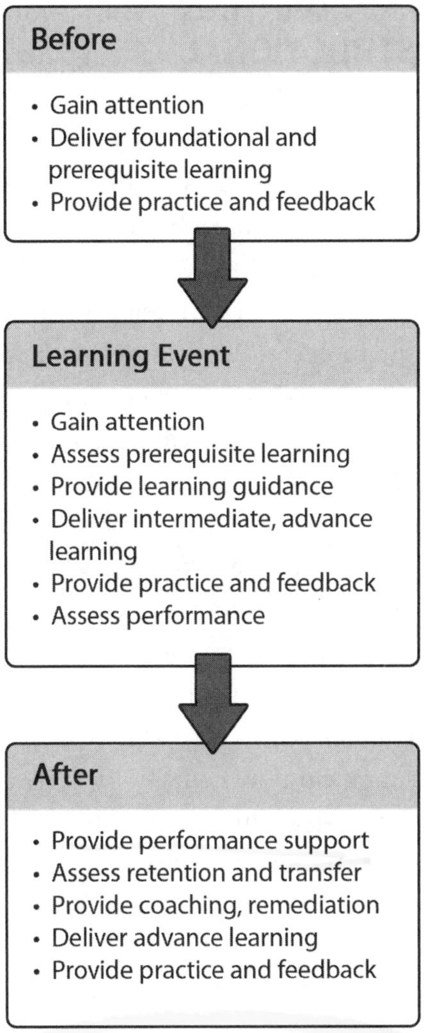

Gagne's original mission more than sixty

Before
- Gain attention
- Deliver foundational and prerequisite learning
- Provide practice and feedback

Learning Event
- Gain attention
- Assess prerequisite learning
- Provide learning guidance
- Deliver intermediate, advance learning
- Provide practice and feedback
- Assess performance

After
- Provide performance support
- Assess retention and transfer
- Provide coaching, remediation
- Deliver advance learning
- Provide practice and feedback

Figure 2. Gagne's Instructional Events Spread Across a Learning Experience

years ago was to find ways to make learning more efficient for soldiers and civilians. Although technology may have changed since then, our objective as learning professionals has not. We must find ways to design learning experiences that leverage the powerful set of tools we have today to make learning more efficient and effective.

ADAPTING INSTRUCTIONAL DESIGN 2: EXPAND THE TOOLBOX I once worked in an organization populated by e-learning addicts. The manager reminded me a bit of Gus from *My Big Fat Greek Wedding*. While Greek Gus used Windex to solve every ailment, e-learning Gus thought every business problem could be solved with an e-learning course. Customers are having problems purchasing on the website? No problem, here's a WBT. We need to roll out a new performance review process to managers? Sure, let's build a WBT and some virtual classroom webinars. Users have no way to access the new equipment manual? You guessed it: e-learning. Over the course of one particular year, we created just shy of two thousand new online courses. In fact, we even had several e-learning courses devoted to train others on how to make more e-learning. We proceeded under the assumption that e-learning could solve any problem, address any need.

As e-learning professionals, we have to be less one-dimensional than Gus and his miracle bottle of e-learning. We have to acknowledge the fact that some business problems—in fact, *most* business problems—may be best addressed using e-learning combined with some other *performance interventions*. In certain situations, e-learning or training in general may not even be necessary. Figure 3 outlines a number of different performance interventions that can be combined with traditional e-learning offerings to address specific business needs.

This notion of developing solutions that include more than just learning is not at all new. Those who subscribe to the principles of *performance improvement* have long professed this approach. A performance technologist would argue that careful, deliberate analysis followed by the thoughtful selection

Performance Intervention	Supporting Products
Classroom Instruction	Instructor guides, learner guides, learner mats, presentations
Coaching and Mentoring	Assessments, coaching guides, observation checklists
Communication	Blogs, email, information briefs, instant messaging, podcasts, video podcasts, or web content through an RSS feed
Knowledge Base	Knowledge management system, wiki
On-the-Job Training	Assessments, checklists, communication tools, performance support tools
Performance Support	Frequently asked help, job aids, online help, wiki, workflow-based support
Simulation	Rapid e-learning, sandbox
Team Reinforcement Activity	Activity guides, employee guides, job aids, problem scenarios

Figure 3. Performance Interventions That Can Be Combined with e-Learning to Create Learning Experiences

of training, support, and just about any other intervention under the sun will better address business problems than training alone.

However, one of the pitfalls of this approach is that we risk becoming mediocre tinkerers at everything and expert at nothing. Even though the list of performance interventions in Figure 3 is not at all exhaustive, it would be unrealistic and costly for any organization to develop core competencies in each intervention and to identify supporting products. It is simply not possible to become an expert at e-learning and job aids and coaching guides and knowledge management and. . . .

Fortunately, you don't have to become one. By and large, most learning organizations serve a specific audience and specific business domain. These boundary limitations can be used to select a pre-defined set of performance interventions that your organization should consider adopting, become very good at, and use in combination with e-learning.

Using the worksheet in Figure 4, you should start by identifying the type of content

your organization is typically responsible for training. For example, a sales organization may typically deal with factual content for its ever-changing product portfolio. A learning organization based in the information technology department may commonly deal with software procedures and business processes. A group supporting a factory likely must support manufacturing processes, equipment troubleshooting principles, and repair procedures. A human resources department may be asked to provide learning for management principles, performance review procedures, or legal and compliance facts.

Once you've identified the type of content your organization generally supports, you should identify performance interventions that would best support the performance of learners as they master this content. In addition, it is useful to identify one or more products to support each intervention that your organization could realistically implement.

For instance, a sales organization may choose to deliver its volatile product informa-

Type of Content	Target Audience	Type of Learning Objective	Performance Interventions	Specific Products
Example: XYZ's family of solar products	• Field sales reps • Marketing execs	• Facts: product specifications • Processes: how do photovoltaic systems work?	• Communication • e-Learning • Performance Support	• Weekly podcasts on new products, product changes and promotions • Web-based training courses on the photovoltaic process • Mobile-enabled wiki with technical engineering specifications

Figure 4. Content-Performance Intervention Mapping Worksheet

Michael Allen's 2012 e-Learning Annual

tion through podcasts that can be produced rapidly and inexpensively. An IT training organization may elect to adopt a wiki with common and uncommon software procedures to provide learners with performance support after they attend the learning event. A manufacturing group could use a blog to allow technicians to quickly capture new repair procedures. They could set up team practice activities whereby technicians gather together to solve case studies that closely mirror recently identified equipment issues. The human resources team could create coaching guides that help managers deal with low-performing employees.

Ideally, you should identify a range of performance interventions that can provide support to learners before, during, and after the learning event. Depending on the content and audience you serve, you may need only a few different performance interventions. In other situations, you may need a dozen or more. Some factors to consider are complexity of the work, content volatility, and size and distribution of your employee base. For example, if your employees work in a fairly rigid, process-driven manufacturing environment where things change on an infrequent basis, it's likely that your organization could rely on fairly conventional interventions like direct communications, job aids, and on-the-job training. On the other hand, if you primarily serve field sales representatives who work with clients on-site to sell the company's latest and ever-changing products, then you

may need to consider a broader toolkit that includes video podcasts updated on a daily basis, performance support systems that can deliver learning at the moment of need, and other mobile learning interventions. The key is to select the requisite interventions to meet your needs and become very good at designing and developing those interventions. Again, don't adopt so many interventions that you are mediocre at all of them but expert at none.

With a toolbox brimming with new performance interventions, you should benchmark other organizations that may have strong expertise in these new interventions, identify any best practices and incorporate them into standards and product templates for others in the organization to follow, and establish internal experts to champion each performance intervention and support their peers as they adopt these new tools.

Finally, focus on how to best combine these products with traditional e-learning to create rich learning experiences. To guide instructional designers and e-learning developers through the selection of the best performance interventions for a given situation, you may want to develop a decision-making process or guidelines. One approach is to create a matrix specific to your organization that outlines criteria for each performance intervention such as the example shown in Figure 5. Such factors may include the type of content, audience size, cost, and other factors.

	Learning Product	Before	During	After	Content
1	Coaching Guide			✓	Fact/Concept **Process** Procedure **Principle**
2	Information Brief	✓		✓	**Fact/Concept** Process Procedure Principle
3	Instructor Materials		✓		Fact/Concept **Process Procedure Principle**
4	Job Aid	✓	✓	✓	**Fact/Concept** Process **Procedure** Principle
5	Learner's Guide		✓		Fact/Concept **Process Procedure Principle**
6	Perf Support: Embedded		✓	✓	**Fact/Concept** Process **Procedure** Principle
7	Perf Support: Workflow		✓	✓	**Fact/Concept Process** Procedure **Principle**
8	Team Reinf Activity			✓	Fact/Concept **Process** Procedure **Principle**
9	Vodcast	✓		✓	**Fact/Concept Process** Procedure **Principle**
10	Web-Based Training	✓	✓		**Fact/Concept** Process **Procedure** Principle

Figure 5. Example of a Performance Intervention Matrix

ADAPT INSTRUCTIONAL DESIGN 3: EMBRACE THE MASSES

Just as some instructors feared that e-learning would signal the death of the classroom, some today fear that Web 2.0 technologies and the learning paradigms they enable may signal the death of e-learning. Why do learners need us if they can share what they know with each other and learn on their own? Why take an e-learning class when they can search for information in a wiki? Why sign up for a class next month when they can read an expert's blog today?

Just as classroom training did not die with the advent of e-learning, it is unlikely that e-learning or training will die with the advent of user-generated content. However, unless we adapt how we design learning and move away from providing stand-alone, isolated, and untimely learning events, we certainly risk being undervalued. More than likely, we will be perceived as slow, out of touch, and eventually irrelevant.

Because of Web 2.0, the world has irrevocably changed. Rather than perceiving this paradigm shift as a threat, we should instead see it as an opportunity. It is a mechanism that allows us to mine the knowledge of the masses. It is an opportunity to mobilize a larger body of resources—learners, their peers, their managers—and deliver more timely and scalable learning experiences with lower cost and fewer resources.

For example, instructional designers have historically relied on subject-matter experts (SMEs) as their primary source of content and information. We have been at the mercy of SMEs' projects, schedules, and competing commitments. We struggle to arrange meetings to obtain the information we need. We send reminder after reminder to obtain the screenshots or process documents promised weeks ago. We wait impatiently to have them review and provide feedback on learning

Brainspace > SMEs ?

materials. When the input finally does come, it sometimes arrives in the eleventh hour or even after the e-learning course has been published to the masses.

In a Web 2.0 world, our elusive subject-matter experts will continue to be a trusted source of information. However, we also have access to a broader source of knowledge: learners. We can review blog sites of well-respected employees to identify best practices. We can reference content posted by employees in the organizational wiki. We can reuse podcasts as part of a structured learning experience, perhaps as a foundational performance intervention before a web-based training or virtual classroom course.

We can also leverage Web 2.0 technologies to support learners before, during, and after learning events. For instance, prior to a course designed to help managers deal with difficult employees, we may require the participants to write an anonymous case study about a difficult employee using a course blog. During the learning event, small groups of managers can collaboratively problem solve and identify strategies on how to deal with the difficult employees described in the case study. They could even then produce low-fidelity videos, post them to a video-sharing site, and watch video case studies from other managers. They could then extract the strategies identified during the course and document those to a wiki for on-the-job reference.

THE GOOD OLD DAYS ARE HERE . . . TODAY

Every once in a while, I look at that first e-learning course I built years ago. The experience is akin to digging up an Atari 2400 game console from the closet and loading up Space Invaders, Donkey Kong, or Pong. While you can't help but feel a little nostalgic, you have to wonder how you ever thought it was cutting-edge.

The e-learning industry has matured since the early days of HTML, crashing corporate networks, and cases of Mountain Dew. Just as we had to learn and adapt back then, e-learning is at an inflection point today where we must do the same.

In order to continue make learning efficient, we cannot simply focus our design energies exclusively on learning events. We must also design and structure learning experiences that intelligently provide learning and support before, during, and long after training is over. In order to do this, we must expand our toolbox beyond e-learning and adopt interventions that we may not be comfortable with, including Web 2.0 technologies. In a Web 2.0 world, we must no longer think of our learners as learners, but as our subject-matter experts, instructors, and partners in the instructional design process.

REFERENCES

Gagne, R. (1985). *The conditions of learning and the theory of instruction* (4th ed.). New York: Holt, Rinehart and Winston.

Internet World Stats. (2010). *World internet usage statistics.* Retrieved September 27, 2010, from www.internetworldstats.com.

Julia Bulkowski

Julia Bulkowski, M.A., works as an instructional designer at Google, Inc. She has worked on the sales training teams supporting Asia Pacific and Latin America and the Americas, as well as the engineering education team. Recent projects have included piloting a mobile learning solution, using an alternate reality game to teach sales skills, and implementing Web 2.0 technologies wherever possible. She has presented at the ISPI, ASTD, and DevLearn conferences. Prior to Google, Julia trained astronauts at NASA, worked as an instructional designer at Informatica, and taught science to sixth graders. She holds a master's degree in education with a focus on instructional technology from San Jose State University and a bachelor's of science in neuroscience. When she's not online, Julia plays the clarinet, practices organic gardening, and enjoys the California sunshine.

WEB 2.0 AND PERFORMANCE:
USING SOCIAL MEDIA TO FACILITATE
LEARNING AT GOOGLE

Julia Bulkowski

One of the latest trends in learning is applying Web 2.0 technologies to enable learners to share their expertise with each other. I'm delighted to have this opportunity to learn from the innovations at Google that Julia Bulkowski shares with us. Julia begins by defining and discussing the benefits of Web 2.0 technology. We then see illustrative examples of how Google's learning and development teams have used these social media technologies to save money and enhance learning and performance. After reading this article, you will be able to decide which Web 2.0 technologies are appropriate for your organization.

WEB 2.0 AND GOOGLE

Examples of Web 2.0 technology include blogging tools such as Twitter, Facebook, Blogger, and WordPress; mailing lists such as Google and Yahoo Groups; knowledge repositories such as Wikipedia; online photo sharing sites such as SmugMug, Picasa, and Flickr; online collaborative documents and presentations; and video sharing sites such as YouTube and Vimeo. Here is one definition of Web 2.0:

> "The term 'Web 2.0' is commonly associated with web applications that facilitate interactive information sharing . . . and collaboration on the World Wide Web. A Web 2.0 site allows its users to interact with each other as contributors to the website's content, in contrast to websites where users are limited to the passive viewing of information that is provided to them." (Web 2.0, n.d.)

This definition came from a Web 2.0 site, which I will discuss below. Collaboration, content, and information sharing are the aspects of this definition that we have capital-ized on for learning at Google.

Web 2.0 sites have many advantages. They enable experts to share their knowledge with novices. When the information is posted online, it is accessible worldwide at any hour of any day for free or at a low cost. Web 2.0 tools also engage young and technologically savvy workers. These sites save employees time and reduce reliance on trainers. Because information is available at the time of need, it can have a positive impact on performance. People around the world are using Web 2.0 tools more and more every day.

In *Wikinomics*, authors Tapscott and Williams note, "This new participation has reached a tipping point where new forms of mass collaboration are changing how goods and services are invented, produced, marketed, and distributed on a global basis. This change presents far-reaching opportunities for every company and for every person who gets connected" (Tapscott & Williams, 2006, p. 10). It is not an unwarranted leap to say that Web 2.0 tools are changing the way adult training and education can and should be delivered.

Using Web 2.0 tools in corporate environments is not a new concept; in the 1990s, Xerox created an online knowledge-sharing system for their field technicians called Eureka. This system enabled employees to search for information and submit examples of how they had fixed technical problems. This knowledge-sharing solution has dramatically increased productivity and reduced costs (Roberts-Witt, 2002).

CASE STUDIES AT GOOGLE | In the rest of this article I will focus on examples of Web 2.0 technologies used for learning. I will show you concrete examples of how we have implemented these technologies at Google. The case studies come from learning and development teams throughout the company. Please note that Google has a unique culture that encourages and expects its employees to innovate, to participate in online communities, and to use new technologies. Since the company has built versions of many Web 2.0 technologies, we use them extensively. It may not be as easy to implement these techniques in every organization.

Wikis. The definition of Web 2.0 above came from a wiki, which is a website where many people can edit the content. Wikipedia, an online encyclopedia, is one of the most well-known examples of a wiki. Several studies have compared Wikipedia's accuracy to the *Encyclopaedia Britannica* and found it to be surprisingly accurate and reliable. The journal *Nature* selected scientific articles on the same topics from both Wikipedia and the *Encyclopaedia Brittanica*, sent them to experts to review, and tabulated the number of errors and omissions in each article. "Among forty-two entries tested, the difference in accuracy was not particularly great: the average science entry in Wikipedia contained about four inaccuracies; Britannica, about three" (Giles, 2005, p. 900). When experts contribute to articles, the errors diminish substantially.

Google engineers use wikis extensively. Because technology changes rapidly, engineers frequently need to learn new languages and technical skills. The engineers tend to either search for study materials on their own, attend live classes, or ask peers to teach them. All of these solutions require a significant time commitment, both from the learner and from the peer/instructor. The learning and development team for engineering therefore launched "Code Labs." A code lab is a collaborative website (or wiki) where experts share examples of code that illustrate best practices. New engineers at Google start exploring these tutorials in their first week. Code lab articles join an online, searchable repository for engineers in all of our offices to access. When code labs need to be edited by adding additional context or changing example code, anyone can either edit them or suggest changes. This prevents misinformation or information becoming outdated. Wikis have impacted performance by decreasing new hire ramp-up time, decreasing time experts spend teaching new hires, increasing the quality of code, and increasing the time experts spend on their core jobs.

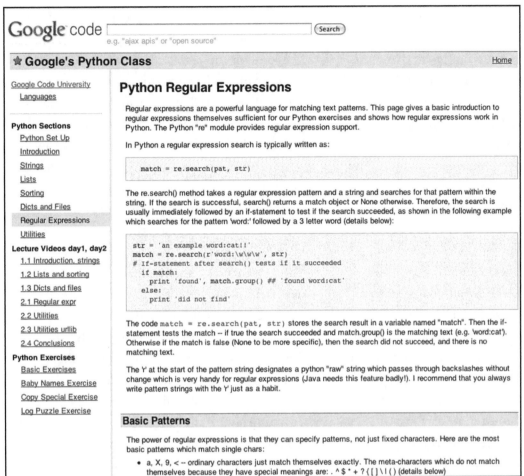

Figure 1. Code Lab Wiki Example http://code.google.com/edu/languages/google-python-class/regular-expressions.html. Reprinted with permission of Google Inc.

Figure 1 shows an example of one of the publicly available code labs. If you have something to contribute to this topic, you can do so through the Google Code University (http://code.google.com/edu)!

Blogs. Blogs are another familiar and popular Web 2.0 technology. The term blog comes from the union of we**b + log.** A blog is a website "usually maintained by an individual with regular entries of commentary, descriptions of events, or other material such as graphics or video" (Blog, n.d.). Blogs provide a quick and easy platform for publishing articles and sparking lively discussions. Authors can contribute to blogs by composing a message through an online interface or by sending an email to the blog's email address. RSS feed aggregators enable readers to make a customized play list of their favorite blog topics and authors; reading a feed is like reading a personalized magazine, with the added benefit of being able to communicate directly with the author and other readers.

Blogs are great tools for communicating information, and executives often use them to communicate with their employees. A Google employee could use blogs to enhance her learning and performance in several ways. She could set up a feed to keep track of trends in her industry (performance improvement, for example). She could also participate in live classes that use blogs for post-class reinforcement. For example, after a class on effective email communication, students were given an assignment: compose an email using the checklist provided in class. The students composed the email in their normal email program and sent it to the address assigned to the class blog. The email automatically displayed as a new entry on the class blog. The students, their managers, their instructors, and people who did not take the class could review all of these messages. They could all comment on the other posts with critiques and praise. Messages were posted in many languages and filtered by language; this enabled and encouraged employees around the world to participate. In this situation, learners practiced an authentic application of the class, created a repository of effective emails, and received feedback from their peers. This reinforcement ensured that learning was not simply a one-time event. Instructors assessed how well the students applied the skills learned in class and adjusted class activities accordingly. Blogs have impacted performance by ensuring emails were written more effectively and efficiently, ultimately saving time and increasing productivity and ensuring the transfer of skills from the classroom to the workplace.

Shared Online Documents. Several online document tools facilitate writing, editing, and collaborating. These tools eliminate the hassle of emailing traditional attachments back and forth. Because the online version is the most up-to-date, no one needs to wonder if he is looking at the current version. Changes are tracked automatically so collaborators can see who has edited each part; previous versions can be reverted to

if necessary. Our training team uses shared project plans hosted in Google documents. Anyone on the team can access and edit the project plan whenever he wishes. The training team also created easy-to-update templates for design documents and facilitator guides using online documents. Productivity savings are incalculable, and multiple editors ensure high quality.

In addition to using online documents for productivity savings within our own team, we also frequently use online documents during and to supplement the courses we deliver. For example, during a "Designing Effective Instruction" class with participants attending from several different geographies, the instructor created an online spreadsheet. The participants brainstormed a list of one hundred different delivery mechanisms for learning simultaneously. Because participants could see what their peers were writing, they could build on each other's ideas. This was an effective and efficient way to brainstorm virtually.

The instructor used another application of online spreadsheets for learning during the same class. As you can see in Figure 2, learners practiced using Gagne's Nine Events of Instruction. In Column A, the nine events of instruction were listed. The instructor's example filled Column B; each participant was then assigned a column and asked to enter information for each class each one was designing. During this activity, the instructor could monitor the learners' progress and assist where appropriate. Learners could look at each other's ideas and learn from each other. The spreadsheet lived on after the class; participants could review their work at any time. Online spreadsheets have impacted perfor-

	A	B	C	D	E	F
1		Instructor's example	Kun	Emma	Ashley	Julia
2		Meetings that Rock!	Product Training: Common Misconceptions	Handling Objections	Selling Seasonal Advertising	Leadership
3	Gain attention	Poll: what % of time do you spend leading/attending meetings? Meetings have a very high cost! (Why we should care about having efficient ones: if 10 team members who average $50,000 in salary spend 2 hours every week in an inefficient meeting, it would cost $25,000)	Come-up with mock scenarios that the participants might have encountered before, i.e. handling tough question from a client	Recall an experience when, as a customer, your objection was handled well.	What's the next big holiday in your country? What advertisements do you usually see around that holiday?	One of the characteristics of successful employees is their leadership ability. What you will learn today will start getting you thinking about how you can be a great leader.
4	Inform learners of objectives	Show objectives on the screen: -Identify when & when not to schedule meetings. -Use the meeting planning template.	Bring-up the PPT deck on screen with 10 misconceptions. Tell them that these will be the main topics we will cover. After this session they will be comfortable explaining the concepts to clients	- be able to deal effectively with common objections	-Identify high potential holidays for advertisers, develop strategies to increase revenue and advertiser traffic and ROI for that holiday season	-Apply leadership techniques -Lead a project
5	Stimulate recall of prior learning	What was the last great meeting you attended?	Ask question: what is the toughest experience they have had when answering customer issues?	What are some common objections you get and how have you dealt with them?	How did you prepare for the Q4 holiday season? What techniques did you use? What worked, and what didn't work?	Think of an example of a stunning leader. Visualize this person in your mind. What made them such a great leader?
6	Present the content	Presentation of key concepts: -elements of great business dialog -when meetings are/are not necessary -who to invite -expectations for participants	Presentation of 10 misconceptions with specific examples to facilitate their understanding	-typical objections and sample answers -framework for responding to objections	Q1 holiday calendar, Market data, Sample strategies from previous successful holiday campaigns, Suggested strategies	-10 tenets of successful leadership

mance by facilitating activities during a class for learners in multiple locations.

Another feature of online spreadsheets is the ability to create, deploy, and collect information through forms and surveys easily. Although numerous online survey tools exist, the form functionality in Google spreadsheets makes it extremely easy to view, share, and parse the raw data. Since the forms can be emailed and embedded easily in websites, survey respondents can respond through their email, via a website, or on their mobile

Figure 2. Online Spreadsheet Excerpt Used in a "Designing Effective Instruction" Class
Reprinted with permission of Google Inc.

phones. Response rates using these forms for level one and level three feedback have increased dramatically because it is so easy for participants to respond. Participants can also view the aggregate survey data, or the raw data, depending on the settings chosen. The impact on performance in this example is that as a training team, we are able to collect more information easily and rapidly, enabling us to improve the quality of learning solutions.

Online Videos. Let's now examine some other collaborative media. Using videos as an instructional medium is not new. What's new, however, is the ubiquity of easy-to-use and inexpensive video cameras. Learners can film themselves, upload the videos to the Internet, and share them with others quickly. In addition to all of the "Cats on Skateboards" videos available online, there are very many educational videos. You can learn just about anything, from how to prune a lemon tree to how to use macros in Excel, through educational videos online. At Google, we have capitalized on this in two ways: by creating a Googler-to-Googler video learning network and by identifying star performers through video submissions.

Our learner-to-learner online video network encourages employees to film short videos illustrating their areas of expertise. Viewers can use a star rating system to indicate how well they like each video, thus providing a guide for other viewers. There are "channels" for different topics, including "How to Use the Customer Relationship Management (CRM) Tool," "Career Development Tips," and "Train-the-Trainer." Employees have taken screen casts to show tips, shortcuts, and best practices on the CRM channel. For the "Train-the-Trainer" channel, experienced trainers and instructional designers offer video tips on topics such as writing instructional objectives, the ADDIE model, and Kirkpatrick's four levels of evaluation. By watching these videos, learners can gain an introduction to basic concepts. They can be used in lieu of an "Introduction to

Instructional Design" class; in-person classes can therefore focus on advanced topics and discussions. Learners sharing their expertise with each other through video results in a significant amount of knowledge being shared throughout the company.

Online video can also help identify star performers by giving an audience an authentic task and allowing others to vote on the best examples of this performance. The YouTube Symphony was designed to identify top performers from musicians around the world, create a collaborative, asynchronous symphony performance, assemble an all-star team of accomplished amateur musicians to perform together, and up-skill musicians who do not have direct access to professional musicians. The Symphony team initiated a competition and invited all of the world's musicians to participate. Professional conductors offered performance support by talking about the submission pieces entrants were asked to play; these were filmed in multiple languages and posted online. Master classes, with professional musicians talking about their instruments and demonstrating techniques/best practices, were also filmed and posted on YouTube. Performance expectations and criteria for judging were provided to participants. Musicians recorded themselves playing and uploaded their videos. Following an initial review by experts, a worldwide community voted on the videos they liked best. The selected musicians came together to perform in a concert at Carnegie Hall. The YouTube Symphony project impacted performance by identifying outstanding musicians from around the world and providing access to master instruction for amateur musicians.

A similar technique could be used for other

skills, such as "Giving Effective Presentations." Imagine a post-class assignment, where participants upload videos of themselves giving presentations. Other participants (and/or presentation experts) could then view and rate the performances and offer comments. The top performers could then be offered additional opportunities to present to their peers or help teach a class. The ease of creating and sharing videos presents an opportunity for learners to share their skills, tips, and best practices with each other.

Google Moderator.

A little-known free online tool enables viewers to vote on submissions from an audience. Have you ever attended a talk, a town hall meeting, a presentation, or a training class during which someone asked questions that you weren't really interested in? Or that derailed the conversation? Have you ever had a question you were too afraid to ask because you didn't think other people would be interested? One of the important components of the Google culture is an ongoing lecture series in which authors and experts in their fields speak about their areas of expertise. We also have frequent town hall meetings with business leaders and executives during which we can ask questions about almost anything! We use a publicly available tool called Google Moderator (http://www.google.com/moderator) in these situations.

Google Moderator allows participants to submit questions, comments, and suggestions in response to a subject or a specific event. During a recent presentation about Web2.0 technologies at a learning conference, the presenters created a Moderator page to take the pulse of the audience. (See Figure 3 for a screenshot of the tool used during this talk.) Participants submitted their questions online

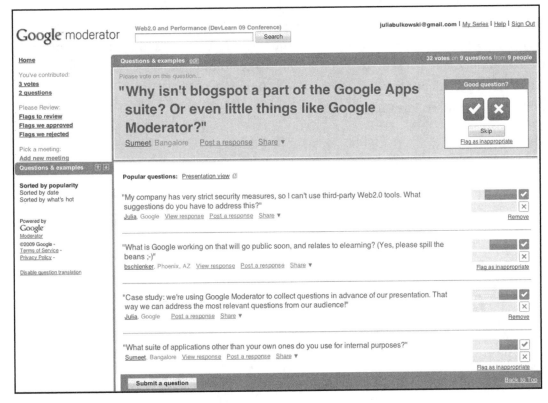

Figure 3. Google Moderator in Action During a Presentation on Web 2.0 Reprinted with permission of Google Inc.

(or through mobile phones). They could view all of the other questions that had been submitted and voted on the questions that were most interesting to them. At the conclusion of the session, during the regularly scheduled question-and-answer period, the session's facilitators addressed the top-ranked questions. Moderator has impacted performance by ensuring an audience's most relevant questions are answered, saving time and keeping participants engaged.

Did you know that President Obama has also used this tool? He used it immediately after the election to collect ideas, thoughts, and suggestions on policy issues from the public. "The Citizen's Briefing Book" enabled everyday Americans to share their opinions, expertise, and insight. "We have had an unbelievable response—over 70,000 people participated, half a million votes, and tens of thousands of wonderful ideas" were submitted, according to Michael Strautmanis, director of public liaison and intergovernmental affairs for the transition (McSwain, 2009). These were compiled and presented to the president. During presidential town hall meetings, citizens submitted questions through Google Moderator and voted on which ones he should answer. The president therefore could ensure that the topics he focused on were the ones that really mattered to his audience. Moderator collects questions from the audience and enables voting so that the speaker can address the top questions and suggestions.

CONCLUSION

I hope that these examples of Web 2.0 tools used to enhance learning and performance have provided inspiration for you to try some of them in your organization. Not all organizations embrace the latest technology, but I encourage you to start small. Perhaps you could run a pilot with your training team or information technology team. Engage your information technology team members and ask them for ways to bring these technologies behind the firewall, if that is a concern. Although I have heard a lot of fears about Web 2.0 technologies, I have only seen tremendous benefits.

REFERENCES

Blog. (n.d.). Retrieved from Wikipedia: http://en.wikipedia.org/wiki/Blog.

Giles, J. (2005). Internet encyclopaedias go head to head. *Nature, 438*, 900–901.

McSwain, D. (2009, January 16). Wrapping up the Citizen's Briefing Book. [Web log]. Retrieved from http://change.gov/newsroom/entry/wrapping_up_the_citizens_briefing_book/

Roberts-Witt, S.L. (2002, March 26). A "eureka!" moment at Xerox. *PCMag.* Retrieved from www.pcmag.com/article2/0,2817,28792,00.asp.

Tapscott, D., & Williams, A.D. (2006). *Wikinomics: How mass collaboration changes everything.* New York: Portfolio.

Web 2.0. (n.d.). Retrieved from Wikipedia: http://en.wikipedia.org/wiki/Web2.0

Clark Aldrich

Clark Aldrich designs and build simulations, and either manages the entire end-to-end process or just takes on the role of lead designer if an external team is already in place. One of his simulation products, Virtual Leader, was the most popular leadership simulation in the world, had rigorous third-party evaluations demonstrating superior long-term behavior improvements, and generated millions in revenue. He is also the author of five books, *Simulations and the Future of Learning* (Pfeiffer, 2004), *Learning by Doing* (Pfeiffer, 2005), *The Complete Guide to Simulations and Serious Games* (Pfeiffer, 2009), *Learning Online with Games, Simulations, and Virtual Worlds* (Jossey-Bass, 2009), and *Unschooling Rules* (2010). Clark also is a consultant. He works on short-term, long-term, and board-level client projects.

His work has been featured in hundreds of sources, including CBS, ABC, *The New York Times*, *Wall Street Journal*, CNN, NPR, CNET, Business 2.0, *BusinessWeek*, and *U.S. News and World Report*. Among other distinctions, he has been called an "industry guru" by *Fortune* magazine.

DEVELOPING SERIOUS GAMES AND SIMULATIONS: | Clark Aldrich
A QUICK GUIDE

Games attract, motivate, and engage people, but many attempts to integrate education or training with games have resulted in applications that neither appeal to learners nor produce targeted learning outcomes. I'm particularly delighted that Clark has contributed to this *Annual* his extensive experience and wisdom based on success in such endeavors. Organizations often need simulations and serious games to build competence and confidence in their workforce and extended enterprise. Clark explains when and how simulations and serious games fit into a learning organization and presents a rigorous process for identifying roles, responsibilities, processes, and time frames for creating them.

SIMS: WHAT AND WHY

A good educational simulation may look a lot like a casual computer game. It may have stylized, fast-moving graphics. There may be a timer during some part of a level and exaggerated consequences of failure. The person engaging the sim may look very much like a gamer, hunched over with a hand tightly grasped on the mouse and eyes riveted on the screen. The student may even be in a flow state—and having a lot of fun.

This has led a lot of people to erroneously conclude that the primary point of simulations, or sims, is to "make content enjoyable" (a skeptic may further and logically intuit) often at the expense of depth and flexibility while increasing the cost of production and time to "play." And if a *designer* of a sim shares this assumption, the formal learning program is unlikely to be successful.

Rather, *the necessary goal of a well-designed sim-based program is to develop in the student a deep, flexible, intuitive, kinesthetic understanding of the subject matter.* Students learn what their real-world options are in situations and earn a conviction in what are often complex and even indirect strategies that lead to positive results. They earn situational awareness.

As a result, students who learn via simulation can improvise better in the real world. They can handle unpredicted situations. The knowledge is not structured around a list of extrinsic "rules" or processes that can be broken if no one is looking (such as posted speed limits), but developed from intrinsic personal experience (such as whether a driver had a few near misses and even accidents with significant consequences). This is knowledge they retain for years or decades.

Forcing Repetition. To deliver this condensed experience, sims have to purposefully present interactive content models, interfaces, and visualizations. Then sims have to entice or force students to repeat patterns of actions in increasingly complex and novel situations—and with rigorous short-term and increasingly long-term feedback.

It is here that computer games, much more than classrooms or books, become the better framework to organize content and motivate students. These games have such useful attributes as being self-paced, easy to access, and good at developing learning through self-motivated repetition without the need for a coach.

Having said that, the content of the sim itself has to reflect the learning goals, not a reskinned game. As a result, an experienced sim designer will *first* identify key learning goals, *then* analyze the content through a simulation lens, and *only then* find a good interactive content model, sometimes inspired by the game world.

Sims in the Context of Enterprise Skills Flow.

Before going into *design* and *end-to-end creation*, however, let's look at the broader contexts of organizational learning into which sims must be designed to fit, shown in Figure 1.

Anyone who is in charge of a training organization has to sweat out the flow of skills in a dynamic entity, looking at the four quadrants of *expert, instructor, student,* and *practitioner,* and the movement of ideas and people between them.

Here are some of the flows:

➤ *Instructors* might learn from *experts,* and format the information for *students.*

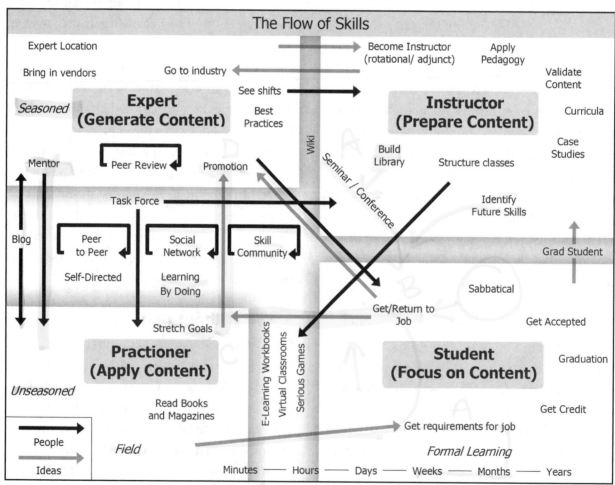

Figure 1. Chart: The Flow of Skills

- ➤ *Experts* might mentor *practitioners.*
- ➤ *Practitioners* might get promoted to *expert.*
- ➤ *Practitioners* may work on special projects, that if successful, then elevates them to *expert.*
- ➤ *Students* might work to get into a class, and get credit for successfully completing it.
- ➤ Peer to peer communities might chew on problems and come to a solution.

The Role of Simulations. Recently, there has been ramped-up focus on dramatically reducing the entire right side of the Flow of Skills chart—the formal role of *instructor* and the role of *student*—while dramatically increasing the areas of overlap between expert and novice (middle left), such as peer-to-peer work and social networking, often labeled as *informal learning.* But very specific content, and the corresponding certification/tracking, are even more necessary for both legal and strategic reasons.

Given this, the new models of sims uniquely fill that razor edge of opportunity and necessity for people responsible for organizational or community learning. Specifically, sims should be used when two or more of the following criteria are met:

- ➤ The application of the content in the real world is critical to an organization or community.
- ➤ Developing a conviction in the content is critical to an organization or community.
- ➤ Certification or other measuring and record-keeping is critical.

- ➤ The content is both important for the student to understand, and other formal learning techniques have failed or are too expensive.
- ➤ The content has a broad, geographically distributed audience.

Structured in chunks no longer than an hour, these new sims develop business-critical concepts and drive long-lasting behavioral changes in a way that is engaging for the user and is reinforced by a deeper understanding of the material. It's also critical for the sims to meet certification requirements and other external measurements for the sponsor. Multiple sims can be chained together for greater depth and breadth. And their visual and kinesthetic nature makes them the perfect choice for global audiences.

CREATING SIMULATIONS AND SERIOUS GAMES What follows is that methodology and identified best practices to produce a sim. Let us first look at a framework to get you through the Design Process in four predictable steps.

Design Step One: Collecting the Top-Down Rules. The first step in designing a sim is to collect all of the top-down patterns that have already been created, including established analysis, best practices, and rules. In this step traditional educational content and linear materials such as courses and curricula, books, reports, famous or inspirational quotes, and rules and policies are very helpful. They also serve to set a scale for what the sim will and won't cover.

If you were building a simulation about composting, you would collect commonly established advice as established by experts. For example:

> ➤ Don't throw in dairy or meat, turn your pile every few weeks, mix in grass clippings to keep the nitrogen at the right level so it doesn't smell, and that people compost to reduce their impact on landfills and improve their land.

Design Step Two: Identifying the Bottom-Up Tiny Relationships.

The second step, after all of the traditional rules and analysis are collected, is to uncover the hundreds of tiny relationships. These tiny relationships should roughly fall into the simulation framework of *actions systems results*. (The form of these tiny relationships is described in detail in *The Complete Guide to Simulations and Serious Games* (Aldrich, 2009).

Tiny Relationships: Actions

One set of tiny relationships concerns actions. *Yell. Beg. Put tongue A in groove B. Invest money. Run*—are all examples of actions.

For *actions*, the biggest questions are: What are the seriously considered options available to an expert? What do naïve people do? Can actions be defined very specifically, including levels of magnitude?

For example, imagine we were creating a sim around end-user computer security. Some of the actions available are a user, when receiving an email, can follow an embedded link to a website (and then perhaps enter personal data), open the attachment, forward an email to a friend, log in or not, even install the suggested program. Or the person can try to figure out whether the email is legitimate or not. Or he can delete the email, or perhaps report it to a manager or the IT department. These are the specific target actions.

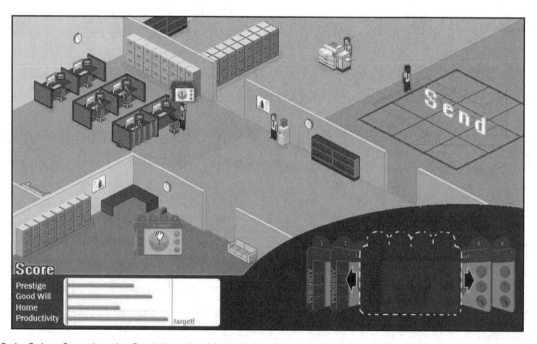

Figure 2. In Cyber Security, the Decisions Are Made in the Context of a Busy Office That May Have to Be Modeled
Screen shot used with permission from Carney Inc.

Further, a sim designer may also have to surface the activities that are done around the target actions in order to provide an accurate context. For our *end-user computer security* example, people have to make the above decisions around potentially fraudulent emails while they are focusing on doing their jobs. These "life" actions might have to be worked into any final set of actions available in the sim, as in the Figure 2 example.

Tiny Relationships: Missions/Results

The second category of tiny relations on which we need to focus is results. For results we ask, What do success and failure look like? Is success all or nothing, such as the accomplishment of a mission? Or are there three or four things that a person is trying to balance and grow? Or is success in the sim (as well as from the sim) the ability to consistently apply an increasingly complex set of competencies?

Again, we look at *target results,* and also *contextual results* if appropriate. The target results for computer security may be a smooth IT environment versus a massive virus infection. But the contextual results are just as important to design: players need to be rewarded for completing their virtual jobs. Another example: being an ethical person or not doping in sports is only interesting in the context of life or an athletic event, which has to be modeled and in which success has to be encouraged.

Identifying and portraying the causes and consequences of *failure* is more interesting, more important, and more counterintuitive for most instructional designers than identifying and portraying success. We have to figure out what the various types of failure one can

experience are and what situations lead to them. What are the immediate wrong things to do, and what are long-term failures?

Tiny Relationships: Systems

The final set of relationships to identify is that of systems. Systems connect actions and systems, and they often get in a person's way between what actions a person is taking and what results she wants. If the collection of all sets of tiny relationships is an iceberg, then systems are the part of the iceberg that is underwater—often a huge hidden mass.

Here are two quick examples: When playing chess, a person may want to capture the other player's king, but the systems of rules and positions and the activities of an opponent on the board have to be navigated and overcome (which is, of course, what makes it fun and interesting). Meanwhile, in leadership, we may want to build a great team, but the rules of accomplishment, personal egos and motivation, and reward need to be navigated (which can be fun, but more likely frustrating).

For *systems* some questions might be: Are there processes or mazes that have to be followed? Are there opponents who are striving to keep the person from being successful? Are there hidden processes that others are following (in our computer security example, bad guys may be taking scraps of personal data and crafting highly targeted profiles for scams)? Are there cycles, balancing loops, or feedback loops? Are there delays? Are there some mathematical relationships?

To return to our composting model, here are some examples of all three sets of tiny relationships:

> *Actions:* Put different kinds of food in compost (egg shells, coffee grounds,

hamburger, plastic, yogurt), turn compost, shovel out and spread compost, put in other organic matter (leaves, branches, weeds), cover pile, start new pile, buy barrels, mixing tools, water pile, sift compost, throw out food as garbage, design compost area

> *Systems:* Rain washes through compost; food breaks down with aeration in about a month, food breaks down without aeration in about a year; nitrogen level imbalances can result in smell and inefficiencies; table of what matter contributes what nitrogen amounts; compost creates better soil, which creates better growing conditions for flowers and vegetables; growing one's own vegetables results in cheaper and healthier food; garbage costs money per pound to put in a landfill; exposed vegetables will mildy attract critters, exposed meat will strongly attract critters; different microbes do different things at different temperatures; earthworms can aerate dirt.

> *Results:* Great soil, smell, less garbage sent to landfills, yellow jackets, great vegetables, critters

Finding Them

Many of these relationships (shown in Figure 3) are so simple that it feels absurd to even capture them in a document. But their power comes in their rigor, volume, and integration. You have to be a detective here, grilling subject-matter experts (and my favorite tool, listening to podcasts), pouncing on every scrap.

Figure 3. The Bottoms-Up Relationships from the Simulation Model

Design Step Three: Find the Closest Existing Toolset, Game or Sim Genre, or Microcosm. We have already identified the high-level rules and the mounds of tiny relationships. Now, find an existing simulation or game that comes close to the framework or spirit of some or all of what you want to accomplish (if you possibly can).

Is it a first-person shooter? Tower defense? Branching story? Then borrow the established format as much as possible. If an engine exists, such as Second Life or Adventure Maker, figure out how to use it (this can save more than 80 percent on the development time). Regardless, use the gameplay and level design conventions. In many cases, you will also draw models from other genres as well, glomming them together.

The Order Matters (a Lot)

While each of the above three steps ultimately should inform the others (as we will soon discuss), the order is actually hugely important. Interestingly, depending on whether you start with step two or with step three, you obtain dramatically opposite effects.

Starting with the identification of the little relationships (step two) often occurs when either a researcher or subject-matter expert starts an effort. But identifying the little relationships before framing the best practices (step one) is a staggeringly complex activity, which (while it satiates the content completists) can take huge amounts of time and overwhelm all but the most intrepid. Projects that start here seldom see the light of day. Even if they do survive, there has been a great deal of wasted effort.

In contrast, starting with the identification of the genre (step three) or sim/game engine and filling in the blanks is a much more typical phenomenon. I often see this when either a vendor has a pre-built engine they are using for a new project, or when an organization has invested in a platform or authoring environment and is trying to push more programs onto it. The results are quick (weeks instead of months), cost-effective, and efficient. The course is spit out on time. The only problem is that the content is flat. Designers end up merely reskinning rather than teaching anything of note. Two or three different programs, ostensibly covering different topics, starting from the vantage of the same engine, all look the same and, more importantly, basically "teach" the same thing. We are seeing this in abundance with sims in Second Life,

but also from small specialty vendors. From a business perspective, this makes sense for them—the vendor's internal cost, time frame, unpredictability, and quality of talent needed are five to ten times greater if they are creating a new engine rather than using an old one. But it can result in a substandard or forced student experience.

Design Step Four: Bring All of the Content into Alignment.

Now, at stage four, we have to bring everything together. Use the best practices in step one to organize the tiny relationships in step two, and then use the genre from step three to frame everything. You will work in from the three corners to the middle. Ultimately, all three should converge (even if there is fear at first that they won't).

Creating Strategic and First-Person Perspectives

The most effective sims use two or more parallel and mutually reinforcing perspectives. This approach is consistent with generations of computer games and flight simulators that have traditionally featured a first-person perspective and a strategic (aka a radar or "mini map") perspective. The protypical example is of driving game, where the screen is used to show the world from the driver's perspective looking out at the highway and other nearby cars, while also showing a top-down perspective on the entire track with all

Figure 4. A Financial Acumen Sim with a Simultaneous First-Person and Strategic View

competitors. Players made decisions based on both perspectives simultaneously.

The first-person perspective presents the actual situations and decisions that the student will see and make in the real world. This often involves interpersonal conversations. The strategic perspective presents the "big picture" and involves a visualization of a system and interactions often not visible in the real world. (An example is shown in Figure 4.)

Other Steps in the Alignment Process

As one closes in on a final design, some tough questions have to be answered. Example of questions include: How broadly can the identified actions be generalized or abstracted? For our computer security example, all of the actions, in both the target set and the contextual set, can be generally abstracted into the core three actions of *accept the incoming request and act upon it, probe the request, or reject the request.*

Coming up with the right level of abstrac-

tion and generalization for the interface is critical, as most sims work best in real time, where the computer does not wait for the student. Ideally, a few actions are applied repeatedly, in different orders and sensitive to timing. Further, abstracting actions can increase the applicability of the sim to wider groups.

Another question we have to answer is how the sim handles little failures. Being inappropriately aggressive to a subordinate, for example, is a bad idea in a leadership sim. But does it stop the whole sim? In real life, plenty of successful people have little slips. Are failures cumulative? Arcade games often have a "three lives" model. Is that appropriate?

You may have a few outlier rules (from step one) at the end of the process that fall outside of the system and level of designs that you have created, but that still need to be included. Here you might use traditional pedagogical technique such as sliders or pop-ups to convey this content. But this should be minimal. You will know you have done a good job when all three perspectives support each other rather than grind. And often, amazingly, you will gain unique and industry-valued perspectives through this process.

In our compost example, my goal is a thriving ecosystem, so I might choose a variation of SimCity or Roller Coaster Tycoon. I might use quality of life, cost, and environmental impact as some core metrics the player tries to optimize. I might create a house area, a compost area, a garden area, and a garbage area and have people be able to move stuff between the four. Finally, moving away from these genres, I might zoom in and allow people to create and modify their own composting structure.

Of course, the design process has to fit into a larger serious game development process. Let me zoom out now a bit and look at the rest of the process.

THE THREE TRIMESTERS OF A SERIOUS GAME DEVELOPMENT PROCESS

The duration of serious game development usually falls into the three trimesters of *create, code,* and *calibrate.* In just a moment, let's look at them in some detail, including key roles and responsibilities.

How Long Does It Take to Create a Serious Game?

Before we dig in, let's talk a bit about end-to-end time frames. Everyone asks about it.

Let me come at this from two sides. On one side, the most effective sims of the next five years, single-player and Adobe Flash or HTML 5 based, will take about nine months to create starting from scratch, and take about

one to two hours of student time; however, most corporations want something delivered within about three months of signing a contract.

These two realities are not incompatible. Thankfully, there are some significant modifiers that are cumulative, so you can get something out the door in weeks, not months, if you have to. Here are the key decisions to both decrease and increase the default nine-month development time:

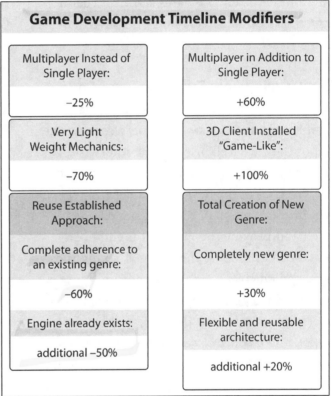

Game Development Timeline Modifiers

Multiplayer Instead of Single Player: −25%	Multiplayer in Addition to Single Player: +60%
Very Light Weight Mechanics: −70%	3D Client Installed "Game-Like": +100%
Reuse Established Approach: Complete adherence to an existing genre: −60%	Total Creation of New Genre: Completely new genre: +30%
Engine already exists: additional −50%	Flexible and reusable architecture: additional +20%

These time modifiers tend to impact all three trimesters evenly. Now here are the trimesters in a bit more detail. Even though I present them as discrete, they really overlap.

Sim Development Trimester One: Create

In the first trimester, the sim is designed using some of the techniques we discussed above. The goal is to produce a great design document, between thirty and fifty pages long. The *lead designer* (such as myself) immerses him- or herself in the content, often becoming an expert.

But yes, there's more to this trimester. The learning objectives and requirements are formalized, often using people in the role of a *client liaison* and *program sponsor*. The look and feel are nailed down, hopefully with the work of a good *graphic designer*. Any technical decisions, including media, authoring environments, engines, and end-user requirements, are established. Steps also have to be taken to set up trimester two.

Sim Development Trimester Two: Code

In the second trimester, the two or three people in the role of *programmers/coders* (one hopes they are well briefed and otherwise involved during trimester one) will program the material in the design document. They will produce much of the core sim engine itself and provide the links to the fluid content, such as graphic files, videos, sound files, text, and entire level designs and sim flow, using industry-standard media and xmls. The *program sponsor, lead designer, graphic designer,* and *client liaison* will be peripherally involved, making decisions and helping flesh out the numerous parts of the sim engine that need refining. Near the end of this process, the *lead designer* will begin inputting as much of the final content as possible. About 70 percent of the project budget is spent in this stage.

Sim Development Trimester Three: Calibrate

In the final trimester, the *lead designer* finishes inputting content into the engine, and

the entire package is put in front of *target audiences* by the *program sponsor* (by the way, finding the right target audience and introducing the experience to them is a surprisingly difficult task). The *programmers/coders* must be available to make core engine changes, but even more importantly, the *lead designer* and *client liaison* have to refine the fluid content. Finally, there can be integration work with the LMS or database.

What are the Skill Sets Necessary to Create a Serious Game?

Finally, here is the breakdown of skill sets needed.

Title: Client Manager/ Sales Person/ Client Requirements

Description of responsibilities: The client manager is the de facto lead of a sim project. They are the people who identify and secure the project to begin with. They then provide a constant voice of the customer throughout the development process. They may or may not be involved directly in the content creation process. They are constantly looking over everyone's shoulders and often making final judgment calls on tough decisions based on what they believe the client wants. The client manager may also assist the project manager and the lead designer in setting up a critical approval meetings, project pilots, and meetings with subject-matter experts.

Percentage of Entire Project: 20 percent

Title: Lead Designer (and Other Designers)

Description of responsibilities: (This is the role I take.) The lead designer can be thought of as, in movie-making parlance, the "director" of the simulation. He or she controls the tone, content, and length of the experience. The lead designer is responsible for all of the necessary research for the simulation, the level structure, the interface, mockups of screenshots using PowerPoint or crayons, identification of users, walkthroughs, meta-coding and framing of underlining systems and mechanics, goal states, all written material including dialogue, and more. He or she often presents all of this in the design document. The lead designer is also responsible for ongoing calibration. (See *The Complete Guide to Simulations and Serious Games* for full details.)

Percentage of Entire Project: 20 to 30 percent

Title: Lead Programmer (and Other Programmers)

Description of responsibilities: The lead programmer is responsible for creating all of the code for the sim. This includes prototyping, piloting, creating any authoring or editing environment, and creating a finished simulation. In many projects, this category also includes skills for evaluating and adopting third-party technology and tool sets. (Most of my projects require Flash or, increasingly, HTML 5).

Percentage of Entire Project: 20 to 30 percent

Note: Programmers may create authoring environments that significantly decrease the time it takes for the designers to input and refine information.

Title: Project Manager

Description of responsibilities: Project managers have to be masters of precision and tact. They have to be there to support all of the other people and talents, and yet at the same time enforce deadlines and budgets through soft and hard power. Ultimately, project managers have to be of high skill level and low ego. They report to the client manager. It is a sure path to failure when project managers try to overreach and seize control of everything, just because they have the role of managing the project's budget.

Percentage of Entire Project: 10 percent

Title: Lead Artist

Description of responsibilities: The lead artist is responsible for all of the art of the project. This includes the aesthetics of the interface, any and all color schemes, drawings, and animations.

Percentage of Entire Project: 10 percent

Title: Database Systems Integrator

Description of responsibilities: The database systems integrator is responsible for all integration of the program into the customer environment. This includes SCORM compliance, LMS integration, database integration, and knowledge of the end-user environments. This role often extends the furthest out, as client implementation environments change months or even years after the simulation has been successfully installed.

Percentage of Entire Project: 5 to 10 percent

Title: Voice Talent

Description of responsibilities: Voice talent provides all of the voices for the sim, including narrator and characters. Typically, voice talent are professional actors. They always come from the outside, are quite expensive, are hired for one or two sessions, and are critical to the ultimate success of the simulation.

Percentage of Entire Project: 5 percent

Title: Subject Matter Experts

Description of responsibilities: Subject-matter experts provide the knowledge that has to be captured and developed in others through the sim.

Percentage of Entire Project: 0 percent

Curiously, subject-matter experts are often not factored into the cost of creating a serious game or educational simulation. This is because they are often provided by the sponsors or even accessed asymmetrically through books or podcasts. Still, given how important subject-matter experts are, and how much most people complain about the lack of cooperation from subject-matter experts, one can't help but wonder whether paying them out of the simulation budget might align motivations over time.

All the roles described above are shown in the chart below.

Role	Percent of Entire Project
Client Manager/ Sales Person/ Client Requirements	20%
Lead Designer (and Other Designers)	20–30%
Lead Programmer (and Other Programmers)	20–30%
Project Manager	10%
Lead Artist	10%
Database Systems Integrator	5–10%
Voice Talent	5%
Subject-Matter Experts	0%

FINAL THOUGHTS | Things have never seemed harder for those tasked with developing the skill sets of organizations. They have to deliver content, and sometimes entire curricula, sometimes with coaching, often with tracking and certification, with a minimum of costs (in terms of development and delivery dollars, student time, and student disruption).

The good news is that simulations and serious games can instruct more, in less time and at less cost. The most successful organizations will either have an internal sim development capability or partner with an external vendor that does. I hope following these steps and processes makes the implementation a bit easier and more predictable.

REFERENCES

Aldrich, C. (2004). *Simulations and the future of learning.* San Francisco: Pfeiffer.

Aldrich, C. (2005). *Learning by doing.* San Francisco: Pfeiffer.

Aldrich, C. (2009). *The complete guide to simulations and serious games.* San Francisco: Pfeiffer.

Aldrich, C. (2009). *Learning online with games, simulations, and virtual worlds.* San Francisco: Jossey-Bass.

Aldrich, C. (2010). *Unschooling rules.* Self-published.

Ken Spero

Ken Spero, MBA, is the co-founder of Humentum. He has focused his career on helping organizations do a better job of critical thinking and decision making. Encouraging mindful behavior with his clients has enabled him to produce measurable improvements in productivity inside many of his clients' strategic initiatives. He has spent the last twenty-one years developing and deploying learning solutions with computer simulations at their core.

Ken brings a strong background in business strategy, leadership, and project management to his work at Humentum. His strengths in problem solving, performance management, team building, global deployment, and relationship management contribute to the value he brings to clients.

Prior to Humentum, Ken was responsible for the chemical and pharmaceuticals practice at Strategic Management Group, where he focused on the application of simulation to the needs of those industries. In that capacity he helped his clients and his team to deploy customized solutions through focused consulting, development, and delivery.

Ken has worked directly with a diverse portfolio of clients, including Dow Chemical, Dow Corning, Schering Plough, Disney, Barnes and Noble, Xerox, and AstraZeneca.

Ken earned his MBA from Columbia University and his undergraduate degree in management science from Case Western Reserve University.

EXPERIENCE DESIGN:
Ken Spero
A PRACTICAL METHODOLOGY FOR CAPTURING, DELIVERING, AND DEPLOYING EXPERIENCE

Experience is the word. I'm so happy to see Ken Spero's emphasis here. Experience is important because experience leads to performance in real-world contexts. Ken puts it this way, "When hiring a new employee or promoting someone from within, most organizations look for experience appropriate to the position and responsibilities. Although skills are an important part of the requirements, experience often trumps skills because it is essential that the candidate be able to utilize those skills in context, applying both experience and critical thinking to work situations. Organizations often use training strategies that are built on instructional design techniques to improve performance. But when the job requires experience and critical judgment to address contextual situations effectively, instruction is not enough." In this article, Ken introduces a methodology that makes experience more accessible and more readily deployed in a scalable manner as part of a blended learning strategy. Using this approach will help organizations to increase the efficacy of their learning efforts and to achieve their strategic and operational requirements more quickly.

Employee and organization development have become critical challenges for companies in the current economic environment. Many companies have reduced their headcount appreciably; however, they have not had a respective reduction in expectations for volume of whatever product or service they provide. There seems to be an explicit assumption that the remaining employees are going to be considerably more productive in order to maintain and/or grow the business. Unless one believes that the employees have been holding back and simply needed the appropriate motivation to significantly increase their productivity, companies are going to have to provide their employees with a new/better way of doing their work. The ideal way to build extra capability is to find an approach that facilitates experience with the issues that need to be addressed. The challenge, of course, is how to provide experience without the risk and

time of learning through the school of "hard knocks." Research has shown that computer-based simulation is one of the best ways to effectively and practically deliver consistent experience across an organization.

Simulations can be very powerful due to their experiential nature. But the benefits can manifest far beyond the "product" or the software. This relates to an overall approach that is driven by "experience." Experience has been shown to be a key driver in the success of both individuals and organizations. The experiences of the respective individuals as well as what lessons they have learned from their experiences are key determinants to the ongoing success of any organization. However, when an organization chooses to invest in building the capabilities of its staff to enable them to do something new, the chosen method tends to revolve around instruction rather than experience.

Instructional design (ID) and it is a very important field for designing really effective *instruction.* The focus is primarily on the *what* and *how* of the content. Good instructional design provides the information that participants need in an orderly and structured manner. The *how* and *what* are both static and not contextual, so instruction can be effective. However, the real challenge is when the *why and when* of the content do not manifest in the neat and orderly manner that was presented in the training. Ideally, learners' experience will provide insight into the *why* and *when* of the content so that it can be applied into any context. Given that instruction is really only good for the *what and how,* when we need to demonstrate *why* and *when,* a more dynamic approach is required—one that takes into account context and interrelationships. In other words, a method for capturing *experience* is needed.

Learning professionals tend to look at the range of solutions they can produce as falling along the following learning continuum, ranging from boring, page-turning e-learning to highly interactive learning.

The highly interactive solutions that are developed stem from a core of instruction oriented objectives. Although exercises and case studies may be incorporated into the programs, the solutions are generally designed around delivering the *what and how* of the content in increasingly creative ways. It seems that in the minds of many learning professionals, learning is synonymous with instruction. It comes as no surprise then that the design methodology is instructional design. The rigor that make ID such an effective method for the design of *instruction* are not conducive to designing *experience,* which is more about capturing a compelling story. This distinction will be elaborated upon later in the article as we distinguish the objectives and outcomes of what we call "experience design."

In the meantime, with respect to the learning continuum, we are left with a dilemma. Given that the learning continuum is focused on instruction, where does simulation fit? I would suggest that simulation is not more pervasive in the industry simply because of our focus on traditional instructional design, even though the efficacy and benefits of simulation and experiential learning have been well documented. When faced with finding solutions to complex problems, many learning professional opt for an approach that is both structured and defined. Falling back on an instructional approach can be comforting. Capturing experience is more subjective and less rigorous. It may require input from non-traditional subject-matter experts to design a simulation. How can we present simulations in a better light and utilize them more appropriately?

Figure 1. Learning Continuum

Figure 2. Revised Learning Continuum

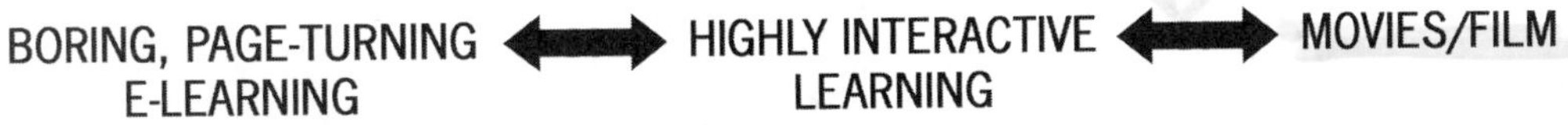

BORING, PAGE-TURNING ⬌ **HIGHLY INTERACTIVE** ⬌ **MOVIES/FILM**
E-LEARNING   **LEARNING**

The answer to the disconnect between instruction and experience lies with the continuum itself. The learning community needs to broaden its perspective on ways they can reach participants. The continuum in Figure 1 is really only half of the picture. In reality, the continuum is more like the one in Figure 2.

Highly interactive learning (H.I.L) is somewhere in the middle. The left side of the continuum shows learning with little entertainment value to drive engagement, and the right side shows efforts driven by entertainment with little learning. Looked at this way, simulation is toward the movies/film side of the spectrum. This expanded perspective shows that instructional design comfortably governs many of the opportunities to the left, while the right is more driven by the power of narrative. The more compelling the story, the more engaged the viewer/participant becomes. He or she has the opportunity to live vicariously or to experience the topics being addressed. Learning is no longer about instruction, but rather about experience.

When experience becomes the frame of reference from a design perspective, it can be focused upon at different levels within the organization, with each level feeding the next. At the individual or participant level, we *deliver the experience* that the person can live through. If there is an opportunity to deliver the experience in a group setting, then participants have the additional benefit of seeing the experience as others do. At the leadership or subject-matter expert level, we *capture the experience* or articulate the way things ought to be done. At the organizational level, we *deploy the experience;* we blend the experiential component with the necessary initiative, learning, or on-the-job elements that enable success. The shared experience across the organization facilitates broader and deeper communication, which fosters effective execution. This method is what we refer to as *experience design:*

1. Deliver the Experience—Individual
2. Capture the Experience—Leadership
3. Deploy the Experience—Organization

EXPERIENCE DESIGN— SIMULATIONS

The focus of this article is on behavioral or branching simulations built using the metaphor of a decision tree. They are focused on providing participants with an opportunity to:

➢ Exercise critical thinking and decision making
➢ Experience consequences
➢ Receive feedback

The model is shown in Figure 3.

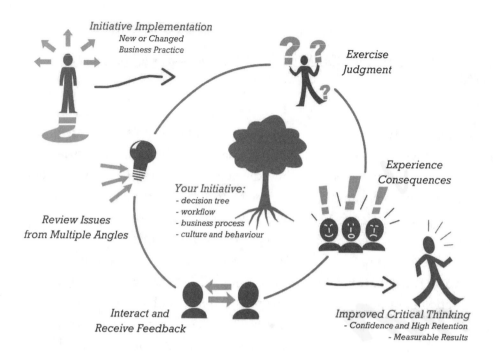

Figure 3.
Initiative Map

Branching simulations manifest as a form of "choose your own adventure" exercise during which the participants are placed into a series of scenarios in which they are challenged with decisions they must make. They then experience the consequences of their choices as the simulation follows that "branch." The scenarios are mini experiences the impact of which is influenced by the depth and applicability of the exercise to participants' lives. For our purposes, simulation can be defined as a complex weave of scenarios put together to capture a period of time in the life of a character. They incorporate content (leadership, ethics, sales, etc.) with context (environment, people, task, etc.) so that it imitates life. This combination of content and context over time enables participants to experience a situation as it could play out in real life.

Using Simulations to Deliver the Experience. *Experience is the best teacher.*
Unfortunately, organizations have neither

the time nor the budget to allow their people to learn through the school of hard knocks. However, simulations allow participants to gain experience without the bruising. They provides an opportunity for participants to engage with the issues both intellectually and also emotionally, allowing for greater depth of processing.

In experience design, it is the experience itself that is important, not whether the participant does it right. Think back to the most powerful lessons you have learned; most likely, they were driven by a failure you experienced. When we face any new situation, we typically are guided by our "gut reactions." We sift through past experiences for relevant instances when we have seen this type of thing. We then garner some insight into the situation we are facing and take action.

What happens when the "experience portfolio" is empty? For example, if an employee has been recently promoted to being a supervisor, he or she is not going to have leadership experiences to draw upon. The experiences he or she does have may be counter to what is appropriate and effective now. A good decision for an individual contributor could be a bad one from a leadership perspective. In this type of situation, simulations are especially effective. Through the experience of leading others and dealing with coaching issues or difficult conversations, participants are able to gain experience that can be called upon in real life. When playing the simulation, participants can practice their decision-making and critical-thinking skills. By choosing among options they are presented with, they gain experience making decisions. Given the context of the simulation, participants make their own decisions, thinking critically about what is appropriate.

When designing a particular experience, we can isolate it from extraneous elements. This enables us to present a topic from beginning to end in accelerated time. Participants can play the simulation in much less time than it would take to actually live the experience. As participants play, they can experience the consequences of their actions right away. In real life, consequences are not immediate and may not manifest until some other issue triggers them.

Experience Portfolio and Critical Thinking. Because of the way that simulations are written, participants are challenged at key times in the narrative to make decisions. Clearly, this is more overt than the way issues present themselves in real life, but through this approach muscle-memory supporting critical thinking is created. When faced with a situation that

requires a decision, we consult our "guts" and take action. The challenge here is whether our gut actually has a clue (whether there is anything relevant in our experience portfolio)—and also whether we have the wherewithal to utilize what is there to make a good decision in the particular situation. In other words, will I be able to consider the issue that is before me, scan my portfolio, and consider alternatives and potential consequences before determining a strategy and taking action? The concept of an experience portfolio is diagrammed in Figure 4.

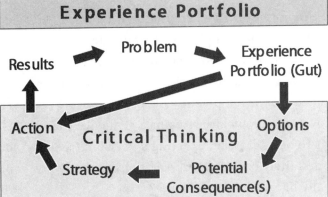

Figure 4. Experience Portfolio
Source: Will Thalheimer, Work-Learning Research

The box in Figure 4 represents critical thinking, which an experience-driven simulation is designed to provoke. Simulations provide an opportunity to see the benefits of thinking first, or at least pausing before taking action, so that better decisions can be made or participants can be better prepared for the consequences of their choices.

From the perspective of populating one's

experience portfolio, a simulated experience can sometimes have an advantage over the real thing. Rarely does any scenario we face happen in a vacuum. Simulation enables us to connect our decisions and their consequences and still see the flow of time. In that way, the file in the experience portfolio will be more complete. By providing an experience in a context that looks like one's own environment and presenting challenges similar to the kinds one might face, simulation designers enable participants to practice thinking critically.

Experience Design.

Given some of the obvious benefits that simulations can provide, why are they not more commonplace? A common reason given are the perceived time, cost, and complexity of simulation development. But with the advent of the many tools available on the market now, time and cost of development have been reduced. However, complexity remains a challenge that has to be addressed. Creating a decision tree is definitely complicated. And does anybody really like to do flowcharting?

Experience design specifically targets the challenge of capturing and deploying *experience*. All that is required from an expertise standpoint is either subject-matter expertise or at least ready access to SMEs. Knowledge of the job/function is also helpful, but that can be described in narrative form, which is a powerful medium. A good story can engage an audience at any level. It simply must reflect the reality that the participants face. Narrative facilitates both the intellectual and emotional engagement that lead to impactful experiences to file in one's experience portfolio.

The most significant distinction between experience design and instructional design is in how success is measured. When dealing with instruction, we want to know whether the participant got it "right." Learners can be tested in some manner to measure success. With experience design, the issue is all about *having* the *experience*. As mentioned before, simulations are appropriate when the goal is contextual and critical thinking is required. Through having different experiences we can understand the nuances and exhibit critical judgment. When playing a simulation, participants do not go through *the* experience, but rather *an* experience. Participants do not have to get it "right"; they simply have to do it. Clearly, it is important that the experience be well articulated, but because the issue is populating the experience portfolio, success is realized by simply completing it.

Authoring Simulations—Capture the Experience.

So far, our focus has been on benefits of simulations for the players. But the benefits go well beyond those playing the game. Organizations can derive significant benefit from capturing the experiences of participants. An example is the field of knowledge management (KM). Traditionally, KM documents the best practices and stores them where they can be readily found. The issue with KM is whether a person can extrapolate the necessary learning from what someone else did and apply it to his or own situation, even assuming that it was well documented.

From an experience perspective, there is opportunity to decide what makes something a "best practice," which is related more to the why and when, rather than to the mechanics of what was done. By capturing the experiences of the best practitioners, an organization has an opportunity to present those experiences in a way that allows others to interact with them. The best *thinking* (why and when) rather than the best *practice* (what and how) can be captured. We want to know when and why the best practitioner made a decision in executing any practice, what the alternatives were, and what the consequences would have been of choosing those alternatives. The outcome is a decision tree that enables other participants to experience the thinking behind best practices and incorporate it themselves. The objective is to enable employees to take the best path in their own situations, which may look nothing like the simulation.

An additional benefit is that best practitioners and other subject-matter experts who are involved in the process will be encouraged to think more deeply about what the experience ought to be like. By engaging them in this way, they can serve as coaches and mentors so that their best practices can be more effectively deployed and executed by the rest of the organization.

Blended Learning—Deploy the Experience.

The final aspect of experience design is deployment. From a design perspective, in *delivering the experience* the focus was at the individual level. In *capturing the experience* the focus was on leadership or subject-matter experts. With deploying the experience, the focus shifts to the manner in which what has been developed will be experienced across the company. The primary activity in delivering is playing. In capturing it is authoring. But in deploying, the primary activity is blending. Even though the *why* and *when*

are critical to improving decision making, they cannot be effectively executed without the *what* and *how*. The experience-oriented components have to be blended with the other critical elements of the initiative. The overall experience all employees have with the content is key. Employees across the organization have a shared experience, which enables better and deeper communication across geographies and functional silos. The experience can be used to propel the organization forward.

EXAMPLES | Here are a few examples of experience design in action.

New Leaders Simulation.

An office equipment company was interested in preparing new service managers for leadership positions. For the most part, they were promoting from within the organization. The technicians who demonstrated the potential for leadership were promoted. Given that these employees were new to being supervisors, their leadership experience portfolios were empty. What made for good decisions when they were individual contributors were the wrong decisions from a leadership perspective. A simulation was developed that captured six months in the life of a service manager. It provided participants with some leadership experience from the perspective of their direct reports, their customers, and their bosses. A performance review question is shown in Figure 5.

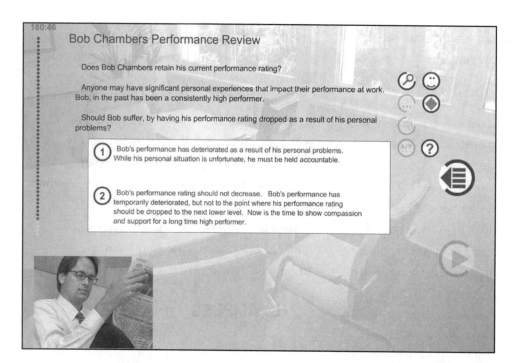

Figure 5.
Performance Review

Performance Management.

A chemical manufacturer was implementing a new performance management process and wanted to provide leaders with experience in the new process. The change was from an employee-driven model to a leader-driven one. Leaders were required to assess their teams using a bell curve. Placement on the curve would ultimately affect pay and promotions. The primary experiential component of the training solution was a simulation of a year in the life of a supervisor who has seven direct reports. Significant benefit was realized from creating the simulation. In formulating where to place different kinds of employees, the company was able to articulate a common experience for their leaders worldwide. The simulation was embedded in a two-day facilitated workshop that combined instruction with the experience of rating employees. We further supported the process with a series of mini-simulations related to each step in the process. They were deployed via the Internet as performance support tools. The training was offered at the beginning of the year. This meant that a significant amount of time would pass before the actual reviews. By our providing performance support, participants were able to try the process out before they needed to use it. By playing through a performance review with a difficult employee (see Figure 6), for example, a leader could get a sense of possible employee reactions. This improved the probability that the leader would do a better job responding to whatever transpires during a real review.

Compliance.

Due to ethical infringements, a pharmaceutical client was required to have its customer-facing employees go through compliance training. The client determined that the issue was more behavioral or contextual, rather than knowledge. The employees might know the correct responses if they were being tested, but when in front of a customer, it was not always so clear-cut. The client wanted to put compliance

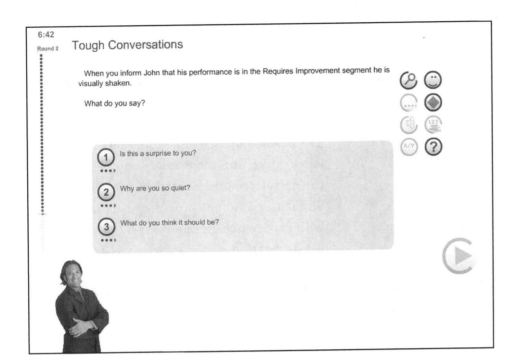

Figure 6. Tough Conversations

training into a more experiential exercise with both good and bad experiences that participants could draw upon as appropriate. Once again, significant value was derived in the development process as resources from different parts of the company came together to articulate the necessary points of view required in compliance. This not only enabled a more rich application (see Figure 7), but also established a group of cross-functional internal coaches who were able to help deploy the ideas more effectively within the organization. The designers used the power of interactivity and storytelling to create a compelling application that was extremely well received in the field and received excellent reviews, even though it was compliance training.

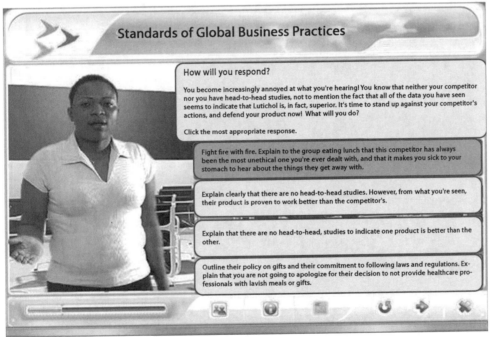

Figure 7. Standards of Global Business Practices

CONCLUSION | Given the current business environment, finding ways to up-skill/re-skill employees quickly is increasingly important. Employees are being required to be more productive without the necessary time to be trained. Given that experience is the best teacher, experience design is an approach that can effectively capture, deliver, and deploy experience to the people who require it. Experience design and simulation combine experience with the power of storytelling to satisfy employee development requirements quickly. Experience design debunks the traditional view that simulations are too complicated and costly. The necessary skills and experience to produce simulations are well within the reach of existing staff. The organizing principle for simulations is narrative, and the primary source for the narrative is the actual job process. Simulation is about providing participants with experience, not about making sure they get it "right." By using experience design, organizations can increase the speed and efficacy of their employee training efforts and speed their way to improved productivity.

Bryan Chapman

Bryan Chapman, M.S., is chief learning strategist at Chapman Alliance, a provider of research-centric consulting solutions that assist organizations to define, operate, and optimize their strategic learning initiatives. As a veteran in the industry, he has more than twenty years of experience and has worked with such organizations as American Express, Shell, Kodak, Sprint, Sharp Electronics, Honda, IBM, Microsoft, Avon, UNICEF, The Food and Drug Administration, U.S. State Department, and many others to help them optimize learning efficiency through the use of innovative learning techniques and technologies.

Bryan was formerly the director of research and strategy for independent research and consulting firm Brandon Hall Research, where he served as the primary author and researcher on numerous high-profile projects and a comprehensive study of custom content developers in the industry. In addition, Bryan was responsible for structuring Brandon Hall Research's consulting practice.

He holds a master's degree in instructional technology from Utah State University, where he was voted outstanding instructional design scholar by the faculty. He also holds a degree in multimedia communications from Brigham Young University.

LCMS:

NOT JUST A TECHNOLOGY, IT'S A STRATEGY

Bryan Chapman

Bryan Chapman is one of our field's most venerable leaders. He balances research and pragmatic approaches in ways that make a true difference. Because my readers tell me they especially appreciate controversy and point/counterpoint articles, I'm particularly pleased Bryan has chosen a topic for which I was able to find a counterpoint author (please see Carla Torgerson's article). Herein, Bryan properly notes that, while learning systems are considered mainstream in many organizations, they have not become mission-critical business systems for many organizations. He posits that today's technology offers much greater organizational utility than we might realize if we were to take a much stronger content-centric approach. Although squarely counter to the learner-centric approach that many of us advocate, Bryan takes an articulate, well-reasoned stance that must be carefully considered.

Learning systems, although considered mainstream in many organizations, still have not reached the same lofty status of mission-critical business systems such as Enterprise Resource Planning (ERP) systems, Human Resource Information Systems (HRIS), or the ubiquitous Customer Relation Management (CRM) systems. Why haven't learning systems reached their full potential and claimed high-profile status within business ecosystems? Perhaps the root cause is learning professionals. Could it be that we haven't been asking enough of our learning systems?

When creating a learning technology strategy, we typically ask questions that focus on administrative tasks, such as:

1. How can we use learning technology to centralize training and make it accessible from a single point of access?
2. How can we provide secure access to training courses, whether taught in a classroom or online?
3. How can we automate tracking and record-keeping?
4. How can we keep track of compliance and certification completions?
5. How can a learning system manage resources used in training?

Although these are good tactical problems to solve, few of these questions really hold learning systems directly accountable for solving mission-critical business objectives. To truly move our learning systems into the category of mission critical, here are the questions we should be asking:

1. How can we use learning technology to decrease development time?
2. How can we increase speed to competency?
3. How do we leverage learning to create new business opportunities?
4. How can we use learning to rationalize business practices across a new enterprise?
5. How can we align the use of mission-critical content across lines of business and departments?
6. How can we use technology to capture and maintain expert knowledge?

The key to achieving greater accountability (and visibility) requires a paradigm shift in the way we approach learning. First, we need to change our emphasis from using technology as a means of automating the administrative aspects of learning to focusing more fully on the strategic value of the learning content itself. Content is what gives a company its competitive edge and allows it to meet organizational goals and objectives. Training professionals must learn to use learning content as a strategic asset.

Learning management systems (LMSs) have been instrumental in streamlining training tasks, such as managing compliance/regulatory training; delivering libraries of off-the-shelf and custom content; and automating training registration and record-keeping. While LMS technology goes a long way to support many training functions, it often falls short of putting proper emphasis on "content" as the most important function of the training department.

By contrast, learning content management system (LCMS) solutions are ideally suited to create content-centric learning strategies, supporting multiple methods for gathering and organizing content, leveraging content for multiple purposes, and operationalizing content for mission-critical purposes.

Once we shift our focus to the strategic value of learning content, we can also shift the way we view, structure, and deploy learning content. In older content development models, learning content is systematically created and structured as courses used for specific learning purposes, which limits the value an organization can derive from learning content. In contrast, a content-centric model of learning allows greater flexibility to leverage learning content—strategic assets—and powerfully connect learning activities with bottom-line business objectives.

This article includes tips and techniques from organizations that have achieved success using LCMSs to deploy content-centric learning strategies and elevate learning to new levels of mission criticality.

LCMS CONTENT TOUCHES MANY PARTS OF THE BUSINESS When your LCMS solution and content-centric learning strategy are in place, people across the company will create, share, and consume learning content, even though they don't know what "LCMS" stands for and don't work in the training department. Consider the following real-world before-and-after examples to observe this ideal in action.

How Can We Use Learning Technology to Decrease Development Time?

Gone are the days when a training department could spend months carefully analyzing, planning, designing, developing, testing, and delivering large, monolithic courses. Adapting to the speed of change is often a common driver that leads a training department to seek out better, more efficient methods to keep pace with the rest of the company.

SITUATION: Each part of our telecommunications business seems to be making big changes—and all at the same time.

Before: The training department had become a major bottleneck, causing some lines of business to be so frustrated with our timelines that some of them have already started going around our group, creating and delivering their own training.

After: The training department used the new strategy to keep up with producing content to support multiple lines of business. They successfully engaged subject-matter experts (SMEs) across the business as ad-hoc content developers, with their central training group orchestrating the effort. They are in a stronger position than ever before to keep pace with the business now and in the future.

How Can We Increase Speed to Competency?

Keeping training current with rapid changes is a challenge for every company. The combination of decreased content development cycle time and increased speed to performance can result in direct, bottom-line impact on businesses in terms of cost reduction.

SITUATION: A business equipment manufacturer primarily sells through an extensive distribution network of partners and resellers.

Before: The company needed to teach and continually retrain eleven thousand learners in its dealer network with a limited staff of twenty full-time trainers. Most classes were taught onsite as instructor-led workshops and, in addition, the staff provided personal phone-based assistance directly to resellers. The training staff could not keep pace with the demand, resulting in frustrated customers who had to wait for onsite training.

After: The company created a blended learning platform, populated with modularized learning content that could be used for (1) structured, self-paced learning, (2) on-demand performance support, (3) elements as part of classroom events, and (4) shared resources to supplement phone-based inquiries. In the first six months of implementation, the same twenty trainers were able to service and reach twice the number of customers as with previous methods of delivery.

How Can We Leverage Learning to Create New Business Opportunities?

Training groups may be the first to experience a reduction in budget, layoffs, etc., because indirect contributions to profitability are sometimes hard to translate to bottom-line figures. Even in difficult times, learning technology can help solve specific business problems by leveraging learning content for multiple audiences and also impact the bottom line by *decreasing cycle time and increasing speed to competence.*

SITUATION: A high-tech computer software company creates training for internal staff that includes best practice use of company-branded software to solve real-world problems. Customers began asking for similar training.

Before: A customer education department was created to develop both instructor-led and e-learning materials to service external learners. There was considerable overlap in development efforts. Content was often first created by internal training and then reformatted for external use by customer education. However, an economic downturn forced the company to make cutbacks in both internal training (cost center) and customer education (profit center).

After: Fortunately, the company decided to use the economic slump to synergistically merge the two groups and work toward a more content-centric approach, eliminating redundancy in development and creating a single, unified process for design, development, and delivery of reusable, modular learning content.

How Can We Use Learning to Rationalize Business Practices Across a New Enterprise? In

the news, we regularly read about new mergers and acquisitions. Learning content repositories are becoming increasingly visible as important business systems by decreasing cycle time and serving as real-time, operational manuals for company-wide operations.

SITUATION: One large bank acquired another large bank. The merger created a new entity of nearly 150,000 employees. One of the first charters was to map organizational efficiency.

Before: Both banks already used LCMS technology independently, with well-defined strategies for not only storing courses within their infrastructure, but keeping content up-to-date. As the acquisition took place, business analysts working on the mapping exercise realized that their task became much easier because the learning systems inside each organization helped them compare and contrast policies and practices.

After: They used the mapping exercise to create a master training program for the newly created entity to acclimate learners from both sides of the acquisition, resulting in a much smoother transition.

How Can We Align the Use of Mission-Critical Content Across Lines of Business and Departments? The following example

illustrates what can happen when learning content extends across the enterprise and links other groups (such as documentation) to further leverage enterprise content.

SITUATION: A software company has content relevant to many different groups and divisions, including documentation, help desk support, and so forth.

Before: Departments with similar types of content worked independently to create deliverables for their own audiences. Documentation was created in isolation, as was the development of training (instructor-led, e-learning, and others).

After: The company created a single-source strategy to centralize and standardize learning content from multiple divisions. Content is stored as discreet learning objects, such as a paragraph of text, a chart, or a diagram, that can be linked with other learning objects to create courseware in a variety of modalities, including print-ready manuals. The company has published over sixty training manuals per year covering more than a dozen major products and created online learning in ten languages in a matter of weeks by reusing learning assets.

How Can We Use Technology to Capture and Maintain Expert Knowledge?

One very important aspect of the content-centric approach is planning for content from a variety of sources. SMEs can use the LCMS to store diagrams, plans, blueprints, and many other learning assets. As workforce demographics change, using a content-centric approach can be an excellent way to capture experts' knowledge.

SITUATION: A pharmaceutical company has a large portfolio of structured learning courses (both instructor-led and e-learning) available from a company-wide learning portal. The training group was asked to provide learning about new, related biotechnologies to keep staff up-to-date on what's happening in the industry.

Before: The training group's first attempt was to create formal courses on several different biotechnologies of interest. They quickly realized that information on the biotechnologies is changing on a daily basis and that the courses required constant updates and maintenance. They found it difficult to keep pace with training requests.

After: The company decided to use a content-centric strategy and, for the first time, allow direct user-generated content within their learning framework. They inventoried the company and found a central subject-matter expert for each of the requested biotechnologies. These SMEs could create and update learning content from their own desktops.

SEVEN STEPS TO CREATING A CONTENT-CENTRIC LEARNING STRATEGY

Next, we will address how to start or improve your strategy.

1. Organize Your Learning Content with Business Impact in Mind.

The first order of business is to gather content that may currently exist in content silos—content that may be trapped on someone's desktop or across a number of web servers. After you have assessed the content, you can begin to associate it with different training purposes, such as a specific learning purpose, an entire group or department, or the entire enterprise. Create a content repository for each of these purposes, and place the content into the proper repository.

Learning Content Management System (LCMS) technology is ideally suited to create a well-organized repository. Beyond simple content organization, LCMSs have out-of-the-box features and functionality that will operationalize your content-centric learning strategy. Here are just some of the functionalities you can expect to find in an LCMS:

1. *Accepts content from multiple sources*—Dedicated content developers and even part-time content contributors can work in their tool of choice, using tools such as Word, PowerPoint, rapid authoring tools, graphics tools, and others and upload content.
2. *Metadata tagging*—As content is imported into the system, it can be tagged for optimal search and reusability.

3. *Automatic features*—An LCMS is a staging mechanism for any type of learning content; it will automatically provide navigational controls, look and feel, and a table of contents.

4. *Delivery player*—Once content is sequenced (often using a simple tree view), content can be quickly previewed and deployed when ready.

5. *Tagging content for different delivery methods*—Learning objects can be tagged for specific output configurations, allowing the same content to appear both as part of an e-learning course and in a paper-based training manual.

2. Position LCMS as the Center of Your Learning Strategy, Automating Development, and Delivery.

Remember that engaging in a paradigm shift takes much more than choosing a new technology. Everyone on the team must completely understand the strategic value of placing "content" at the center of your learning platform. Each new learning initiative can be measured against business objectives by asking critical questions:

1. Can we decrease cycle time for this project? Can we base the learning on existing material or create the material so that it will decrease cycle time for future projects?

2. Can we increase speed to competency? Can we test for prior knowledge? Can we shorten the delivery cycle by making some modules mandatory and others optional?

3. Is there a new business opportunity with this initiative? Can we approach content development so that content is also useful to our customers, partners, and others?

4. Can we draw on content from other divisions of our company? What content do they have that will help us? And what content do we have that will help them?

5. Can we create content in such a way that it could be simultaneously used for instructor-led training, e-learning, synchronized PowerPoint slides, manuals and other print-based materials?

6. What best practices, procedures, and policies can we capture that will benefit the business as a whole?

3. Modularize Learning.

For years, training professionals have been creating and storing content in small chunks that could then be clustered into learning objects, or five- to fifteen-minute modules.

There are several key reasons for keeping content modularized:

1. Small modules of content can be assembled and deployed almost instantly without having to create an entire, large course.

2. Modules can be used as entry points from dynamically generated table of contents.

3. Modules can be updated and maintained without pulling remaining learning content offline.

4. Small modules make natural entry and exit points for bookmarking an online course.

5. From an instructional perspective, modules can cover a single enabling objective. When clustered with other modules, they can work as prerequisites for accomplishing a terminal objective.

4. Move Training Closer to the Point of Performance.

With traditional authoring techniques, the training professional constructs courses page by page to create a course. To create just-in-time learning, he or she cuts out the desired content from the larger course, pastes it into a new mini-course, and then publishes it through the learning system. With a content-centric approach, the learning content already exists in the repository. To create new just-in-time learning, the training professional simply reuses the learning content and creates a new derivative version. Any changes to the learning will be automatically updated in both locations.

5. Benchmark Metrics on Decrease in Cycle Time.

Do you know your current cycle time for creating and deploying learning? How about maintenance time for keeping existing content up-to-date? While most people don't have these training statistics readily available, you probably have a good idea of how long it takes from the time a training need is expressed to the moment it is delivered.

To gather metrics on decreased cycle time, start by estimating the cycle time on your last ten training development projects. Use these data as a benchmark to measure the success of your content-centric approach to learning.

After implementing the new approach, you will notice that some projects, such as a major software rollout or a leadership development curriculum, may have lengthy cycle times when first developed. However, when it comes to updating and delivering content for minor rollouts, you will see huge decreases in cycle time. In addition, decreased cycle times can be achieved once there are many "reusable" modules in the system and you identify patterns for reusability, such as creating multiple, derivative versions of courses for different audiences.

6. Benchmark Metrics on Speed to Competency.

Metrics on speed to competency are one of the absolute best ways to show the strategic value of learning content. If you can demonstrate that training is being delivered most efficiently, leaving workers to focus on their daily job functions, your learning system will enter the upper echelon of business systems.

7. Encourage Reusability.

As you read through the mini-case studies and examples above, you quickly saw that organizing the content alone is not enough. You also need your training team to completely buy into the strategic value of content and, once your strategy is in place, you need to educate the rest of the organization on the possibilities that exist. You may need to be the champion for change in your organization.

CONCLUSION | Learning technologies can be used for much more than automating the administrative aspects of learning. The time is right to ask our learning technologies to do more—much more—and by so doing, we can elevate the status of learning systems to new levels of visibility and mission criticality. We can learn from those who have been successful at decreasing cycle times, increasing speed to competency, finding ways to leverage content to create new business opportunities, sharing best practices across companies and throughout our own enterprises, and capturing and retaining knowledge as a valuable asset for our organizations.

The challenge is to think of learning as transactional and not as a one-way communication from the training department to learners everywhere. Learning systems grow, adapt, and change with the business needs of our organizations, which are reflected in training needs. In order for learning technology to become mission critical, it must be seen as completely transparent and allow users to focus on strengthening their overall business—not on the business of creating training alone.

REFERENCE

Chapman, B. (2010). *LCMS KnowledgeBase.* Sunnyvale, CA: Brandon Hall Research. Available www.brandon-hall.com/publications/lcmskb/lcmskb.shtml.

Carla Torgerson

Carla Torgerson, M.Ed., has a bachelor's and a master's degree in education, both from the University of Alberta in Canada. Her master's degree is focused in multimedia design and development. Carla has more than ten years of experience in the field of e-learning and instructional design. She was the founding director of the Center for Teaching and Educational Technologies at Penn State Erie, The Behrend College, where she worked with faculty members to improve their teaching online and in the classroom, ultimately improving student learning. In that role she also taught undergraduate courses in multimedia development.

Currently, Carla is an interactive training designer for a Fortune 500 company where she develops new employee training curricula. Previously she was a senior instructional strategist with Allen Interactions, where she worked with Fortune 500 clients to design learning solutions that change behavior. She was also a primary instructor of the e-learning instructional design and the advanced e-learning instructional design certificate courses offered by the American Society for Training and Development.

Carla is very interested in using training to meet businesses' strategic needs and is currently finishing an M.B.A. from the internationally accredited G. R. Herberger College of Business at St. Cloud State University.

LCMS: | Carla Torgerson

NOT JUST A TECHNOLOGY,
IT'S A STRATEGY — A REBUTTAL

This article provides an alternate perspective to Bryan Chapman's article about using reusable learning objects as a way to make training more efficient and effective. I'm grateful to Carla Torgerson for sharing her thoughts here, in particular because readers have told me they especially enjoy rebuttal articles. Carla is not ambivalent on the topic: "Reusable learning objects do not give appropriate context for the learner, which makes them less effective. While they may make development faster, they are not likely to produce better learning outcomes nor will they increase speed to competency." While one might too easily conclude this is a conflict between what's expedient for the organization's budget versus what's best for the learner, Carla makes the business case for investing in learning content that is customized to the learner.

In his article, Bryan Chapman makes some excellent points about how training can and should provide a strategic value to the business and connect "learning activities with bottom-line business objectives." I agree wholly with his points about the importance of using training to push organizations to better efficiency, productivity, and profitability. However, that's where our agreement ends. While I agree with the goals Chapman identifies, I disagree with the methods he recommends.

Chapman suggests that training is best developed when we use shared learning objects on a learning content management system (LCMS). That is, training modules and content documents are repurposed and repackaged for different learner groups. Ultimately Chapman's vision is to create reusable, modular learning content. He suggests that this decreases development time, increases speed to competency, makes training available across departments, and enables the training department to capture expert knowledge.

AN OMELET BAR AND WHY MODULARIZED LEARNING TASTES BAD

Imagine that we are going out for breakfast. I'll take you to my favorite restaurant down the street where they have a fabulous omelet bar. There's a friendly chef who will cook my omelet to order. I can choose from a host of things to have in my omelet: mushrooms, spinach, ham, chicken, tomatoes . . . and of course the cheese!

On the surface this may sound like the learning that Chapman is proposing—a host of learning morsels for the learner to enjoy, all culminated in a single dish. However, what he's really proposing is that the chef make a plate of scrambled eggs and sprinkle the ham, tomatoes, and cheese on top. I'll be lucky if the cheese is even melted. There will be no blending of foods or tastes. No culinary contribution, really. Ultimately, I will have a plate piled with food, but not the omelet I was expecting. If I finish it, I certainly won't be back for seconds. I didn't want groceries; I wanted a carefully conceived, constructed, and integrated dish.

Instead (thankfully!), the chef will take all of the food items I've requested and stir them in with the eggs, integrating the ingredients into the tasty omelet I desire. Ultimately, the omelet tastes better because all the pieces were cooked together. They were combined thoughtfully, with the flavors of each ingredient impacting the others. Just as you cannot have a delicious omelet by piling ingredients on top of the eggs, you cannot have an effective learning experience by stringing learning objects together. There needs to be a unity in the learning experience—where things from later in the course reference things from earlier and the whole course works together to optimize my time and experience.

I am not saying that we should not reuse learning content. Absolutely we should, as it is more efficient. However, an instructional designer should be like your omelet chef, taking individual ingredients and shaping the content mixture to create a complete course for the learner, just as the chef takes your desired ingredients and delivers a delicious whole omelet just for you. Careful integra-tion complete with helpful transitions allow the course to flow together in ways that are relevant to the learner. They allows the course to build on previous learning activities rather than just being a number of discrete learning objects placed together.

REVISITING CHAPMAN'S ADVANTAGES OF LEARNING OBJECTS

In the article, Chapman makes a strong business case for the use of learning objects. However, I'd like to look at some of his points and offer an alternate strategy.

The Overall Case. Time and again, Chapman insists that content is the key. Certainly, having the right content is important, but for people to learn the content, *context* is the real key. If Chapman were right and just having access to information was all that learners needed, then we wouldn't need training at all. We would simply provide employees with Google and access to a central repository of proprietary content.

Certainly, much learning could happen in such an environment. There is a lot of excite-ment and interest in informal learning—the learning employees do when quickly searching the Internet, talking to a colleague, or read-ing something on LinkedIn. (For more on this, create your own informal learning experience by doing a Google search for Jay Cross!) How-ever, there is still a place for formal learn-ing—learning that is directed by outcomes and perhaps even by a manager to whom the employee is held accountable.

Formal learning is most effective when there is a context. If you strip away the con-text, you make it much harder to keep the learner engaged and for the learner to transfer the learning to her work. For example, let's say I was going to design a course on sexual harassment. I could simply put the corporate policy on my LCMS and expect people to read and interpret it, as Chapman recommends. Instead, I recommend designing a course that has the learner apply the policy to common situations and learn about the nuances of the policy from the feedback in those activities. The feedback will be adapted to what the learner may already know and do. This would be more interesting and engaging and would also enable the learner to practice efficiently and to a point of mastery. If learners don't have the opportunity to practice the behaviors you want them to exhibit, they are unlikely to be able to perform those skills on the job. Chapman seems to confuse reading content with the learner's ability to apply it.

Even if the learning object is interactive and enables the learner to practice and apply learning, it must be applicable to her. If you teach me a number of things without relating them to my specific job role, I may not be able to apply them when I get back to my work. Creating learning objects before you even know who will use them will force you to create something so generic that it's really not helpful to any learner.

Similarly, learning must be customized for the knowledge expected of the learner and the tools and resources at his disposal. Let's say I need to learn how to change a flat tire on my car. I can watch a number of YouTube videos about how to change a flat tire, but I may still not find the information that I need. What if I told you the car is in my garage and I have a hoist? Would that change what I needed to learn? Of course. I need to learn

how to change a tire for a car on a hoist, not a car on the side of the road. When the training department doesn't recognize the different environments that learners are in and the different tools they use, then the training is not likely to meet their needs. Just one learning object may not meet all learner needs, and it would be foolish to assume it could. Trying to make content elements generalized and reusable almost certainly guarantees lesser impact for all learners.

Does It Really Decrease Development Time?

Reusing learning objects can decrease development time, but it may not allow you to bring in the unique contexts you need, or to customize them for each learner group. Chapman is right that it can be *faster*, but is it *better*? There are many cases for which we could do things faster, but we don't because quality is also important. For example, would you want to fly in a plane if I told you it was assembled in just two days? Would you want to drive across a bridge that had been constructed in just a week? Of course not. In both of these cases you would fear the corners that might have been cut to finish the product quickly. Even at the omelet bar, my omelet could be delivered more quickly, but then it would be undercooked. It wouldn't taste very good, and worse, it might be very unsafe for me to eat.

The same is true of learning. We need a certain level of quality to ensure the learner actually learns. A course that is thrown together too quickly will not provide adequate teaching, the learner won't learn from it, and the learner will hate the experience. If students don't learn, then we've wasted our time and our learners' time. There is no efficiency in this. We should not be measuring courses by the amount of time it took to create them, but rather by the amount of learning that took place from them and the strategic value of that learning to the organization.

For example, at Allen Interactions, we developed a piece of e-learning that was very successful. The client's research found that the training decreased lab breakage by 12 percent and decreased error re-dos by 17 percent. This resulted in $7M in annual savings! If I told you I needed more than a week or two to design and create that training, would you allow me the time to make the right solution? Of course you would. The payoff of quality is simply too great for you not to.

Certainly Chapman is right that longer development times can create bottlenecks. We must always review potential courses and prioritize those that have the most strategic value for the organization. This allows us to create the most strategically significant training and use learners' limited time most wisely.

Will Learning Objects Deliver Increased Speed to Competency?

Chapman suggests that learning objects will increase speed to competency. In his examples, he's showing how learning objects can speed up development time. Truly, it is unfair to say that just because you have a course ready sooner, the learner will be able to become proficient sooner. It depends on the effectiveness of the courseware. Certainly, you lose the bottleneck that Chapman talks of, but the learner's time to competency is still the same.

Chapman also suggests that *shorter* courses create increased speed to competency. While it is an excellent business goal to make learn-

ers proficient faster, learning takes *time.* Performance proficiency requires cognitive effort, thinking, synthesizing, and practice. A short course does not necessarily mean the learner will learn something faster or even to adequate proficiency at all. It's a poor tradeoff to provide a host of short courses that fail to bring learners to proficiency when a well-designed program could actually achieve proficiency. While at Allen Interactions I designed a forty-five-minute e-learning course on how to be a better manager. There is some theory about leadership and team dynamics, but mostly practice activities wherein the learner applies this material. Could I have made it a five-minute course? Absolutely. Would the learner be as proficient after completing the course? Absolutely not.

Organizations need their staff to be at high levels of proficiency. Precluding learners from adequate practice, application, and processing time is detrimental. If we don't consider this, we have wasted both our time and the learner's and have lost an opportunity to actually change behavior.

Can We Use Mission-Critical Content Across Lines of Business and Departments? Again, I agree with Chapman's goals, but not his methods. Of course we need to leverage mission-critical content and share it as widely across multiple groups as we effectively can. However, we need to show the learner "What's in it for me?" That is, we must provide context and meaning to make this learning apply to learners and show why they should care. Appropriate contexts are likely to be different within the various business units and departments, and as learning activities

are created for each different context, other elements will likewise need to be differentiated for each context. Some sharing of objects will no doubt be possible, but many will need to be edited and revised to provide the most relevant context and support for the learner.

Chapman recommends having content stored as discreet learning objects, such as a paragraph of text, a chart, or a diagram. These are then linked together in different ways to create courseware for different learner groups. But without appropriate context, this content just becomes corporate speak. Without context to give the content meaning ("Let me put that into context for you"), the learner must figure out what's important and how to apply it in her work. This is neither efficient nor effective. It's not efficient because it may be difficult for the learner to connect the content with her work, which will make the learning esoteric and difficult. More importantly, it's not effective because you are leaving it to the learner to determine what's important. If the organization has a strategic need for the training, then you need to design the training to ensure the learner recognizes that strategy. Without that, chances are slim that the learner will integrate the content in ways that meet the organization's strategic goals.

Can Learning Objects Capture and Maintain Expert Knowledge? Is it important to capture and maintain expert knowledge? Absolutely. However, I would

not use learning objects for this purpose. Chapman seems to want subject-matter experts (SMEs) to just upload documents they use in the normal course of their jobs. These are rarely good teaching tools. Teaching tools need to be carefully thought out and structured to show key points and then explain those points. Just tossing a document on the LCMS won't teach much.

Further, if you ask SMEs to actually create proper teaching in their learning objects, then you require SMEs to be instructional designers. It's better to make use of your SMEs by creating a two-way conduit for open communication with learners. Have SMEs maintain a blog whereby other SMEs can correct each others' comments, share current thinking, respond to learners' clarifying questions, and so on. We can often make SMEs into helpful teachers by having them answer questions from learners. But please, be very careful in assuming all SMEs can teach.

Often SMEs are not the best teachers. One reason for this is that they have trouble understanding the learner's novice perspective. So we should create environments in which learners can ask for clarification. Ultimately, this makes the learner the instructional designer, creating the learning experience he or she needs by asking just the right questions for him or her. SMEs often become stronger teachers when they can interact with learners. To reduce an SME to only posting learning objects removes much of the value that SME can offer learners and the organization.

THE RISK OF CHAPMAN'S VISION (OR "PLEASE, PLEASE DON'T CREATE A CONTENT-CENTRIC LEARNING STRATEGY")

I hope I have shown the importance of thinking about context and the quality of training, not just putting content into a repository for learners to access. This is like giving a learner a library card or access to the Internet and believing your work as a training professional is done. Learners often need more than that—they need courses that teach them how to apply their learning to their work, that show them the value of changing their behavior, and most importantly, that enable them to add increasing value in the most strategic ways for the organization.

Sadly, if you offer training that lacks these characteristics, learners know it. They label it "bad training." Learners will get through their courses as quickly as possible and take as little of your training as they can. Interestingly, a lot of people want to learn at work. They want to grow and become better at their jobs. If you can't give that to them, they will go somewhere that will. If you offer bad training, you don't just get bad business results, you may end up with turnover problems as well.

Instead, we should seek to create an environment in which training is like my favorite omelet bar. Not only is the omelet made for me and with my needs in mind, but it is also so enticing and so delicious that I can't help but come back for another helping—and I won't be looking for a new restaurant any time soon.

Clive Shepherd

Clive Shepherd, M.A., is a consultant specializing in e-learning, blended learning, and business communications. He works with a broad range of public- and private-sector organizations, helping them to effectively harness the benefits of technology for workplace learning. He established his interest in interactive media while director, training and creative services, for American Express in EMEA. He went on to co-found Epic, one of the UK's major producers of custom e-learning, where he won many industry awards. He is widely acknowledged as one of the UK's foremost experts in e-learning, with hundreds of published articles and many books and e-books to his name. He speaks regularly at major international conferences and contributes regularly to his blog, Clive on Learning. He was recognized for his outstanding contribution to the training industry at the World of Learning Conference in 2004 and for the past three years has been chairman of the eLearning Network. Clive is a director of Onlignment Ltd, which provides expertise in all aspects of online communication.

RETHINKING THE SCOPE AND NATURE OF INSTRUCTIONAL DESIGN

Clive Shepherd

Most definitions of e-learning are broad and inclusive. Most simply require the use of technology to aid in the delivery of instruction. A broad array of approaches is available. An important responsibility of instructional design begins with a good choice of instructional paradigms. Clive Shepherd alerts us to a common pitfall. Once designers become proficient in a paradigm, they tend to stick to it without carefully evaluating its appropriateness and selecting another when warranted. "It's just possible that the requirement we're faced with would be better served with an alternative strategy, perhaps not instruction, perhaps not self-directed, perhaps some mix, perhaps not learning at all." The professional designer has to be savvy enough to pick the most appropriate solutions, even when different skills to design and build them may be required. In this article, Clive gives us structured approaches for selecting appropriate solutions.

TIME TO RETHINK

If you are an instructional designer who makes his or her living designing highly structured, self-directed learning materials that are delivered online, then it becomes pretty easy to behave like a hammer—somehow, every brief that's brought to you looks like a nail, another opportunity to bash out some more highly structured, self-directed online learning materials. There are good reasons why we do this, not least of which is self-preservation. Basically, we're looking for business, an opportunity to impress with our talents and put food on the table.

Sometimes, however, we have to be more professional than a hammer; we have to rise above the temptation to do what we always do and to suggest something different to our clients. My guess is that only a small proportion of requirements are best met by self-study materials alone and we should be savvy enough to pick the most appropriate opportunities, while suggesting something else to meet the rest of the requirement. We may be able to contribute to the development and delivery of those alternative approaches; if not, we should be big enough to step back.

LEARNING ISN'T ALWAYS NECESSARY

In many jobs, it is increasingly difficult, if not impossible, to know everything there is to know. Even if, through prolonged study and training, you were lucky enough to get to know everything that was required for your job, you'd soon find that most of it had changed. There's too much to know and it changes far too quickly. In the knowledge economy, it is more important to know where to look—or who to talk to—than it is to have the knowledge yourself.

The abundance of information is weighing heavily on the knowledge worker. The statistics are frightening, as Jay Cross reports:

➢ "In many professions, knowledge workers spend a third of their time looking for answers and helping their colleagues do the same.

➢ "Only one in five knowledge workers consistently find the information they need to do their jobs.

➢ "Knowledge workers spend more time re-creating existing information they were unaware of than creating original material."

(Cross, 2007)

When there is too much to know, instructional designers have to be discriminating in deciding what has to be learned in advance, on a just-in-case basis, and what can be accessed on-demand, just-in-time. You could argue that on-demand learning isn't learning at all, because the objective is to support performance rather than to teach. There's no guarantee; indeed, there may be no real concern that an employee acquires in any permanent way the knowledge needed to carry out a task, just so long as he or she can do it right now. After all, a task may need to be carried out only once or only so rarely that the effort required to retain the knowledge may not be justified.

However, there's a blurry line between just-in-time performance support and learning. The information itself is likely to be the same; the same people may be approached to provide this information; the same materials may be used in each case. The main difference comes with the strategy:

➢ When the goal is simply performance, the information must be available at the point of need for easy reference.

➢ When the goal is learning (a more or less permanent set of new connections in the brain), the intervention must go beyond providing information to include practice, assessment, and feedback.

Another way to reconcile the concept of performance support with learning is to conceive that knowledge can exist beyond the individual, in his or her own personal network of digital and human connections. The idea of the "outboard brain" is closely associated with a relatively new theoretical perspective to learning called connectivism, as articulated by George Siemens:

➢ "Instead of the individual having to evaluate and process every bit of information, she/he creates a personal network of trusted nodes: people and content, enhanced by technology. The act of knowledge is offloaded onto the network itself.

➢ "Connectivism places new demands on the L&D professional who, as a facilitator of learning networks, helps to provide the infrastructure that enables employees to more easily make connections with sources of expertise. Underpinning this role is a realization that the connections that enable us to learn more are more important than our current state of knowing. 'Knowing where' and 'knowing who' are more important today than knowing when and how"

(Siemens, 2006).

So what are the situations in which performance support can substitute for good old-fashioned training? Alison Rossett and Lisa Schafer have identified a number of situations in which performance support makes particular sense:

> *When the performance is infrequent:* There's no point learning how to carry out a task if you rarely perform it, not least because, with insufficient repetitions, the information is unlikely to stick. An example might be setting up a home office network—chances are, you'll only have to do this every four or five years, with little reinforcement of the information in between. An exception would be a task that, although carried out rarely, simply has to be carried out proficiently from memory, the most obvious example of which is an emergency procedure.

> *When the situation is complex, involves many steps, or has many attributes:* The more complex the task, the less likely you are going to be able to remember every important detail. Even if you have been trained formally, performance support materials are a good backup.

> *When the consequence of error is intolerable:* Highly critical skills may need to be formally developed through intensive training, but when every detail is important, it pays to provide clear instructions at the point-of-need, just to make sure.

> *When performance depends on knowledge, procedures, or approaches that change frequently:* There's no point acquiring knowledge that is soon outdated. Take that example of the home office network—five years ago

you'd have been laying Ethernet cables, but now it's all wireless.

> *When there is a high turnover and the task is perceived to be simple:* It's not only information that's constantly changing, it's people too. In some industries with high employee turnover, there's little point in devoting training time to simple tasks—just provide clear instructions.

> *When there is little time or few resources to devote to training:* In other words, if all else fails, at the very least make sure you provide a decent job aid. (Rossett & Schafer, 2007)

STRUCTURED INSTRUCTION ISN'T THE ONLY ROUTE TO LEARNING

Let's assume, then, that at least some part of the requirement you are faced with depends on the target population acquiring new knowledge or skills rather than just accessing information on demand. Does that mean we can now set about designing those interactive e-learning lessons that we all know and love? Not really, because structured instruction is only one of a number of strategies for learning—and not always the most appropriate.

Formal learning comes in many shapes and sizes. The effectiveness and efficiency with which a formal learning intervention is delivered depends to a large extent on whether the shape and the size are appropriate for the job. Clark and Wittrock (2001) devised a useful model for analyzing training strategies according to the degree of control imposed over the learning process by the trainer and/ or the student (see Figure 1). At the most

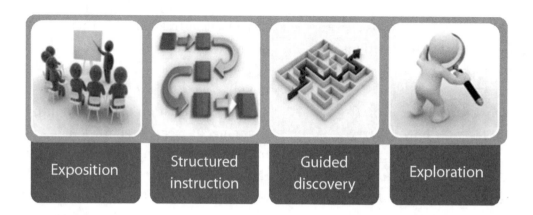

Figure 1. Model
for Analyzing
Training Strate-
gies
From Clark and
Wittrock, 2001

trainer-centred end of the spectrum is simple *exposition*—you tell the learner things, using methods such as lectures, presentations, or prescribed reading; no interaction is expected or required, except perhaps some Q&A.

Exposition might seem an anathema to the instructional designer; after all, surely interaction and feedback are critical to the learning process. Well, for novices and dependent learners, this is a safe assumption; but those with a great deal of experience in their area of specialty and/or a high degree of metacognitive skills (they know what they know and what they need to know; they're able to figure out for themselves how to bridge any gap) will get by just fine with exposition.

The second strategy—*structured instruction*—is still under the trainer's or the author's overall control, but is much more interactive, allowing the trainer or the software to fine-tune the process to the needs of the particular audience. Structured instruction is, of course, widely used in training and includes most classroom sessions and most e-learning materials. Novices will rely on this degree of structure; independent learners can often do without.

A more learner-centred strategy is *guided discovery*. In this case, learners engage in tasks that have been specially designed to provide them with opportunities to experiment with alternative approaches. Learners improve their skills or understanding by reflecting, with the help of facilitators or well-designed software, upon the outcomes of these tasks and, as a result, draw general conclusions that they can apply to future tasks. Guided discovery allows learners to try things out and to learn from their mistakes. This strategy can be deployed in the classroom, in outdoor settings (as with adventure-style courses), or through computer-based scenarios, games, and simulations.

The final strategy in Clark and Wittrock's model is *exploration*. Here each learner determines his or her own learning process, taking advantage of resources provided by trainers and others, and takes his or her unique learning out of the process. Exploration may seem a relatively informal strategy, but it can be integrated in a blended solution.

A formal learning intervention may rely on just one of these strategies, but increasingly will use a combination. The choice of strategy will depend on the nature of the learning objectives, the prior knowledge and the expectations of the target audience and, to some extent, the preferences and values of the trainer (Clark & Wittrock, 2001).

SELF-DIRECTED LEARNING WON'T ALWAYS DO THE JOB

We all know that self-study e-learning is growing in popularity, and that's primarily because it's efficient. It helps employers by cutting travel costs and allowing more training to happen more quickly, but in some respects it is welcomed by employees as well. In a survey conducted in 2009 by Siemens of more than two thousand employees from eight different European countries, an overwhelming majority (87 percent) reported that they most liked to learn at their own pace. This should not be that surprising; after all, self-paced learning is highly flexible (you control when, where, and how often) and low-stress (you are not pressured to keep up with the pace set by an instructor). This and other surveys have also shown that employees like to learn in small chunks (a sensible preference, because this is much more brain-friendly) and on-demand, that is, without having to wait for a scheduled intervention. So self-study is more than just a tonic for the CFO; it works for learners too.

But, of course, nothing is that simple. First, self-study is limited in its application, because it doesn't address all learning requirements—in some cases the desired results simply cannot be achieved without interaction with experts, coaches, and peers. Above all, self-study does not meet all of the needs of learn-

ers. However, many learners want flexibility and control. They also want support, collaboration, and community. They want access to real human beings so they can ask questions, share experiences and perspectives, benchmark their skills, and both give and receive encouragement.

There are four social contexts for learning, and each has its place:

> *Self-directed:* Self-directed learning is highly flexible, low-stress, quick, and low-cost; on the other hand, it requires the learner to exert considerable self-discipline and, if unsupported, can leave the learner isolated.

> *One-to-one:* One-to-one learning is highly tailored, intensive, and potentially very effective; unfortunately, it's inconsistent in quality and highly expensive.

> *Synchronous group:* Synchronous (live) learning in groups provides the opportunity for learners to share perspectives and experiences, to practice together, and to provide each other with support, encouragement, and a little healthy peer pressure; unfortunately, it also requires a commitment by the whole group to a particular time and the session is one-paced, sometimes too fast for some and too slow for others.

> *Asynchronous group:* Asynchronous (self-paced) group collaboration, using tools like forums, wikis, and social networks, provides the advantages of working with a group, but with greater flexibility; on the other hand, it can require a great deal of facilitation.

	Exposition	Structured Instruction	Guided Discovery	Exploration
Self-directed	Books, videos, pod-casts	e-Learning modules, workbooks	Scenarios, games, simulations, projects	Reading lists, links, search
One-to-one		On-the-job instruction	Coaching, mentoring	
Synchronous group	Presentations, lectures, webinars, webcasts	Classes, workshops, virtual classroom sessions	Multi-player games and simulations, class and outdoor activities	Unconferences
Asynchronous group			Action learning, collaborative online activities using forums, wikis, etc.	Social networking, social bookmarking, blogging

Table 1. Educational and Training Method by Social Context

Table 1 shows how the array of available educational and training methods can be mapped against these four social contexts, as well as against the four strategies for learning discussed earlier:

NOT ALL LEARNING IS BEST DELIVERED ONLINE If you're sure that self-directed learning using a strategy of structured instruction is appropriate to meet the need, you still have choices when it comes to the medium you employ. Of course, we want to deliver this online if we can, because it improves accessibility for the learner, facilitates the maintenance of content, and allows us to record progress using an LMS, but there will be occasions when this just won't work.

The digital divide is certainly narrowing from a gaping chasm into more of a crack, but it can still trip us up. First, we still have to contend with that small band of learners who can't tell one end of a computer from another. This is a problem we can and should solve, but in the meantime it gets in the way. Second, even a willing and able online user will be confounded by the absence of an Internet connection, whether fixed line or mobile. Sometimes, you just can't get around this problem in the short term, particularly in remote areas and parts of the world still relatively unconnected.

Your choices? Well, if IT literacy is not the problem, then resort to CD-ROM or download material in advance, as you would do with pod-casts. No chance of using computers in any way? Then you still have the option of a workbook.

One factor you can safely ignore is that of learning styles—the idea that some learners inherently prefer being face-to-face to using a computer, or that they prefer one media element—such as audio—to another, such as text. There's absolutely no scientific evidence for any of this, and too often it's just used as a rather lame excuse.

NOT ALL CONTENT REQUIRES AN INSTRUCTIONAL DESIGNER

Here's where I risk incurring the wrath of some of my readers by suggesting that not all learning content has to be created by skilled, professional instructional designers.

Well, not all learning interventions are equal. Some are business critical, address the needs of large populations, and have a shelf life of many years; others are aimed at smaller, more specialist audiences and may be required to meet a short-term business requirement; still others are confined to the very particular needs of individuals and small groups of employees, when information is required on-demand. These three types of interventions can be shown diagrammatically in the form of a pyramid in Figure 2.

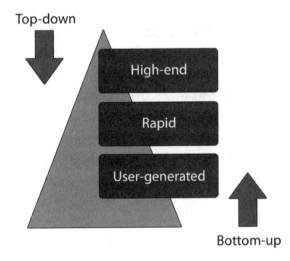

Figure 2: Learning Interventions Pyramid
With thanks to Nick Shackleton-Jones of the BBC.

High-end interventions demand the highest budgets and the attention of skilled professionals. They are the equivalent of the Hollywood blockbusters. The attention to detail and lengthy development schedules can be justified by the large numbers that will benefit from the end results. These are the exception, not the rule. Most needs cannot possibly justify this much effort and time.

Plan B is the rapid intervention, where the emphasis is on developing content that is good enough to do the job and no more. Plan C requires the help of more experienced or knowledgeable employees who help their peers by contributing the simplest of resources, often just text. So don't over-engineer. Match your production values to the requirement.

The phrase "the long tail" was first coined by Chris Anderson in 2004 to describe the niche strategy of businesses, such as Amazon.com, which sell a large number of unique items in relatively small quantities. Whereas brick-and-mortar bookshops are forced, by lack of shelf space, to concentrate on the most popular books (shown on the left of Figure 3 on the next page), retailers selling online can afford to service the minority interests shown tailing off to the right. Interestingly, for a retailer such as Amazon, the volume of sales for minority titles exceeds that of the most popular; yet before the advent of online retailing these needs would have been very hard to service (Anderson, 2004).

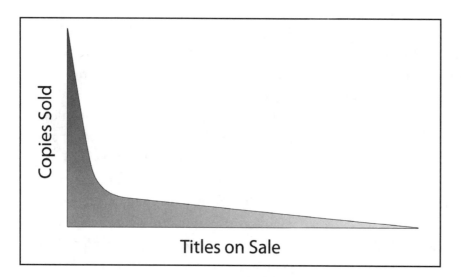

Figure 3. Long Tail—Copies Sold Versus Titles on Sale Source: Anderson, 2004.

The concept of the long tail can be applied as well to training needs as it can to sales of retail products; just substitute "learning needs" for "titles on sale" and "audience size" for "copies sold" (Figure 4). However hard we try, as trainers we cannot hope to respond to the long tail through formal, top-down efforts. We can begin to address the middle reaches of the tail if we are prepared to delegate some of our responsibility for top-down interventions to generalist trainers and subject experts. In e-learning terms, that means rapid development processes making use of rapid development tools.

At the far reaches of the tail, we have to rely on bottom-up approaches to meet the needs of small numbers of learners. In a way this has always been the case—in the absence of any other help, an employee has never had any option but to ask for help from co-workers and supervisors, or at least just copy what they do. But learning and development professionals can help the process along in a number of ways. First and foremost, they can ensure that employees are aware of their responsibilities as teachers as well as learners and are cognizant of the most effective ways to pass on knowledge and skills. And where

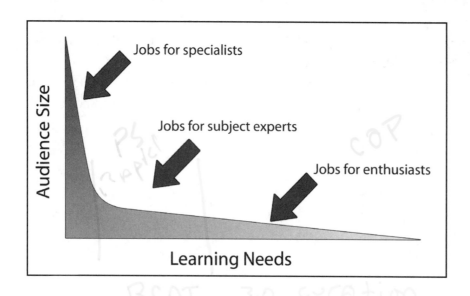

Figure 4. Long Tail—Audience Size Versus Learning Needs

employees have access to the appropriate technology, they can make available tools that smooth the way for bottom-up learning— tools like forums, wikis, and sites that enable employees to connect with experts and others with similar interests.

Good managers have always known that they cannot accomplish great things if they try to do everything themselves so they empower others and then encourage their efforts. Trainers who try to control all aspects of the training process and deny others the tools to make their own contributions will never satisfy the needs of the long tail and risk being bypassed in the rush to get things done in a fast-changing work environment.

CONCLUSION
Professionally designed, interactive, online, self-study materials clearly have a useful role to play in education and training, but they are not always necessary, nor are they always

appropriate. Use them in these situations and you won't go far wrong:

➤ When the material must be learned and performance support would not suffice.
➤ When the target population is comprised of relative novices in the subject matter and/or dependent learners.
➤ When the learning process doesn't depend on immediate access to tutors or fellow learners.
➤ When the target population has IT skills and access to adequate network connectivity.
➤ When the subject matter is of sufficient importance and/or there is a sufficiently large target audience to justify professional design and development.

And there are plenty of these situations. So if you're an instructional designer you can relax; you're going to be in demand.

REFERENCES

Anderson, C. (2004). *The long tail: How endless choice is creating unlimited demand.* London: Random House Business Books.

Clark, R., & Wittrock, M. (2001). Psychological principles of training (p. 51). in *S. Tobias & J.D. Fletcher (Eds.), Training and retraining.* New York: Macmillan.

Cross, J. (2007). *Learning is strictly business.* [White paper]. Retrieved from www.internettime.com/2007/09/feedback-and-transparency/.

Rossett, A., & Schafer, L. (2007). *Job aids and performance support.* San Francisco: Pfeiffer.

Siemens, G. (2006). *Knowing knowledge.* www.lulu.com

SkillSoft survey. (2009, June). Rethinking learning.

Martyn Sloman

Martyn Sloman is a research academic who specializes in learning training and development. He has extensive practical experience as a training manager. He is a visiting professor at Kingston Business School, Kingston University, and a teaching fellow in the Department of Management and Organizational Psychology, Birkbeck College, University of London. Martyn is principal consultant to the TJ (*Training Journal*) L&D2020 project.

From 1997 to 2000 he worked as director of management education and training for Ernst & Young, one of the largest business advisory firms in the world. Between 2001 and 2008 he was adviser, learning, training, and development, at the Chartered Institute of Personnel and Development (CIPD), where he produced groundbreaking work on the shift from training to learning.

As author, lecturer, and conference speaker, he has made a significant contribution to the development of modern human resource concepts and practice. He has lectured and presented to conferences and colleges in nineteen countries across five continents. He has been the keynote speaker at the European Commission Training Day in Brussels and spoken by invitation to the Central Training Committee of the Chinese Communist Party.

E-LEARNING: A POSITIVE SKEPTIC'S JOURNEY INTO NIGHT?

Martyn Sloman

I have daily angst regarding e-learning. What we do in education and training is important. Performance abilities can have profound effects on individual lives as well as the organizations to which they belong. But are we really helping people all that we can, or are we short-changing them? Author Martyn Sloman states bluntly, "Progress to date on implementing e-learning has not reflected well on practitioners; the debate has been about technology rather than learning." Martyn feels we have not capitalized on the potential and that our failure is due in large part to misplaced focus. He draws on research and experience at the UK Chartered Institute of Personnel and Development to identify a set of key principles for effective e-learning and also considers the new challenges posed by Web 2.0 Social Networking. I appreciate his critically important commentary.

The title of this personal reflection on e-learning is taken from the name of a play by Eugene O'Neill, the great American playwright. To quote from Wikipedia, nearly all O'Neill's plays involve some degree of tragedy and pessimism; the characters in *A Long Day's Journey into Night* "constantly conceal, blame, resent, regret, accuse, and deny in an escalating cycle of conflict with occasional desperate and half-sincere attempts at affection, encouragement, and consolation."

After more than a decade of monitoring and recording the progress of e-learning from a European vantage point, I have frequently felt irritated and frustrated at the misunderstanding of fundamental principles and the associated hype or over-selling. In this article I will try, by outlining progress and offering illustrations, to explain why I think this has happened and what we need to do if we are to move forward on a sounder basis. I remain convinced of the enormous potential of e-learning and, despite the opening paragraph, describe myself as a positive skeptic.

AN OBJECTIVE ASSESSMENT

The term e-learning first emerged in the fall of 1999 (Overton, 2009). There followed a period of great optimism. At the height of that period the management guru and author of *In Search of Excellence*, Tom Peters, addressed the Conference of the American Society for Training and Development (ASTD) in Florida in June 2002. Urging his audience to progress more rapidly, he argued that the goal should be that 90 percent of training in organizations should be delivered electronically by 2003.

In fact e-learning certainly has not, and will never, amount to 90 percent of training in organizations, however the term is defined. What we have witnessed is a gradual and probably irreversible growth in "learning that is delivered, enabled, or mediated using electronic technology for the explicit purpose of training in organizations," to draw on the definition advocated by the Chartered Institute of Personnel and Development (CIPD, 2008a).

Between 2001 and 2008 I worked as a full-time researcher at the CIPD, the 130,000-member-strong UK professional association for those involved in personnel management and development. During this period we monitored the progress of e-learning through surveys, case studies, and forums. Together with ASTD we produced a useful body of information and some reliable statistics.

Each year in its State of the Industry survey, ASTD reports on the percentage of training delivered through learning technology. Their reporting began in 1997 with under 10 percent. The percentage then plateaued, then noted steady growth to just over 36 percent for 2009 (the latest available at the time of writing) (ASTD, 2010). This progression is reproduced as Table 1 below.

Similarly, the Chartered Institute of Personnel and Development conducts an annual survey of their (mainly UK) members to monitor and chart progress of training and learning in the workplace. Every third year (most recently in 2008), an extended section on e-learning is included. The 2008 survey results offer a comparison with the 2005 and 2002 figures and the opportunity to reflect on progress and make some more general observations on technology in the workplace.

The news is mixed. There has been steady progress and good practice can now be identified, illustrated in Tables 2 and 3. The 2008 survey shows that more than half of the respondents (57 percent) reported that they are using e-learning (CIPD, 2008b). Moreover, of those who were not using e-learning, more than one quarter (27 percent) planned to do so in the next year. This proved beyond any doubt that e-learning has arrived. It is firmly established as a key part of training delivery. No questions were asked in the survey on the type of e-learning that respondents are implementing in their organizations. However, we acquired a good base of knowledge that suggested that the predominant form of e-learning is a web-based module format, normally produced for the organization concerned. Customized or bespoke e-learning applications have become predominant.

Percent of Training Delivered Through Technology

Year	Percentage
1997	9.1%
1998	8.5%
1999	8.4%
2000	8.8%
2001	10.5%
2002	15.4%
2003	23.6%
2004	27.0%
2005	Not available
2006	30.5%
2007	32.7%
2008	31.8%
2009	36.3%

Table 1. ASTD State of the Industry Reports on Percent of Learning Technology Used in Organizations, Primarily in the United States (Figure 15, p. 16)

Percent of UK Organizations Using e-Learning

Year	Percentage
2008	57%
2005	54%
2002	31%

Table 2. CIPD Annual Learning and Development Survey: Percent of Organizations Using e-Learning, Primarily in the UK

It is important to note that the percentages reproduced in Tables 1 and 2 are not in any sense comparable. The U.S. data relates to the percentage of learning hours available through technology. The UK data relates to the proportion of organizations that are making e-learning available to their workforce. There is no established data available on the UK percentage of learning hours delivered through technology. However, less formal

indications uncovered in the course of CIPD research have suggested that progress in the UK has not been as dramatic as in the United States. For example, using returned data from the 2008 annual survey, CIPD researchers estimated learning hours delivered through technology to be 12 percent, compared with a U.S. figure of above 30 percent (CIPD, 2008a).

One other insight can be drawn from the CIPD surveys. In 2008, 2005, and 2002, respondents were presented with a series of statements on e-learning and asked whether they strongly agreed, agreed, neither agreed nor disagreed, disagreed, or strongly disagreed. Table 3 shows the extent of agreement for the five statements that appeared in all five surveys. It can be seen that two statements have emerged as representing shared wisdom on e-learning. The first, "e-Learning is more effective when combined with other forms of learning," is the acceptance of the importance of what has become known as

Extent of Respondents' Agreement with Statements on e-Learning

Table 3. CIPD Annual Learning and Development Survey

*In the 2005 and 2002 surveys, the statement used was "e-Learning demands an entirely new skill set for people involved in learning and development."

**In the 2005 and 2002 surveys, the statement used was "e-Learning is the most important development in training in the past few decades."

% of respondents indicating "strongly agree" or "agree" with the statement:	Year	Percentage
"e-Learning is more effective when combined with other forms of learning."	2008	95%
	2005	94%
	2002	63%
"e-Learning demands a new attitude to learning on the part of the learner."	2008	92%
	2005	86%
	2002	90%
"e-Learning demands a new skill set for those who are involved in learning and development."*	2008	80%
	2005	63%
	2002	65%
"e-Learning is the most important development in training in the past few decades."**	2008	48%
	2005	23%
	2002	23%
"e-Learning involves the possibility of wasting a lot of money."	2008	38%
	2005	51%
	2002	54%

"blended" learning; the second, "e-Learning demands a new attitude to learning on the part of the learner," emphasizes the need for a learner-centric approach to the subject. We need to act on as well as recognize this finding.

WHAT MUST WE LEARN?

So, after a shaky start, we have witnessed a gradual but inexorable rise in e-learning. However, such progress bears little relation to the wild optimism evident in the late 1990s and early 2000s. Actors in e-learning may not have "constantly concealed, blamed, resented, regretted, accused, and denied." However, many of them have consistently oversold and overstated the advantages of e-learning; many more have ignored the need to proceed from an understanding of the basic principles that must underpin any intervention to promote training and learning in a corporate organization. Certainly, in the UK, government has behaved particularly badly as it has seized on e-learning as a cheap and easy way to encourage skills development (as one of the three illustrations below will demonstrate).

In the next section of this article, three short case cameos are presented. Taken together they provide the backcloth for an articulation of the basic principles that must govern any learning intervention.

Cameo 1. The first of the three cameos is hypothetical and is a direct quotation from a 2002 UK government publication (Transforming the Way We Learn, 2002).

"After assembly, the first period is GNVQ Science, in which digital learning materials on the school's intranet feature prominently. Currently, pupils are working through these in a three-week block. Uzman works independently on the unit on physical forces and regularly discusses his experiences with other pupils doing this through a virtual community of which he is a member. However, he knows that he can e-mail his science teacher to seek help with any assessment he has not understood. He also knows that, for this lesson, the teacher has prioritized direct support for another group of pupils who are having rather more difficulty with some of the ideas than he is."

GNVQ is a UK vocational qualification and the assumption must be that Uzman is a sixteen-year-old school student.

Cameo 2. This cameo, which has the advantage of being true, is drawn from a family experience. My wife and I live in Norfolk, an agricultural part of the country, and she has a large extended family living nearby. One of her cousin's children was facing major problems at school. At the age of eleven he had difficulties reading and writing and his classroom behavior was unruly; the school was contemplating serious action. Matters were due to come to a head at the forthcoming parents' evening, when the teachers were due to give feedback to the mothers and fathers. To avoid what would be a very uncomfortable experience, the young man in question constructed a letter to the school, purporting to come from his parents. This stated that they would be unable to attend the parents' evening due to a death in family and went on to ask the school not to reply or contact them because they were so upset about the tragic occurrence. Not a bad achievement for someone with literacy problems!

Cameo 3. I know this cameo to be true but did not personally witness it. It concerns the introduction of e-learning through the distribution of CD-ROMs in a medium-sized UK supermarket chain. A PC was made available in each of the stores, relevant product dispatched, guidance material issued, and a telephone help-line established. An early call was received from an enthusiastic manager in a Midlands store who said: "We've hit a major problem. It says in the guidance you should look on the desktop. We didn't have any desks here, so we've put the computer on a table. What do we do now?"

LESSONS LEARNED— LEARNING VS. TRAINING

What should we take from these cameos? The Uzman cameo is hypothetical nonsense. It may be attractive, even inspiring nonsense, but it is nonsense nonetheless. Uzman is from a different planet from the teenage boys who attended a North London School with my two sons. Left to themselves with a PC and asked to work independently on the unit on physical forces, they would have done no such thing. They would have discussed the Arsenal score from the night before (and may well have accessed the site on the web). Getting them back into line would have demanded time from the teacher at the expense of the direct support for the other group of pupils.

The story of my wife's delinquent relative

brings us to an important reality. It focuses on the distinction between ability and motivation and the importance of the latter in many situations. The boy was highly motivated by fear of consequences and produced a coherent letter (alas, in this case it was not coherent enough). This was something no one thought he had the ability to do and was not a skill he was willing to deploy in "normal" circumstances.

In our third cameo, the supermarket, the learners were motivated, but the interventions that were put in place simply did not take adequate account of their prior knowledge or starting-point.

Please note that all three cameos are about learning not training. This difference is absolutely fundamental. The 2004 CIPD Research Report "Helping People Learn" offered precise definitions of the terms training and learning: *training* was defined as "an instructor-led, content-based intervention, leading to desired changes in behavior" and *learning* as "a self-directed, work-based process, leading to increased adaptive capacity" (Reynolds, 2004). Training and learning are related, but conceptually different activities.

The critical point is that the same considerations apply to e-learning as to any other form of learning in the organization. Learning is a discretionary activity that takes place in the domain of the learner. Learning activities, of whatever form, will only receive managerial support if they are seen to add value to business and its customers or clients. They will only receive support from the learner if the learner is motivated and feels capable of undertaking them. Simply making content available on a personal computer and hoping that something will happen is not good enough. It has taken us far too long to grasp this essential truth. It forms the basis of a set of guidelines issues by the CIPD in a fact sheet and are listed below in Exhibit 1.

Exhibit 1. Implementing e-Learning—Key Lessons to Date

As e-learning has progressed, there has been a growing understanding of the steps that need to be taken to make it effective. Based on the experience gained over the last decade, the CIPD view is that the following principles should underline any strategy for e-learning.

➢ *Start with the learner*—Recognize the limitations of the population that you are trying to reach.

➢ *Drive out resistance with relevance*—If the e-learning material is seen as relating to something that matters in the organization, people are more likely to try to use it.

➢ *Take account of intermediaries*—Much learning requires an intermediary to advise and direct the learner. This is just as true of e-learning; it will not be successful if taken in isolation from other learning.

➢ *Embed activity in the organization*—This is a subtler point, but follows from the previous one. e-Learning modules should be seen as one element in an organizational learning strategy; where possible their use should be linked with instructor-led courses and other human resource management systems (for example, performance appraisal).

➢ *Support and automate*—This final catch-all point reinforces and underlines the others. e-Learning does not offer us the opportunity to automate all our learning processes. Instead, it is a powerful new element in a wider strategy, which requires support for learners in the context in which they learn.

GOING FORWARD IN DAYLIGHT We have not made a good job of implementing e-learning for two reasons. First, we have been overly optimistic; we have allowed overstatement and hype to develop. Secondly, we have neglected basic learning principles and have been seduced by the technology. "Start with the learner—recognize the limitations of the population that you are trying to reach" rightly appears first on the list of principles set out above.

The most important challenge facing the training professional is to gain a better understanding of how people learn in his or her organization. Given that this is still true, we have not made a good job of the introduction of e-learning over the last decade. If we do not understand how people learn and impress our colleagues with that understanding, we are indeed likely to embark on a "long day's journey into night." This has become particularly urgent with the emergence of what is now known as Web 2.0. It is essential that we do not repeat our mistakes now at a time of considerable new opportunity.

Over the last few years we have witnessed a series of interrelated factors that make collaborative learning using technology look like a more attractive option. Quite simply, people are likely to be more comfortable with this style of working. More people use a PC at work; broadband penetration is increasing—

and it's a global phenomenon.

The second half of 2007 witnessed a huge increase in the use of the term "social networking." The term is used imprecisely and often interchangeably with Web 2.0. At present there seems to be a clearer definition of Web 2.0 than of social networking. Web 2.0 is a term given to the second generation of Internet-based communities that encourage collaboration between users. A 2005 conference developed the idea that there were emerging changes in the way software developers and end-users were using the web as a platform:

"Web 2.0 is the business revolution in the computer industry caused by the move to the Internet as platform, and an attempt to understand the rules for success on that new platform."
(From Wikipedia and attributed to Tim O'Reilly, a well-known U.S. writer and author)

For the advocates, there has been a sudden emergence of new opportunities for collaboration, co-creating and sharing of content, and enhanced communication. Wikis and blogs have entered the vocabulary of the learning and development manager. Certain activities, which can be included in social networking, have shown exponential growth. Among these are the networking sites like MySpace, Facebook, and LinkedIn.

A 2009 research report, "Web 2.0 and Human Resource Management" asks:

"Groundswell or Hype?" Working for the CIPD, Martin, Reddington, and Kneafsey offered the following working definition of Web 2.0 for HR professionals:
"Web 2.0 is different from the earlier Web 1.0, which focused on the one-way
generation and publication of online content. Web 2.0 is a 'read-write' web providing a democratic architecture for participation, encouraging people to share ideas, promoting discussion and fostering a greater sense of community." (emphasis in original)
(Martin, Reddington, & Kneafsey, 2009, p. 2)

Although the authors recognized the limited applications of Web 2.0 to HRM practice to date they identified the following as one of five ways in which Web 2.0 could add strategic value to organizations:

"Supporting employees using Web 2.0, such as wikis, employee discussion forums, and virtual reality sites, tools to help them to learn and share knowledge and experience." (p. 32)

So does Web 2.0 mark a significant breakthrough in e-learning? Does it transform opportunities by creating a new environment in which the expert tacit information held within the firm could be widely shared, creating a powerful business advantage?

More sophisticated technology and more confident users certainly create new opportunities. However, these will not necessarily translate into activities that develop the knowledge and skills that deliver added value to a business and its customers or clients. Whether this welcome outcome occurs must depend on the nature of the business and the way it generates value through its people. Again, this is about learning, not about technology. Unfortunately, to date, the Web 2.0 vocabulary has developed from technology not from training or learning. "Blog," for example, is an abbreviated form of weblog; "wiki" (a Hawaiian word meaning very quick) was coined to describe a type of computer software. These two terms and others are being used very imprecisely in a learning context as applications and understandings evolve.

There is a need to develop a better vocabulary if we are to grasp and address the implications for learning. This process must proceed by asking learners what mechanisms and practices they use themselves to acquire knowledge and skills. We can expect their answers to embrace less formal categorizations, for example, studying manuals, books, videos CD-ROMs or online materials; accessing information from the Internet; watching and listening to others at work; doing a job or similar work on a regular basis. This will take us in a learner-centred rather than a technology-centered vocabulary. Training and learning professionals must recapture the

FINAL THOUGHTS

initiative from those who would promote technology for its own sake.

In some sense, little has changed since the arrival of e-learning in the late 1990s. Technology may have advanced and new potential opportunities created as a result. Learners may have become more sophisticated and confident in using the personal computers that are now on their desks. However, it is their preferences, attitudes, and motivation that must be understood if their learning is to deliver value to the organization. Our ten-year CIPD research program concluded that the best definition of the role of the trainer was: "supporting, accelerating, and directing learning interventions that meet organizational needs and are appropriate to the learner and the context." This is as true of e-learning (whether Web 2.0 or previous applications of technology) as it is of the classroom.

REFERENCES

American Society for Training and Development. (2010). *State of the industry report–2010,* Alexandria, VA: ASTD. See www.astd.org.

CIPD. (2008a). CIPD fact sheet, e-learning: Progress and prospects. Accessible at www.cipd.co.uk/subjects/lrnanddev/elearning/elearnprog.htm.

CIPD. (2008b). CIPD annual survey report: Learning and development. www.cipd.co.uk/subjects/lrnanddev/general/_lrndvsrv08.htm?IsSrchRes=1

CIPD. (2008c). CIPD research insight: Supporting, accelerating, and directing learning: implications for trainers. www.cipd.co.uk/subjects/lrnanddev/general/_sadlrng.htm.

Martin, G., Reddington, M., Kneafsey, M.B. (2009). *Web 2.0 and human resource management: 'Groundswell' or hype?* London: CIPD.

Overton, L. (2009). 10 years on . . . the e-learning debate continues. Retrieved March 25, 2010 from www.towardsmaturity.org/article/2009/10/29/10-years-on-the-elearning-debate-continues/.

Reynolds, J., (2004). *Helping people learn.* London: CIPD.

Sloman, M. (2009). Learning and technology—What have we learned? *Impact: Journal of Applied Research in Workplace e-Learning.* Inaugural issue.

Patti Shank

Patti Shank, Ph.D., CPT, is the president of Learning Peaks LLC, an internationally recognized instructional design consulting firm that provides learning and performance consulting and training and performance support solutions. She is listed in *Who's Who in Instructional Technology* and is an often-requested speaker at training and instructional technology conferences. Patti is quoted frequently in training publications and is the co-author of *Making Sense of Online Learning* (Pfeiffer, 2004), editor of *The Online Learning Idea Book* (Pfeiffer, 2007), co-editor of *The e-Learning Handbook* (Pfeiffer, 2008), and co-author of *Essential Articulate Studio '09* (Jones & Bartlett, 2009). She was an award-winning contributing editor for *Online Learning Magazine,* and her articles are found in eLearning Guild publications, *Adobe's Resource Center, Training* magazine's *Online Learning News and Reviews,* and *Training Directors' Forum e-net,* Magna Publication's *Online Classroom,* and elsewhere.

Patti completed her Ph.D. at the University of Colorado, Denver. Her interests include interaction design, tools and technologies for interaction, the pragmatics of real-world instructional design, and instructional authoring. Her research on new online learners won an EDMEDIA (2002) best research paper award. She is passionate and outspoken about the results needed from instructional design and instruction and engaged in improving instructional design practices and instructional outcomes. Her website is www.learningpeaks.com/

LEARNSANITY: Patti Shank
THREE DO-IT-RIGHT STRATEGIES TO GET NEW E-LEARNING INITIATIVES OFF TO A GOOD START

If you are new to e-learning, getting your first e-learning initiative(s) off the ground can be overwhelming. There's a lot to consider, much of which can perplex and worry novice designers. You may feel you don't yet have the skills needed to make good decisions. It's true. There is a lot to consider, and it can be overwhelming to start. The good news is that veteran Patti Shank has identified some specific strategies you can use to make your first e-learning initiatives go more smoothly. These strategies build on her many years of experience as well as on what early adopters have learned and will help you get off to a good start, even before you understand everything you need to know. Patti's advice will help you avoid costly mistakes that folks who don't use these strategies too often make.

LET'S GET STARTED If you're new to e-learning, you may feel overwhelmed and vulnerable. It may seem as if the advice you hear from different sources is contradictory and the list of acronyms and new words never ends. Should you hire consultants? Buy a learning management system (LMS)? Lease a webinar application? And what authoring tool should you buy? Although every organization's situation is different (which is why you need to be wary of any one-size-fits-all solutions), there are some general strategies that will make the leap to e-learning easier and with better results.

Let's start with some very good news about getting started with e-learning now. The authoring and development tools available for use are far easier to use and create materials that are much better than the old, clunky, and hard-to-use tools of the recent and less recent past. Many of the commonly used tools today can build decent e-learning in weeks and months, rather than months and years. And by not starting until now, you have avoided the does-this-e-learning-stuff-work questions that early adopters had to contend with. Plus, isn't it more fun to let others make mistakes that you can learn from than to make mistakes that others can learn from? Uh huh. I thought so.

In this article, I'll discuss four critical strategies you and your organization can use that build on what early adopters have learned so you can wisely and thoughtfully initiate e-learning projects with less pain and better results.

THREE E-LEARNSANITY STRATEGIES FOR A GOOD START I'll describe three interdependent strategies that can help you get off to a good e-learning start and reduce some of the hassles. Some may seem obvious, but do people always do the things that will obviously help them? Not so much.

Strategy 1: Really Understand Your Company's Most Critical Information and Instruction Needs.

"Measure twice, cut once," is a proverb that carries a lot of wisdom. Obviously, it should be applied quite *literally* when cutting wood or other materials. Measuring twice, when it comes to e-learning, means beginning with knowledge of what's *really* needed. This strategy will force you to *systematically* gather and analyze information *before* committing to expensive tools, technologies, additional staff, consultants, or vendor services. Because of the many complexities involved, this wise strategy is particularly important in e-learning design and development.

Understand Your Organization, Industry, and How Training Supports Them

The best place to start before jumping into e-learning is to determine the most critical information and instruction needs of your organization. These are the information and instruction needs that *directly support the mission of the organization*. Businesses survive by providing goods or services that are valuable enough to its customers to pay for them. Your job, then, is to help make this happen.

So step one is making sure you understand the business your business is in and how that business is done. Go find out what people do in your organization. Don't wait to be invited. Shadow people in the front lines of your organization, observe what they do and their challenges, and ask questions. Talk to people in operations functions to find out how your business determines whether it is financially healthy. Read industry trade journals. Identify the major forces shaping your industry and

the expected future issues. Does your training (including e-learning) revolve around your organization's most critical business needs? It should.

In addition to understanding your organization and industry, you should determine the training outcomes that are most valuable to people who care about the results from information and instruction projects you work on and who will ultimately determine whether the work your department does is worth the cost. As they say, perception is reality, and knowing this information up-front means that you can better target your efforts. These people may include people who request training (such as supervisors, executives, and others), learners, internal customers (people in the organization who are impacted by the work and results of others in the organization), and external customers (the people who pay for your organization's goods and services).

Gather Information

Table 1 lists some of the information that is valuable to gather from stakeholders in order to assure that your efforts are aligned with your organization's most critical information and instruction needs.

Because e-learning is often time-, cost-, and resource-intensive, *especially during start-up*, it's more important than ever to understand the information and instruction needs of your business in detail. You'll want to be able to justify any extra time, costs, and resources in terms of expected results.

The next section will help you connect your organizations' most critical information and instruction needs to technologies that can be used to satisfy them.

Information	Training Needs
1. Problems to be prevented or solved	Training should help prevent or solve important business problems such as gaining and maintaining customers.
2. Needed organizational results	Training should be aligned with the results that are valuable to stakeholders. This result—making sure that the information or instruction has been completed (for example, compliance training)—requires a different approach and level effort than this result— reducing the incidence or severity of problematic (or worse) circumstances.
3. Needed job results	Training should be designed to improve job results, which in turn help the organization fulfill its mission. You almost always must watch people do their jobs and ask questions to get this right.
4. Time constraints	You need to understand learners' time constraints before you start building instruction, especially e-learning.
5. Technology constraints	You'll need to know whether there will be any technology issues that may impact the success of your e-learning programs. For example, what types of media can your servers handle? Do learners have needed players (the small applications that help the browser play media)?

Table 1. Information to Gather from Stakeholders

Strategy 2: Consider How Technology Can Be Used to Meet These Needs.

Previously, many training organizations and higher education institutions adopted e-learning because they wanted to be seen as forward-thinking or they believed the initial hype about the wonders of e-learning. Over time, we've come to understand that the *most* important reason to adopt e-learning is because *it can get needed information and instruction to the folks who need it, when they need it.*

This is important—You do not have to make a choice between e-learning and classroom learning, but you *should* determine when e-learning makes sense and when it does not (or at least on its own). The truth is that, in many cases, a combination works better than either alone. Even when face-to-face instruction makes the most sense, it often helps to provide electronic work support materials so they can be used during and after training. Even when using self-paced e-learning, it often makes sense to provide support from a live human being.

I've already discussed analyzing the most critical information and instruction needs of your organization (Strategy 1). Now we can analyze how different learning modes will best support these needs. Each different learning modes has attributes that can be employed to meet organizational and learner needs.

Attributes	Classroom Instruction (Face-to-Face)	Synchronous e-Learning (Live Online/Webinar/Web Conferencing)	Asynchronous e-Learning (Self-Paced Online)	Work Support (Job Aids, Templates, and Documentation)
Time and place	Specified time and place. Need to wait for the course to begin.	Specified time but any place (with access). Need to wait for the course to begin.	Any time and place (with access). Can begin any time.	Any time and place (with access). Can use as needed.
Costs	Costs for instructors, building/meeting rooms, materials, travel, and learners' time away from work.	Costs for instructors, materials, and learners' time away from work. Also costs for tools and technologies (for example, a webinar application).	Costs for software and learners' time away from work. Costs for tools and technologies (for example, server space and authoring tools).	Costs for materials, tools, and technologies (for example, a database application and documentation authoring tools).
Benefits	Potential for immediate learner support. Social aspects can improve individual learning and increase motivation. Time set aside for instruction improves learner focus.	Learner support and feedback can be immediate (with fewer participants). Social aspects can improve individual learning and increase motivation. Time set aside for instruction improves learner focus.	Allows for self-pacing and ability to practice and review as needed. Asynchronous learning environment of feels less intimidating when learning about difficult or dangerous situations.	Helps people perform their jobs at the moment that help is needed. Can support knowledge and skills gained in instruction when on the job. Can be much cheaper (and sometimes more effective) than training.
Challenges	Specific dates and times mean courses may not be available when needed. In addition, travel costs may be prohibitive. With a larger number of participants, immediate support, feedback, and social interaction are less likely.	With a larger number of participants, immediate support, feedback, and social interaction are less likely. Specific dates and times mean courses may not be available when needed.	Any time/any place often triggers procrastination and non-completion. Lack of social interaction, support, guidance, and help often reduces motivation and increases frustration.	Only as good as the materials that are easy to find and use at the moment they are needed.
Best uses	Best used when motivation is important, immediate feedback and support are critical, the ability to work through difficult considerations in the same time and space is needed, or in other situations in which face-to-face is valuable.	Best used when motivation is important, interaction with the presenter and possibly other learners is desirable, or in other situations when being live is valuable. Also best when learners are widely distributed geographically.	When information or instruction needs to be available as needed, strict standardization of content is imperative (for example, for compliance training), and when content changes quickly. Also best when learners are widely distributed geographically.	To support knowledge and skills that cannot be committed to memory, such as when information regularly changes or is used rarely.

Table 2. Typical Attributes of Classroom Learning, Synchronous e-Learning, Self-Paced Online e-Learning, and Electronic Work Support

Table 2 shows some of the differences between classroom (face-to-face) instruction, synchronous (live and online) e-learning, self-paced online (self-paced and online) e-learning, and electronic work support materials. The attributes listed are for typical uses of each modality.

An obvious insight from Table 2 is that, because the different modes have different attributes, some modes will likely be a better fit for some information or instruction than for others. What might not be as obvious is that the attributes of the different modes are complementary. In many cases, it is advantageous to combine some or all modes in order to gain the benefits of and mitigate the challenges of each.

For example, a management development program may start with a kick-off webinar (synchronous e-learning) to acquaint all participants in the organization's locations with the topics that will be covered, work through a compelling case study to engage participants, and answer questions about the program. Self-paced online modules may allow participants to work through important concepts (for example, how to provide performance feedback), use self-check practice activities (to determine whether they understand the concepts), and interact with realistic scenarios (to see whether they can apply what was learned in realistic ways). Monthly webinars may be held to field new questions and discuss problems that learners are currently facing on the job. Work support materials such as performance discussion templates may be made available for learners to use during the self-paced scenarios and on the job. And monthly face-to-face brown-bag sessions

may be held in each location to discuss real-life situations, practice skills, and gain immediate feedback.

Strategy 3: Don't Reach for the Moon (Just Yet).

If you have ever updated a kitchen or bathroom, you have probably wished afterward that you had the knowledge you gained *during* the project *before* you started the work. Unfortunately, we all learn by making choices with imperfect understanding or too little data and seeing the results of those choices. We can't know what we don't know in advance, so these kinds of problems are normal. (We can also learn from others' mistakes, and this article and others in this *Annual* should help you do that.)

If you've analyzed your organization's most critical information and instruction needs (Strategy 1) and thought through how technologies can be used to meet those needs (Strategy 2), you're going to make better choices. But some data points don't show up until you make choices and see the results of those choices.

e-Learning involves tons of choices—synchronous and/or asynchronous online learning, what synchronous tool to use, what authoring tools to use, and so on. You probably don't yet know enough, despite doing the work in Strategies 1 and 2, to assure that *every* choice will be spot on.

As a result, it often makes sense to start out small and manageable and learn from it. Then add on and learn from that. And so on. Don't run out and spend a fortune. Start small and gather critical information as you go so you know what you need.

Don't Buy a Learning Management System (LMS).

If you are just getting started, don't run out and buy an LMS or ask five LMS vendors to come in for demos. As I said earlier, you really don't know what you need yet (or even *if* you need something), and vendors can take advantage of that. Plus, buying an LMS before you know what you need will constrain everything you do from then on.

Enterprise LMSs are quite expensive and very complex. Organizations that "do it right" often create committees and advisory groups with representatives from across different units to define requirements, business needs, learning processes, standards, guidelines, and selection criteria, and create vendor evaluation checklists. Successful implementation involves complex issues that few training organizations can handle without IT help.

If and when you determine that an LMS is needed (and again, many organizations do not need one, even if they want to track learners), the right approach is to start by building detailed requirements. After a detailed set of requirements is built, organizations can then create specific workflows that vendors need to demonstrate.

Again, buying an LMS is a complex decision that should involve numerous stakeholders, and making this choice when you are just getting started can be a disaster. Many, many organizations don't have the need for the capabilities of an enterprise LMS. There are simpler, easier, and less complex ways to track test scores and the completion of courses.

Be Prudent About Buying Applications.

Strategies 1 and 2 will help you consider whether live webinars makes sense for your organization's information and instruction needs. But delivering webinars requires rethinking how to present, engage, and determine understanding. They require behind-the-scenes tech support (more than you might imagine). So it's a good idea to attend webinars to see what works and what doesn't work. Attend webinars that use different webinar tools so you can see what they do well and less well. Ask people who do webinars regularly what is involved.

When starting out, it doesn't make sense to spend a fortune on synchronous applications until you understand how they work and what features you most need. You can get a free trial for a variety of webinar applications such as GoToWebinar (www.gotomeeting.com/fec/webinar), Adobe Connect (www.adobe.com/products/acrobatconnectpro), or WebEx (www.webex.com) and rent webinar space as needed until you know what application makes sense for you. You can also use free tools, such as the free version of DimDim (www.dimdim.com) or Adobe ConnectNow (www.adobe.com/acom/connectnow), to get started and learn the ropes.

One of the most exciting things happening in the e-learning field today is the availability of much easier-to-use asynchronous authoring tools that allow us to do much more development on our own, without having to understand the underlying code and technologies. Many of these tools allow instructional designers, trainers, and subject-matter experts (SMEs) to build attractive content quickly, with or without additional help.

Authoring tools are primarily used to create self-paced online information and instruction, and Strategies 1 and 2 will help you consider whether self-paced e-learning makes sense for your organization's information and instruction needs. Remember that it often makes sense to start small and learn. Here are two ideal initial self-paced online e-learning projects:

> - Short application demos using Captivate (www.adobe.com/products/captivate) or Camtasia (www.techsmith.com/camtasia.asp). Or start by using the free screen casting tool, Screenr (wwww.screenr.com).
> - Simple narrated slides using Articulate Presenter (www.articulate.com/products/presenter.php) or Adobe Presenter (www.adobe.com/products/presenter). Or start with a free PowerPoint-to-Flash tool (such as iSpring Free (www.ispringsolutions.com/products/ispring_free.html).

Many other tools are available for these types of projects. I have just listed some of the most popular.

If you have completed Strategies 1 and 2 and you have a good idea of how e-learning fits into your training plan, purchasing a few tools seems like a no-brainer. But it may not be a good idea to spend a *lot* on tools yet because you very well may find yourself tweaking the plan over time and tweaking the tools as well. (Most organizations use numerous tools and, over time, you will likely do so as well.)

IT'S A WRAP The *most* important reason to adopt e-learning is because it can get needed information and instruction to the folks who need it, when they need it. The three interdependent strategies discussed in this chapter will help reduce problems and make successes far more likely.

Determining the most critical information and instruction needs of your organization forces you to systematically gather and analyze information *before* committing to expensive tools, technologies, additional staff, consultants, or vendor services that are often used in new e-learning implementations. Only then can you determine when e-learning makes sense (for those critical information and instruction needs) and what mode(s) of e-learning is/are best for a given information or instruction project.

e-Learning can involve many choices so it often makes sense to start out small and manageable and learn as you go. Starting with smaller-scale webinars using lease-as-needed synchronous learning applications and smaller-scale asynchronous projects using PowerPoint-to-Flash and screen-capture-to-Flash tools are often a good strategy because these projects typically don't require a great deal of money and time and will provide you with ah-has that will make larger scale projects more successful down the road. There are some amazing tools on the market that make these projects easy to develop, but you might also want to start with some of the free versions of these kinds of tools before committing additional money and time.

Not taking learners' needs into consideration can reduce the impact of otherwise good e-learning projects. Your learners have to be able to use your e-learning with minimal frustration. This is a larger consideration than you might think. e-Learning should fit your learners' needs, in terms of support, level of information, style of delivery, and so on.

And, finally, don't forget that the Internet, by itself, is only a delivery mechanism.

To make the learning experiences that are delivered engaging and meaningful requires thought and an understanding of what works. Leaving good design to chance is like leaving a good education to chance. Could happen . . . or not.

Getting started with e-learning? C'mon in! "Doing" e-learning is less difficult than in the past. Which makes now a great time to begin.

REFERENCES

Jane Hart's directory of learning tools: c4lpt.co.uk/Directory/index.html

Tom Kuhlmann's Rapid e-Learning Blog: www.articulate.com/rapid-elearning

Patti Shank's Resource links: www.learningpeaks.com/resources/

Patti Shank's blog: www.learningpeaks.com/category/blog/

Reviews of web conferencing tools: www.webconferencing-test.com/en/webconference_home.
html (note relationship with Citrix, site provides helpful information nonetheless)

Training Media Reviews Authoring Tools Reviews: www.tmreview.com/Editorial.asp?ID=1718

Tina Kunshier

Tina Kunshier, MA, is learning and development director for Boston Scientific. Tina has been with this company since 1997. She holds a bachelor's degree in business management and a master's in adult education and distance learning. Before joining the corporate learning management system process and services group, her primary focus was in supporting the manufacturing and quality functions of the business developing classroom and online learning solutions to enable learners to meet strict federal regulations.

Tina has more than ten years of experience in representing Boston Scientific training processes, systems, and standards with auditing bodies. She has served as the audit resource representing learning and development for specific manufacturing locations and now for the corporate learning and development function. As learning director she is responsible for implementing and maintaining the protocols in place at Boston Scientific, which ensure learning programs adhere to and support the external regulations associated with medical devise manufacturing, including e-learning methodology.

CHALLENGES OF DEVELOPING E-LEARNING IN A REGULATED ENVIRONMENT | Tina Kunshier

Tina Kunshier couldn't make a truer testament: "Creating e-learning in a regulated environment is not easy. The time and resources invested to develop and deploy an e-learning program on a learning management system validated to FDA regulations can be daunting." I confirm this by having watched my own studios working in similarly regulated environments. What is of particular insight in this fascinating article is Tina's ability to find advantages to working under such extreme constraints. "However, the effort spent on maintaining programs after deployment can be much more efficient and cost-effective due to the rigor required in development and deployment. The end result should offer a more controlled, documented, and robust system that accommodates current standards for electronic records and holds up to the scrutiny of an FDA audit." The author outlines challenges developers face when developing and deploying e-learning in a regulated environment and also offers tips and best practices for avoiding some common pitfalls.

OVERVIEW OF REGULATIONS

As a leading manufacturer of medical devices, Boston Scientific is required to adhere to myriad regulations from a range of government regulatory bodies worldwide. The most critical of these is the U.S. Food and Drug Administration (FDA), which specifies regulations through dozens of the organization's offices, centers, and divisions. Medical devices are specifically regulated under Title 21 of the Code of Federal Regulations (CFR), which contains laws and regulations for medical device testing, approvals, labeling, reporting, and recalls. The CFR also details requirements for quality systems, electronic records, and validation of learning management systems (LMS), including e-learning. All processes associated with developing, testing, and deploying an e-learning system must adhere to these rigorous standards and be validated through audit by the FDA.

BOSTON SCIENTIFIC'S LEARNING MANAGEMENT SYSTEM

Boston Scientific's internally branded LMS is called "LearningConnect." Training content delivered through LearningConnect includes online, classroom, and self-certification instruction, all of which is recorded as part of an individual employee's training record. As part of the company's corporate quality system, LearningConnect was validated to be in compliance with existing federal regulations, which involved a comprehensive series of functional tests critical for successful FDA audits. The validation process included establishing and implementing certain standards (described below) to ensure ongoing FDA compliance of the LearningConnect system.

ESTABLISHING STANDARDS FOR E-LEARNING DEVELOPMENT

Instructional Designers.

When developing e-learning coursework, Boston Scientific's instructional designers are required to adhere to a set of minimum standards that ensure the training functions as intended in the LearningConnect system. The first step typically involves working with an external developer to "build" the e-learning content. Instructional designers work exclusively with approved, reputable e-learning vendors experienced with regulated environments, especially the requirements of FDA's 21CFR Part 11 on electronic records and signatures. Careful consideration is also given to the vendor's area of content specialization (marketing/sales, quality, production, etc.). Boston Scientific requires all potential e-learning developers to pass a rigid qualification process before being added to the list of approved vendors. By establishing and abiding by a set of comprehensive and documented e-learning requirements, the company can be more assured that e-learning courses will function as intended in a validated LMS. Following this process also ensures that a learner is able to launch, navigate, and successfully complete the course, as well as provide his or her e-signature in compliance with electronic signature requirements. Boston Scientific's instructional designers are also required to use only those e-learning-related desktop applications and components supported by the company's information technology (IT) support services. Maintaining a list of approved applications ensures that every e-learning course is compatible with standards for the Boston Scientific IT infrastructure. For example, if a course is developed using Internet Explorer 8.0, currently an unsupported browser platform for Boston Scientific, several problems can result for learners attempting to launch and complete an e-learning course that requires IE6.0 compatibility.

Content Development.

Delivering effective e-learning content in a regulated industry poses specific challenges in regard to content. Regulatory bodies are constantly updating laws and regulations, and internal processes are also rapidly changing to keep pace and stay in compliance. As a result, e-learning content in a regulated environment may require frequent and far-reaching updates that can overwhelm internal resources. A best practice used to manage this complexity is to reference or provide direct links to the internal documents housed in Boston Scientific's content management system instead of embedding a static, controlled document. However, including URLs or links to websites outside the company's control should be avoided because any changes could result in unavailable or inaccurate information for the user.

Developers must also carefully select appropriate authoring tools to create the desired content in order to comply with all the requirements of the internal IT systems and infrastructure.

Deployment.

Instructional designers responsible for creating and deploying e-learning content must be effective project managers who can communicate effectively, manage the required testing, and provide hands-on assistance in deploying the program. They are responsible for selecting and managing professional testers who supplement internal personnel to test new training prior to deployment. Operating in a regulated industry adds complexity to the process by requiring additional documentation, reviews, and checkpoints, which contribute to a longer deployment process compared to unregulated industries. For smaller courses and basic certification tests, the typical deployment process can be as long as the course development process. Team members, collaborators, and reviewers are often new to the e-learning deployment process and may be surprised by the complexity of deploying a basic course or test. In order to avoid lengthy delays, the course developer must set clear expectations and explain the interdependencies between developing approved content and deploying it for robust, widespread use.

Testing.
The process of deploying e-learning course content requires rigorous testing that must be properly documented at each step to ensure a validated LMS. Thorough testing of course content and functionality also minimizes delays and the need for rework. The actual deployment process will typically span an additional four to six weeks to accommodate this rigorous testing process and to confirm reliable functionality in the LMS. Some of these steps include:

➤ Functionality testing in the development environment with a defined set of testers, including a professional tester

➤ Testing against the test script in the user acceptance testing environment, which requires a minimum of four testers to gain geographic feedback from results

➤ Final testing in the production environment to a sample of the target audience

Any unexpected result during testing necessitate a complete restart of the test procedure after the problem is fixed in order to ensure the program functions as intended. Proper planning, development, testing, and deployment of custom or off-the-shelf courseware can take months to ensure the content and functionality meet the company's stringent requirements and perform as expected on the LearningConnect system.

STEPS TO A SUCCESSFUL E-LEARNING PROGRAM While every company will follow a slightly different path to creating an e-learning program, several key steps are essential to any successful strategy. The following steps may seem obvious, but they should not be underestimated in the value they provide to keeping a project on schedule and ensuring overall success:

1. *Know your entire e-learning development and deployment process.* Before you even consider starting a project, become familiar with your company's e-learning development processes, standards, and responsibilities. When you are familiar with these elements, you will have realistic expectations of the resources needed and the time it will take to fully deploy your

program. With clear expectations for each stage in the process, you will improve the probability of on-time project completion.

2. *Develop to your baseline settings.* Now that you are familiar with the overall process, ensure the program is developed to the baseline settings or minimum standards. Don't include extra bells and whistles at the expense of meaningful content and interactions. For example, if your baseline settings do not support audio, you will need to provide text as an option for those end-users without audio capability. This does not eliminate audio as a possibility, but it does present the need for optional methods to participate in that part of the program. Baseline settings exist to ensure we develop to the least common denominator, thereby ensuring everyone can experience the full program.

3. *Test to ensure the program performs as expected.* Prior to the pilot launch, rigorous testing is required to ensure the program functions as intended to the baseline settings and that all content is appropriate. At this point, the use of a professional tester and a content subject-matter expert is strongly recommended. A professional tester will check for errors in grammar, punctuation, and interactive functionality, while a subject-matter expert will verify appropriate content and context.

4. *Pilot the program with an appropriate sample from the end-user group.* Once final testing issues have been addressed and testing is complete, pilot the program with a subset of the target audience. These resources should already be identified and ready to begin. The pilot launch is per-

formed on a development server to ensure the validated environment is not adversely affected. After successful pilot completion, the program should be retested to check for any required fixes.

5. *Test in the production environment.* The program is now ready for testing in the production environment. However, do not move the program to the production site until it has been successfully tested and piloted to ensure there are no adverse affects to the validated environment.

6. *Monitor for future improvements.* After the program is made available to end-users, you should continue to monitor all feedback systems for improvements. This process could include data gathered from support functions that troubleshoot e-learning issues, direct email inquiries from end-users, or assessment results. By close monitoring data and application of improvements, you can help to ensure a successful e-learning program.

TIPS AND BEST PRACTICES The requirements of creating and deploying e-learning in a regulated industry present some common challenges. The following tips and best practices may help you avoid setbacks and make the process less burdensome.

➢ *Use pre-screened vendors.* When considering vendors to build and deploy an e-learning program, select from an existing list of qualified vendors who know your company's processes and systems and have a track record of success and intimate knowledge of industry standards, regulations, and subject matter.

➤ *Identify key stakeholders.* Once you have selected the appropriate vendors, it is critical to identify all key stakeholders and reviewers early enough to determine all relevant requirements, content, and functionality prior to full-scale development or deployment. Uncovering issues late in the process will only cause setbacks and delays.

➤ *Obtain legal and regulatory reviews.* In a regulated industry like medical devices, internal legal and regulatory reviews are required for content that may be communicated externally. If this applies to your course content, involve the appropriate legal and regulatory reviewers as early as possible. Seeking approvals late in the deployment, user acceptance testing (UAT), or pilot stages could require changes that set the project back weeks or months.

➤ *Review "deployment-worthy" content.* Before you begin to route a course through final review, UAT, and pilot to a live production server, thoroughly review and update course materials to reflect what you believe to be content worthy of deployment. By eliminating even small errors, you will reduce the iterations and rework required in the final review and testing stages—and keep the project on schedule.

➤ *Avoid "project creep."* Once you begin the deployment process, avoid starting over to accommodate "nice-to-haves"

or minor content edits that would otherwise go unnoticed. A course will never be absolutely perfect in every reviewer's eyes. Submitting even a small change through a complex deployment environment can result in significant delays. At this stage, hold out for "showstoppers," inaccurate information, or broken functionality.

➤ *Maximize the ROI of e-learning development efforts.* Training in a regulated industry typically involves content that requires precise documentation, updates, and compliance records. In some cases, the documentation changes faster than the training process can accommodate it. When choosing course topics, select content areas that are more stable, less likely to require frequent updates, and ideally intended to reach a broad audience. For courses with frequent content changes, consider linking to reference documents or external sources that are consistently and independently updated in a timely manner. This will allow you to avoid course re-deployment each time the content changes.

➤ *Stay current.* Know and follow the program development standards. These requirements are created to ensure your program is compliant with external regulations and can hold up to the system strain of potentially thousands of end-users. Always keep a current version of the requirements available for reference.

CONCLUSION The following quote about Genentech, a leading biotechnology company, is one example of how companies are moving to an LMS to solve perceived compliance training issues, especially when paper records cannot meet the scale of their business requirements.

"Any company regulated by the FDA is required to adhere to many regulations, so performance evaluations and assessments are important to its learning and documentation strategies. Several years ago, internal and external audits showed Genentech to be at potential risk during a good clinical practice (GCP) audit. Although their compliance training was successful and accepted within the company, they were required to create a solution to handle thousands of completed employee assessments in order to maintain its LMS. They recently passed the FDA's audit of their development organization for the GCP audit. The process for solving the compliance problem allowed online completion of the basic level of training. While initially paper-based, the electronic version now provides for automatic assignment to groups, online completion, scoring, and entry into the LMS."
(Parker, 2006)

Recent industry conferences on this topic have featured speakers discussing how to effectively respond to information requests through the use of an LMS (MTLI). Auditors are increasingly recommending electronic learning records to provide greater confidence in identifying training requirements, tracking assignments, recording course completion, tracking change control of training resources, and retaining records. Furthermore, they suggest establishing a controlled training and qualification process that is appropriate to the size, organization, and complexity of the company. While the benefits are clear for utilizing an LMS for maintaining individual training records, it comes with the added burden of rigor imposed by the need for regulatory compliance.

Creating e-learning in a regulated environment is not easy. The time and resources invested to develop and deploy an e-learning program on an LMS validated to FDA regulations can be daunting. However, the effort spent on maintaining programs after deployment can be much more efficient and cost-effective due to the rigor of this progress. In fact, e-learning programs developed to these standards have traditionally yielded an internal error rate of less than 2 percent of all weekly course completions.

This article not only outlined the challenges to e-learning development and deployment in a regulated environment, but also offered tips and best practices to avoid some common pitfalls. The end result should offer a more controlled, documented, and robust system that accommodates current standards for electronic records and holds up to the scrutiny of an FDA audit.

REFERENCES

2010 MTLI Conference. (2010, March 23–24). Creating and maintaining robust training programs, Washington, D.C. www.advamedmtli.org/download/file/agendas/Employee_Training_Agenda5.pdf.

Parker, L. (2006). Online events archive: Assessment strategy in a highly regulated biotechnology environment. www.elearningguild.com

T. Craig Montgomerie

T. Craig Montgomerie, Ph.D, is a professor emeritus of instructional technology in the Department of Educational Psychology at the University of Alberta and president of Mentat Consulting Services Ltd., a firm of educational consultants. He has been involved in the application of computer technology to education since the early 1970s. Craig's interest in using computer networks to support distanced students began in the early 1980s with the development of an online support system for extended campus students. He co-developed the first web-based instruction course at the University of Alberta with Dwayne Harapnuik. It was subsequently selected as the "best educational website—single course" by the North American Web Developers Association in 1996. Craig was a founding member of the board of the Netera Alliance, whose core role is to design and implement the next-generation Internet in Alberta. Craig was the principal investigator on the Rural Advanced Community of Learners (RACOL) project (www.racol.ualberta.ca). The essence of RACOL was the development of a model of teaching and learning that exploits the potential of broadband networks and advanced technological capabilities such as broadcast quality video, collaborative environments, and educational objects to create effective learning environments that addresses the needs of students in rural and remote school districts.

Craig is currently involved in evaluating the Canadian Space Agency/Alberta Education use of videoconference technology to provide distance education opportunities for Alberta schools, developing a course "Introduction to Current Distance Education Technologies" for Athabasca University, and helping the Town of Three Hills to realize the potential of the Alberta Supernet for all residents.

Cathy King

Cathy King, MBA, began her professional career as a project manager and communications specialist for academic research projects at the University of Alberta. Specializing in collaborative technologies, Cathy became known as a power user and videoconferencing guru in Alberta's education system. Coordinating Alberta's Videoconferencing Regional Leads Network (www.vcrln.ca) and providing leadership to educators in both K-12 and post-secondary institutions, Cathy loves to translate the complexities of technology into useful training opportunities and mentorship to encourage the functional usage of technology tools. Cathy now provides strategic consulting and integration services for K-12 and post-secondary institutions. Founder of King's Court Communications, Cathy enjoys helping solve technology problems for clients to create efficiencies, learning opportunities, and better service. She is also the former vice president for Netera Alliance (now www. Cybera.ca), where she played a leadership role in bringing world-class researchers in ICT together to build Alberta's Cyberinfrastructure Task Force. Her work has provided support for educators and researchers across the province of Alberta and has helped to encourage organizational change to ensure all technology tools for teaching and learning are integrated into the greater system.

Cathy is currently completing the implementation of a 114 endpoint videoconferencing network for Alberta's Community Adult Learning, Literacy, and Volunteer Centres (www. iccan.ca), working with the province to create a provincial digital resource system for all libraries and developing training workshops and online resources for organization technology integration.

EDUCATIONAL VIDEOCONFERENCING:
CRACKING OPEN THE CLASSROOM DOOR

T. Craig Montgomerie
Cathy King

For a very long time now, teachers have entered a classroom, closed the door, and shared their knowledge with their students. Videoconferencing is one tool helping to "crack open the classroom door" and allow geographically separated students to experience sights, sounds, and interactions with real people in real time. I'm delighted to have the eye-opening, pragmatic content this chapter explores on educational videoconferencing. The authors discuss the history and types of videoconferencing and how these educational tools have evolved. They then explore the educational uses and supports required to ensure maximum effectiveness in the classroom. I have extremely high regard for the works of Montgomerie and King and am delighted to have their contribution to the *Annual*.

In the past, teachers entered a classroom, closed the door, and shared their knowledge with their students. Occasionally, the school or classroom doors were thrown open to visitors for special occasions, such as career days, "bring your parent to school" days, science fairs, or visits by athletes, astronauts, or other dignitaries. Field trips have taken students out of the classroom and to locations where they can engage with different experts in a different environment. But these were special occasions and not part of the normal educational experience.

Technology is changing this isolation in the classroom: motion pictures and educational television brought the world to the classroom, while the Internet allowed interaction between students in the classroom and others outside the classroom—even outside the planet. Videoconferencing cracks the classroom door even further by bringing sights, sounds, and interactions with real people in real time into the classroom. Recent developments such as broadband to the classroom, less expensive dedicated room-based videoconference equipment, and free personal videoconfer-

ence capabilities on desktop computers, have produced exponential growth in the use of videoconference in educational settings. In this chapter we examine the different kinds of videoconferencing systems, discuss the different ways videoconferencing is being used in educational settings, and provide links to videoconference resources and directories of services.

A SHORT HISTORY OF EDUCATIONAL VIDEOCONFERENCING

Videoconferencing has been used in education since the 1980s, when, in order to facilitate the transmission of a reasonably good picture and sound, a number of POTS (plain old telephone system) lines were multiplexed to provide the necessary bandwidth. The cost of the audiovisual equipment, telephone line multiplexor, codec (the video encoder/decoder), and the charges for multiple long-distance circuits made videoconferencing a very expensive endeavor. The use of videoconference was limited to cost-effective installations such as allowing distant experts to present to large gatherings with audience interaction by two-way videoconference or by audio-only audience participation, or corporate training whereby student time and travel is a real cost to the corporation. IBM, for example, made extensive use of different types of videoconferences for internal training in the 1980s (Scott, 1993).

In the late 1980s costs came down as technologies matured and ISDN (integrated services digital network) telephone circuits made connectivity more convenient in large cities. As a result, universities and colleges began to investigate the use of videoconferencing between classrooms and between institutions. For example, the Universities of Alberta and Calgary joined forces in 1993 to offer joint classes in biomedical engineering. Jointly, institutions had more expertise, but costs were still prohibitive for any large penetration in K-12 education.

It wasn't until the development of videoconferencing over the Internet (IP videoconference) in 1990s that the technology began to be considered a viable technology for use in everyday K-12 classrooms and distance education. (See, for example, Broadband Enabled Lifelong Learning Environment at http://belle.netera.ca/.). The development of Cu-SeeMe at Cornell University in 1992 was the initiator for a number of trials of desktop videoconferencing in post-secondary education. The adoption of the H.323 standard by the International Telecommunication Union in 1996 had a great effect on the development of IP videoconferencing. While there were a number of projects in the late 1990s and 2000s that investigated the use of higher quality (MPEG-2; Montgomerie, Davenport, & King, 2003) and Access Grid (www.accessgrid.

org)) videoconferencing, H.323 became the common standard.

In the 2000s, videoconference became much more common in post-secondary and K-12. Many organizations offer videoconference experiences for students, and state governments have developed provincial standards, developed high-speed, videoconference networks, and sponsored organizations like the Alberta Video Conference Regional Leads Consortium to provide leadership and professional development to teachers. In the rest of this article, we concentrate on IP videoconference and discuss these developments in more detail.

TYPES OF IP VIDEO-CONFERENCING

All IP video-conferencing is not created equal. Videoconferencing can be divided into three, relatively arbitrary, types. There is quite a bit of overlap between the different types, and there are applications that allow users on different types of systems to interconnect.

Personal videoconference is designed to allow one user to talk to another user while also seeing a video image of the other person. Originally, dedicated devices called videophones provided this service, but a number of personal videoconference programs work on desktop computers. Personal videoconference systems can be OS dependent like iChat on the Macintosh (www.apple.com/macosx/features/ichat.html) or Live Messenger (http://windowslive.com/desktop/messenger) on Windows. Third-party products, notably Skype (www.skype.com), which originated as "free" Voice over IP (VoIP) software, allow personal videoconferencing between users of disparate systems. As well as providing point-to-point (two-person) videoconferencing, these programs usually allow limited multi-point videoconferencing, but the pictures tend to degrade as more users are added.

Web conferencing is a collaboration tool that provides users with shared whiteboards, applications software, presentations, and so forth, while also being able to communicate with each other via real-time chat. Most web conferencing systems also allow the broadcast of audio although a number rely on a separate teleconference convener. Again, most web conferencing systems permit at least one web-camera feed—usually the current presenter—and a number provide multiple web-camera feeds. Web conferencing programs operate via a web browser, hence are independent of the user's platform. Users configure their personal computers, which should be equipped with microphones and web cameras, to use the web conference program. Examples of web conferencing programs that are used by educational institutions include WebEx (www.webex.com/), and Elluminate Live! (www.elluminate.com/). Because web conference systems operate through a central server, each user's bandwidth requirement is limited to his or her connection to the server. This means that there is no degradation of signal as more participants are added to a web conference. Many institutions license web conferencing programs to deliver distance courses.

Whereas personal videoconference and web conference systems are oriented toward individuals, **room-based videoconferencing systems** are oriented toward larger groups of participants. Room-based videoconference equipment differs in that it tends to use dedicated hardware (called an encoder/decoder or codec), rather than personal computers to encode and decode the audio and video feeds and to provide the connection to the network. In most integrated room-based systems, the device that contains the codec also controls microphones, cameras, display monitors, and peripheral devices. Room-based videoconference systems are available from a number of companies, including Polycom (www.polycom.com), Tandberg (www.tandberg.com), a division of Cisco (www.cisco.com/), Sony (http://bssc.sel.sony.com/), and LifeSize (www.lifesize.com/). A minimal room-based system usually consists of a codec, one camera, a microphone, two video monitors, and a speaker system. Some room-based systems also include peripheral devices such as integrated computer input, an electronic whiteboard, a visualizer, multiple microphones, multiple video displays, and surround sound audio.

Personal and web-based videoconference systems usually utilize proprietary protocols. Users of room-based systems often need to interoperate between systems; hence they demand that their systems subscribe to a standardized protocol. A number of protocols can be used for room-based videoconferences, but the protocol most commonly used by education institutions is H.323 (www.openh323.org/). The demand for individual presenters to participate in H.323 videoconferences has resulted in software products such as the Polycom PVX (www.polycom.com/products/telepresence_video/video_conference_systems/personal_systems/pvx.html) and XMeeting (http://xmeeting.sourceforge.net/pages/index.php) that allow personal computers to connect to conferences.

MAJOR USES OF VIDEO-CONFERENCING IN EDUCATION

Videoconferencing is a group endeavor with complex requirements for equipment, technology, experts, users, support, and resources. The use of videoconferencing in education can be categorized into four major areas: full course instruction, curriculum enhancement, professional development, and administration.

Full Course Instruction to Remote Students.

Some schools, due to rural and remote locations, lack local expertise to teach certain subjects. Subjects such as science, math, second languages, and music require teachers with extensive backgrounds to provide expertise to students to facilitate the learning process.

As an example, the Grande Yellowhead Regional Division, in the mountains of western Alberta, offers up to forty courses per year using videoconferencing, ranging from science and ecological studies to guitar and choral music to French and Spanish classes. Remote students in Grande Cache receive Cree language instruction from a teacher in Edson, about three hours away. Videoconferencing allows students and staff to work together to provide quality educational programming from communities across the school division. In this example the school division has experienced much success in providing valuable learning opportunities to students regardless of geographic location.

Curriculum Enhancement.

Bringing experts and opportunities into the classroom allows educators to enrich learning experiences for students and enhance curriculum outcomes. Videoconferencing gives students the opportunity to interact and engage with experts, go on virtual field trips, participate in simulation exercises, try their hands at scientific experiments, and collaborate with other schools on joint research projects.

For example, students in Grade 11 in Alberta schools worked via videoconference with Dr. Margaret Ann Armour, a world-renowned chemist and chemistry educator, to present their research findings on DDT (see Figure 1). The opportunity for the students to work with a world-renowned chemist gave them motivation to carry out their research project and enhance their presentation skills. Dr. Armour was able to give the students first-class advice on their findings, encourage them to dig further into their research, and provide them with constructive feedback that they would not otherwise receive from their teacher.

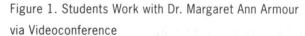

Figure 1. Students Work with Dr. Margaret Ann Armour via Videoconference

Figure 2. Royal Tyrell Museum Videoconference Program

Other examples of videoconferencing for curriculum enhancement are virtual field trips to places like the Tyrell Museum (see Figure 2) or the Cleveland Museum. Students participating in these sessions could interact with a host from the museum and "visit" institutions they might otherwise never have the opportunity to visit.

Simulation opportunities like the interactive Challenger Learning Centre Programs or Canadian Space Agency (see Figure 3) workshops offer sessions to students, which bring real-world experts right into the classroom.

Figure 3. Canadian Space Agency Scientist Interacting with Students

Professional Development. The ability to use videoconference in teaching and learning is not a common skill among teachers. Even though videoconferencing technology and network support are in place, teachers need informal and formal venues to learn, grow, and sustain their use of videoconferencing. Organizations such as the Videoconferencing Regional Leads Network operated by the 2Learn.ca Education Society (www.2learn.ca/vcrln) provide in-services, workshops, and mentorship to assist teachers and increase their comfort level with videoconferencing with learning opportunities such as these:

> Participating in a Multipoint Session
> Coordinating a VC Session with Multiple Sites
> Tips for Developing Peer-to-Peer Classroom Collaborations,
> Developing a Network of Experts
> Pedagogical Strategies and Best Practices
> Ten Ways to Ensure Your VC Is a Success
> Breaking the Ice the VC Way

Educators can also learn from their peers through communities of practice wherein teachers learn new methods of engagement and interaction using videoconferencing from one another based on real-world experiences. Educators can also access outside resources for formal professional development workshops such as those offered by the Center for Interactive Learning and Collaboration (http://cilc.org), where teachers can gain skills to enhance their teaching via videoconferencing. All of these resources feed into the use of videoconferencing and expand the nature of its use. There are also professional development events for teachers and students during which the videoconference is centered around a learning theme such as Earth Day, La Fete Du Printemps (the French Spring Festival; Figure 4) and even "lunch and learn" sessions such as *Learning About Damsel Flies* from leading expert Dr. John Acorn, "The Nature Nut."

Administrative Uses. School and jurisdictional administrators use videoconferencing to support administrative

Figure 4. La Fete Du Printemps

meetings, staff development sessions, and consultations. This allows for staff spread across jurisdictions to meet more frequently, minimizing costs and driving time required by staff. It also mitigates any safety concerns for school staff having to drive extras hours in the winter evenings and bad weather.

SUPPORTING THE USE OF VIDEO-CONFERENCING IN EDUCATION

Videoconferencing is a group endeavor, a network of equipment and people. Being a member of this group brings some constraints, but it also allows the combining of resources to create something that is bigger than the resources of the individuals—a gestalt. At its core, videoconferencing is the synchronous communication between two or more groups. A significant structure is required to support users. The effective integration of infrastructure, technical support, professional development, leadership, collaboration, support resources, and service directories all act as systematic enablers for the effective use of videoconferencing in education (Figure 5).

Infrastructure. Three key infrastructure elements are critical to create an effective, user-friendly videoconferencing network for education. *Equipment* must be easy to use and allow for interactivity and engagement for the learner. Classroom and desktop equipment must be integrated into a *network* with quality broadband connections and easy dialing schemes in order to allow users to interact with other users on both private and public networks. Finally, access to *multipoint control unit (MCU) or bridge* enables seamless connection of more than two (multipoint) sets of videoconference equipment.

Technical Support. Successful videoconferencing requires a technical support team that not only understands the technical possibilities and limitations but also has the ability to communicate effectively and to assist users in how to best utilize the technology. Technical personnel also need to understand how the technological

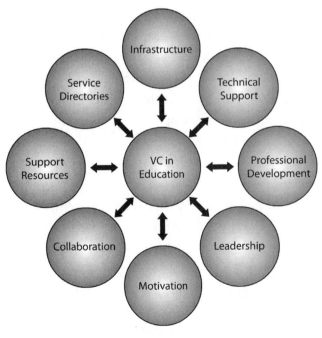

Figure 5. Educational Videoconference Support Model

infrastructure of videoconferencing works in the classroom, jurisdictional, and network environment and how users, management, and administration can effectively utilize this infrastructure.

Professional Development. Educators
need access to advanced videoconferencing users who can provide guidance on how they might use videoconferencing within and outside of the classroom to support student learning and development, access content experts, and create peer-to peer-classroom offerings. One way to expedite this is through the creation of a formalized professional development program that is implemented and supported by regional personnel who are experts in the use of videoconferencing in education.

Leadership. Effective educational use
of videoconferencing depends on effective leadership. Leaders must be willing to encourage innovative and adaptive change in practice and pedagogy as well as provide the technology and support requirements. Administrators need to be educated about and understand what videoconferencing can and cannot do in order to support their teachers in the delivery of curriculum to the classroom and provide professional development opportunities for the educator community.

Educational leadership has the opportunity to facilitate and embrace the power of accessibility and distance collaboration that videoconferencing has to enable their colleagues within and beyond traditional jurisdictional boundaries.

Good infrastructure, technical support,

professional development opportunities, and organizational leadership motivate individual teachers to act as peer leaders on the effective use of videoconferencing in their respective content areas.

Collaboration. Historically, teaching is
an individual practice. Videoconferencing encourages collaboration between classroom teachers and fosters broader engagement opportunities for students and teachers with outside experts. Activities such as cyberbridges and videoconference cafes encourage teachers to become involved in formal and informal communities of practice and to grow in educational facilitation skills. These collaborative opportunities can enhance curriculum outcomes and reenergized educators with tips for enriching learning outcomes.

Support Resources/Directory of Services. A number of online and offline
resources are available to assist in the usage of videoconferencing in the classroom. These provide links to forthcoming curriculum-specific sessions and collaborative classroom opportunities. Often, classroom teachers are not aware of, or do not check for, new opportunities, so someone, often a central coordinator, may need to bring new opportunities to their attention.

BUILDING A VIDEO-CONFERENCE NETWORK
In 2000 the provincial government of Alberta, Canada, announced that they would build the "Alberta SuperNet"—a high-speed broadband network to every

hospital, school, library, and government facility in the province (Alberta, November 2, 2000). This network was completed in 2005, with "approximately 4,200 connections in 429 communities" (Alberta, September 30, 2005).

The government of Alberta realized that the provision of the network was insufficient to encourage the effective use of new technologies. Videoconference was chosen as a "killer app" that demanded the kind of bandwidth that the SuperNet made available and that could be demonstrated as useful in a number of different areas (for example, health, justice, education, and social services). Various provincial government departments funded a number of initiatives to encourage adoption of the SuperNet in general and videoconferencing in particular, including:

➢ 10 Mbit basic SuperNet service was provided to every school and post-secondary institution in the province.

➢ H.323 was chosen as a provincial standard for videoconferencing.

➢ A provincial videoconference network center was set up to provide a multipoint control unit that could connect up to ninety-two locations in various configurations. The provincial network center also provides bridging between SuperNet and a number of other networks, including the consumer Internet, the research Internet, and the ISDN telephone network.

➢ A videoconference network center that is similar to the provincial videoconference network center was set up specifically for the use of educational institutions. Among other services, staff at this center handles all the technical tasks of arranging connections between schools on the SuperNet and schools or providers on other networks.

➢ Each school district was given a grant of $60,000 for videoconferencing hardware, training, or support.

➢ Funding of the development and delivery of "SuperNet Technical Training courses to IT personnel" by the Northern Alberta Institute of Technology (www.nait.ca/supernet/). Creation and funding of VcAlberta. ca, "your one-stop videoconferencing resource in Alberta. It helps you find and connect to other sites in Alberta's K-12 and post-secondary system. Highlights of the site include, tools, resources, best practice videos, research, and a social network where educators, technical personnel, and administrators can connect to others across the province." (http://vcalberta. ca/).

➢ Creation and funding of the Alberta Video Conference Regional Leads Network, "a program established by Alberta Education and administered by the 2Learn.ca Education Society. The purpose of the VC Regional Leads Network is to *support SuperNet and videoconferencing-enabled learning* across Alberta's K-12 education system" (www.2Learn.ca/vcrln/rlnannounce. html).

➢ Funding of *Elevate 2008* (Alberta Education, Stakeholder Technology Branch, 2008), which featured renowned speakers from around the world and included eighteen live videoconference sessions that connected the delegates in Banff to places such as Hong Kong and Australia. Delegates included teachers, principals, technical staff, professional development providers, and administrators. Sessions featured videoconference content providers, best practices for using technology in the classroom, and discussions on the technology trends that will impact education.

Significant funding was put into the creation of the technical components that allow videoconferencing in education in Alberta. There were still significant gaps in both the preparation and the confidence of teachers and others who wanted to use videoconferencing. It is the human connections, provided through VC Alberta, the VCRLN, Elevate 2008 and the staff at the education videoconference network centre who enabled the success of the endeavor. These people provided a number of resources that aid the front-line educator. Some examples of resources, which aid in videoconferencing usage:

Professional Development/Programming.

A number of organizations provide professional development to educators. These resources provide curriculum linkages, one-stop access to content area experts, notification of peer-to-peer educational collaborations, and opportunities for professional development and engagement. Through these resources educators receive another layer of support in a holistic videoconference support mode.

2Learn.ca Educational Society (www.2learn.ca)

"The mission of the 2Learn.ca Education Society is to initiate, advocate and share with educators technology-enriched teaching, learning and leadership options of tomorrow, empowered by unique alliances with educational and community partners" (2Learn.ca). Table 1 gives a list of the kinds of resources provided by 2Learn.ca.

Table 1. Resources Provided by 2Learn.ca

Ongoing Opportunities	Sessions on different course delivery methods and formats, and an educational technology series
Specialized Opportunities	The home page highlights upcoming PD sessions that are not part of their regular programming
Social Network	A network of educators supporting technology in the classroom in a collaborative online environment. The network offers lists of events, collaboration opportunities, and news geared toward educators. www.2.learn2gether.ca
Calendar	Highlights upcoming events and programming

Alberta's Videoconferencing Regional Leads Network (VCRLN) (www.2learn.ca/vcrln)

The Alberta Video Conference Regional Leads Network is a program established by Alberta Education and administered by the 2Learn.ca Education Society. The purpose is to support SuperNet and videoconferencing enabled learning across Alberta's K-12 Education System. The network provides expertise within regions and throughout the province, so as to supplement professional growth of videoconferencing practice in individual jurisdictions.

Centre for Interactive Learning and Collaboration (CILC) (www.cilc.org)

The Center for Interactive Learning and Collaboration (CILC) supports and advances education through videoconferencing and other collaborative technologies. A nonprofit, CILC offers access to quality professional development and student educational content, as well as consulting and technical assistance. This helps schools leverage technology to improve educational outcomes, while saving time and money (http://www.cilc.org/c/about/about_cilc.aspx). Table 3 gives a list of the kinds of resources provided by VcAlberta.

Table 2. Resources Provided by VCRLN

Collaboration	Highlights opportunities of collaboration for Alberta's teachers
VC Opportunities	Shares opportunities for classes to coordinate events with other classes in Alberta
Resources	Links to related sites and other 2Learn sites, resources created by 2 Learn, and resources and materials hosted by VCRLN from other organizations (teacher/student VC etiquette, collaboration tips, etc).
Calendar	Highlights upcoming events and programming

Table 3. Resources Provided by CILC

Content Providers	Over 1,200 teacher evaluated programs from over 170 providers worldwide in alignment with K-12 curriculum standards
Collaboration	Offers a venue for educators to meet, to create collaborative projects, and to share methodologies
Professional Development Programs	An online marketplace to find experts and programs for educators
VC Directories	Directories for content providers, professional development providers, and videoconferencing sites

Table 4. Resources Provided by TWICE

Content Providers	Database of virtual field trip providers and rated list of favoured providers
Curriculum Enhancement	Streaming samples of VC field trips
Professional Development	Workshops, online courses, teacher demonstrations from content providers
Resources	A large source of links to general videoconferencing information, case studies, research, articles, and content information
Collaboration	Lists ongoing and upcoming projects and possible collaborative opportunities

Two-Way Interactive Connections in Education (TWICE) (www.twice.cc)

Two Way Interactive Connections in Education (TWICE) is Michigan's organization for videoconferencing in K-12 education. TWICE promotes and supports collaborative connections for the benefit of all students. Table 4 gives a list of the kinds of resources provided by TWICE.

Organizations like the ones described above are critical to offer continued holistic support to teachers in the area of videoconferencing programming and professional development. Two key recommendations identified in the Videoconferencing Regional Leads Network Evaluation (Alberta Education, 2010) may assist others in ensuring that videoconferencing continues to be successfully integrated into teaching and learning. These recommendations were:

1. Continued targeted funding for initiatives that promote VC technology implementation for K-12, including:

   a. Targeted funding to support VC opportunities for teachers and students.

   b. Templates to assist schools and school districts to provide technical support and minimum infrastructure for VC.

   c. Update and validation of the VCAlberta database of VC sites in Alberta, and promotion of its use among K-12 schools and schools systems in Alberta.

   d. Implement a centralized scheduling system to oversee scheduling and access to Alberta Education VC meeting rooms.

2. Continued support and coordination of a provincial professional development team to:

   a. Provide teachers with ongoing support in order to continue and increase the effective use of videoconference in the curriculum.

   b. Maintain an online list of videoconference opportunities containing Alberta curriculum–specific information, with Alberta and Canadian opportunities identified.

   c. Provide a provincial clearing house to catalogue and promote course delivery via videoconference.

TECHNICAL RESOURCES

VcAlberta is designed as a one-stop videoconferencing resource in Alberta. It helps people to find and connect to other sites in Alberta's K-12 and post-secondary system. Highlights of the site include, tools, resources, best practice videos, research, and a social network where educators, technical personnel and administrators can connect to others across the province. VcAlberta.ca also provides a searchable content provider and VC research database. You can even get advice on videoconferencing standards in Alberta (http://vcalberta.ca/). Table 5 gives a list of the kinds of resources provided by VcAlberta.

classrooms in different parts of the world to work together, and allowing teachers to collaborate on teaching and professional development.

Videoconferencing alone, however, doesn't open the doors nor transform teaching. Systematic supports such as technical expertise to operate equipment, curriculum experts to assist with resources, leadership to enable integration, professional development to enhance teaching and support funding for commercial presentations are all required to ensure the successful integration of videoconferencing into the classroom.

Educational videoconferencing does require an investment in equipment, networks, technical support, and professional development,

Table 5. Resources Provided by VcAlberta

Resources	Provides links to research pertaining to videoconference, checklists and technical information, tip sheets, and videos
VC Directory	Multiple search options: K-12, post-secondary, by city/town, grouped by province, by IP system, by ISDN system
Content Providers	Provides links to searchable lists of content providers in Canada and the U.S.
Social Networking	Offers a social network where educators, technical personnel, and administrators from across the province can connect with one another
Extra Information	Shares event information, news, opportunities, and what VC sites are doing

CONCLUSION

Videoconferencing has taken teaching from a solitary occupation to a generation of global collaboration. It has broken down the walls of the traditional classroom by inviting outside experts in, taking classroom students on virtual fieldtrips, allowing students in different

but these costs pale in comparison to the cost, safety, and organizational problems of physically transporting experts to the classroom or students to other locations. The investment in videoconferencing, if done right, opens classroom doors to the rest of the world and creates a bountiful world of virtual educational opportunities for student learning.

REFERENCES

Alberta. (2000, November 2)."SUPERNET to connect communities to the 21st century at warp speed. Available: www.alberta.ca/acn/200011/9894.html.

Alberta. (2005, September 30). Alberta SuperNet now operational throughout the province. Available: www.alberta.ca/acn/200509/18828F93E02E6-F2D6-4F55-99D3CC5C2E0424EF.html.

Alberta Education. (2010). Evaluation of the Videoconferencing Regional Leads Network (VCRLN). Unpublished report. (Permission to reference this report has been granted.)

Alberta Education, Stakeholder Technology Branch. (2008, September 30). *Tech. News, 8*(2). Elevate 2008. Available: http://education.alberta.ca/media/848933/8-2%20newsletter.pdf.

Andberg, S. (2008). Videoconferencing in distance education. University of Helsinki, Department of Computer Science. Retrieved April 24, 2009.

Grande Yellowhead Regional School Division. (2009, April 14). Available: https://docushare.gyrd. ab.ca/docushare/dsweb/Get/Document-129906/09-04-14%20-%20Board%20Key%20Messages. pdf.

King, C. (2008). Identifying critical success factors for the strategic implementation of a videoconferencing professional development program in the education sector. In *Proceedings of World Conference on Educational Multimedia, Hypermedia, and Telecommunications 2008* (pp. 154–165). Chesapeake, VA: AACE.

Kullman, C., & King, C. (2007). A professional development model to integrate videoconferencing in K-12 education. In R. Carlsen et al. (Eds.), *Proceedings of Society for Information Technology and Teacher Education International Conference 2007* (pp. 3073–3076). Chesapeake, VA: AACE.

Montgomerie, T. C., Davenport, M., & King, C. (2003). Providing quality and equitable distance education. In *Proceedings: PTC2003: Global broadband/global challenges.* Honolulu, HI: Pacific Telecommunications Council.

Scott, B. (1993). IBM distance learning developments using videoconferencing. In K. Harry, M. John, & D. Keegan (Eds.), *Distance education: New perspectives* (pp. 224–229). New York: Routledge.

Belinda G. Smith

The teaching philosophy of Belinda G. Smith, Ph.D. is founded in the belief of giving learners an opportunity to learn at a time and place convenient for them. As an assistant professor with American InterContinental University, corporate educator, and community presenter, Belinda is aware that learners construct their own meaning and realities of their learning environment. It is her goal as a facilitator to make the learning event relevant to learners.

Belinda has presented to local, national, and international audiences about how to employ computer technology within a training program. She is a member of the American Society for Training and Development (ASTD) Speakers Bureau. Belinda has published several articles and a case study about employing computer technology within training programs. The topic of Belinda's dissertation is engaging adult learners in an e-learning environment. Belinda's articles and presentations are based on research as well as more than fifteen years of experience facilitating and developing courses that employ computer technology.

ENGAGING ADULT LEARNERS USING SYNCHRONOUS E-LEARNING MEDIA | Belinda G. Smith

Sometimes it's the little things that veto otherwise superlative efforts in planning, design, and opportunities for success. No car key, phone battery, salt, pencil. While we may focus on what seem to be the "big" challenges of instructional design, programming, graphics, and data tracking, adult learners can be put off by the slighted "little" things—passwords, who will answer their questions, what "submit" means, where they are supposed to type. While facilitators may have the equipment and Internet access required to present e-learning, the question they face is how to use that technology effectively to engage their adult learners. Belinda Smith provides guidance for them.

Adult learners can be engaged using asynchronous and synchronous e-learning technology. In this article I discuss how to employ synchronous e-learning media within a course. Synchronous e-learning media is Internet-based media used by learners to engage their facilitator and other learners in real time. Synchronous e-learning media permits this engagement at a place convenient for both the facilitator and learners. Instant messaging, synchronized chats, and live online conferences are forums that permit adult learners to access their facilitator and other learners from home, work, Internet cafés, parks, or anywhere they may have Internet access.

Interaction and collaboration have been identified as the fundamental building blocks for engaging learners. Learning media allow learners to interact and collaborate with others in a social environment that encourages critical thinking. In e-learning environments, facilitators must consider learners' backgrounds, knowledge, and beliefs, as well as provide discussions that allow learners to use self-reflection. Multiple opportunities for formative and summative feedback from learners and facilitators should be incorporated in the e-learning event.

URGE THEM TO ATTEND

Facilitating e-learning forums begins with an invitation. We cannot assume because learners know about the forum that they will come. Facilitators should take the first step to engage learners before the event occurs. Sending an e-mail invitation to learners will announce the synchronous e-learning event. The e-mail should advertise an event that is informative and fun.

In addition, the forum can be promoted on an online announcement board or the company's bulletin board. In announcements and invitations, state how the learners can assess the event. Include a link to the online forum in the e-mail inviting them to the event. Place the web address to the online forum on the announcement. The time of the event and the topics discussed should also be identified within the e-mail and on the announcement. An example of an e-mail is shown in Figure 1.

Acquiring a promotion, obtaining a new position, starting a new career, or maintaining a current job are all important to adult learners. In addition, adult learners have family

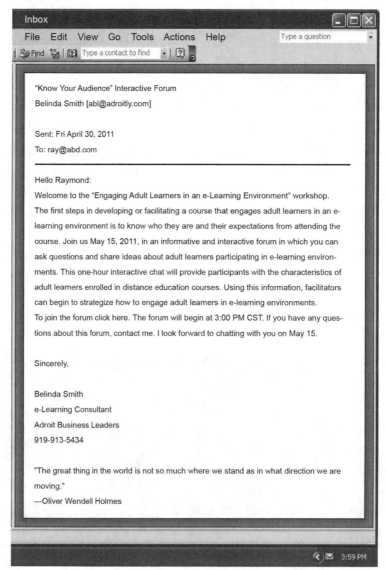

Figure 1. e-Mail Announcing Forum

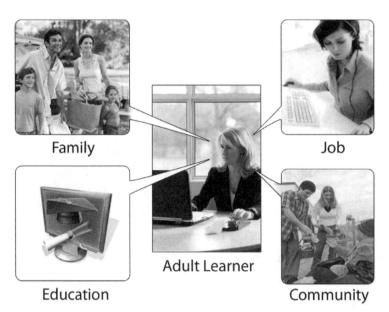

Family

Job

Education

Adult Learner

Community

and community concerns. In invitations and announcements, let learners know that the event has been developed to address a need they may have. Adult learners are busy people with multiple concerns; however, they will attend learning events that are convenient and important to them.

FIRST IMPRESSIONS

When learners enter the forum, it should appear informal, flexible, and non-threatening. An informal e-learning environment suggests that the facilitator knows the material well enough to communicate with learners in a conversational tone. Flexibility proposes that the facilitator has an outline, but is willing to address the learners' needs first. A flexible facilitator can return to the outline after addressing learners' needs. A non-threatening environment implies that learners and the facilitator demonstrate respect for

each other. Both should feel free to ask and answer questions without repercussions.

When adult learners enter any forum, it's smart to welcome them with a greeting and to use their names. State that their time is valuable and that you appreciate that they have decided to attend the forum. Respond immediately to questions. If you have more than one learner in the forum, make sure each person's questions are addressed. Once learners are comfortable and know the forum has been designed around their needs, active engagement is possible.

First impressions are important. Facilitators should not assume that because they are not seen or heard that their personalities are not being transmitted to the learners. In chat and instant messaging forums, participants are aware of each other's personalities by the words they use. Learners will notice how the facilitator responds to others and surmise the passion and desire he or she has to provide helpful information. Forums conducted using online video conference software can provide not only an area for participants to chat, but also a place for the facilitator to have an electronic slide visible that welcomes participants. While participants are gathering in the forum, play music. First impressions are important and set the tone for engagement. The forum should make a statement that learning will occur and that participants will enjoy the experience.

ENGAGING THE ADULT LEARNER USING SYNCHRONOUS E-LEARNING MEDIA

Internet capabilities continue to evolve. Individuals are transitioning from dial-up Internet access to fiber optics Internet services for their homes. Communities are providing free high-speed Internet access. Hotels, restaurants, bookstores, and cafés are promoting their free high-speed Internet services to their customers. Cellular Internet companies are offering wireless Internet cards, and automobile manufacturers are including Internet technology in their automobiles. Mobile devices, such as laptops and net books, are being used by facilitators and learners to participate in online e-learning events at a place convenient for them. Learners and facilitators have the equipment and the Internet access. The question for learners and facilitators is how to use Internet technology effectively to engage each other.

First, software employed in online forums should be intuitive. If learners are new to the e-learning environment, you might send them a one-page, graphic instruction sheet that indicates how to use the software before the online forum begins.

Learners must be comfortable with the software as well as the procedures to follow during the discussion. Facilitators should help learners become aware of the procedures for engagement. For example, the facilitator may state: "If you have a question, type a question mark (?) before asking the question." This gives the facilitator an opportunity to recognize the learner and request the question.

Before the forum begins, facilitators should establish a learning strategy that provides learners with an opportunity to develop critical thinking skills through self-reflection. In order to do this, the facilitator must know something about the learners attending the forum. This way, the facilitator can introduce concepts, facts, and ideas using examples and words that learners can connect with their experiences. For example; in the late 1980s, computer data were stored on magnetic disks. When comparing magnetic disks to vinyl records, the facilitator was able to help learners understand how information was read on a magnetic disk by stating that the needle on the record player was similar to the needle on a hard drive. To remove the magnetic disk while information was being read was similar to removing a vinyl record from the record player while the vinyl record was playing. Both the magnetic disk and the vinyl record would acquire a scratch and therefore be damaged.

Facilitators should provide opportunities for engagement that address each type of learner. Learners have preferences for acquiring knowledge. *Visual* learners prefer information presented visually and in written form. Graphical information can help visual learners understand concepts and ideas. *Verbal or auditory* learners understand information presented to them orally. Verbal learners prefer listening to lectures and participating in group discussions. The *tactile or kinesthetic* learners prefer hands-on activities, to touch and manipulate materials.

Using videoconferencing software, facilitators can address each learner type. For example, electronic slides and/or documents can be incorporated into the online forum for the visual learner. You can include audio when discussing topics for auditory learners, incorporate polls into the learning event for tactile learners, and actively engage learners using synchronous e-learning software to address each learning style. There are many ways to present facts, concepts, and ideas. Facilitators must be advocates for learning by addressing different learning styles.

To increase active engagement, facilitators should use software that permits learners to see other learners' names appear when they enter the forum. Facilitators should greet each learner as he or she enters the forum. In addition, they should allow learners to greet each other to form the basis for learners interacting with each other.

Online forum software should let others know when someone is typing or wants to speak. Some learners type fast and some learners type slowly. The facilitator must give both an opportunity to communicate. Facilitators should ask questions, give learners time to think, and wait while they type their responses. Keep learners engaged by displaying electronic slides and documents. Point to information on these displays and ask learners whether they see what you are pointing to. Have learners participate in an online poll that reinforces the topic being discussed. These polls can be prepared ahead of time or you could create a poll when necessary. It's obviously quite important that the facilitator understand how to use the e-learning software.

Facilitators should orchestrate discussions between learners. Keep learners focused on the topic and do not allow conversations that are distracting to others. Personal experiences should be welcomed as long as they are related to the topic being discussed. Adult learners enjoy learning from each other as well as sharing their experiences. However, e-learning events are not the appropriate arena for learners to vent their frustrations about work, home, and family situations.

Keep learners coming back by letting them leave when each discussion is complete. Do not try to make a discussion longer just to fill the scheduled time period. Facilitators can let learners know the discussion is over but remain in case someone has more questions or information to share. If it appears that the forum members want more time to discuss the topic, and all are in agreement, extend the forum time. If not, reschedule a time to continue the discussion.

Each forum will have a personality of its own. The mix of individuals participating in the online forum and the topic being discussed determine that personality. Be flexible and observant of the character of the group. Engagement does not mean anything goes; however, it does mean that adult learners must have some control of the learning event.

As a side note: Just because a learner is not typing or speaking does not mean he or she is not engaged. Of course, it does not mean that the person is engaged either. When presenting information, randomly say the names of those who are not visually interacting. Ask them whether they understand. You may be surprised by a learner's response or there may not be any response. The person may have signed into the online forum to earn credit for attending; but is not engaged in the learning event.

CONCLUSION

Engaging adult learners using synchronous e-learning media requires the facilitator to develop a strategy for learner engagement. Begin by inviting learners to the forum. Provide information about how to use the e-learning media as well as rules for interacting within the online forum. When learners enter the forum, welcome them and ensure them that the forum will be informative as well as fun.

Facilitators should consider the learning style of each of their learners and address their needs. Deliver information in a conversational tone and be flexible. Facilitators must be advocates for learning. Give learners the incentive to learn. Make online learning events informative as well as fun.

Final Word

What have I learned in the compilation of this *Annual?* I've learned that we have moved beyond two important sticking points in our field: (1) thinking that distribution of information is equivalent to teaching and (2) letting the ways we can use technology provide direction. We may have just barely moved off these inhibiting speed bumps, but I think they're in the rear-view mirror more than blocking our movement. Let me take up each point briefly.

INFORMING VERSUS TEACHING There will always be a need for people to be informed. Sometimes just telling people what's expected or how to do something is enough to enable performance improvement. *Even if you have to put a current call on hold, never let an incoming call ring more than three times before you pick up.* As instructional designers, it's our job to match appropriate solutions to performance needs. The simplest effective solution is nearly always the best solution. But when skills need to be developed to perform a task, just telling someone what to do isn't a solution.

Clearly, some design decisions will be mistakes. We all make them. But it seems to me that we've actually moved past this broad and frustrating misunderstanding. Finally, most people—not just designers—realize that when real learning is needed, the preferred solution is a learning experience. And there's awareness that our technology is up to the task of delivering learning experiences.

Work is still needed to help people construct effective learning experiences. And this takes me to the second sticking point, technology in the lead.

TECHNOLOGY VERSUS VISION As a number of our authors point out and demonstrate, there are often great solutions that low-level applications of relatively simple, commonplace technology can assist with. Our challenge is not how much technology we can implement in our solutions, but rather how effective our solutions can be. Technology can be a great solution, but it comes with both limitations and costs. If our thinking is technology-centered, we won't be learner-centered or experience-centered, and we'll undoubtedly miss the mark.

I constantly see both sides of technology—its benefits and its weaknesses. Getting them in balance is much harder than it appears. The key to me is to be mindful of my focus. Is it on the benefits being provided to the learner or is my focus on utilization of technology? If it's on learner benefits, I have a real chance of success. But I can so easily miss the mark if I let the challenges of technology deployment distract my focus.

WHAT HAVE I LEARNED?

Each author has, from his or her perspective, given me aids to focus on the learning experience while also showing me the range of ways technology can help me enrich that experience. For example, our contributors taught me to think about the importance of conscious and unconscious learner identity. What?! Oh, yes! Personal and social identities, too!

I was reminded that if authors are focused on the speed of their authoring, they're probably focused on the technology and the value of their time, not the quality of the experience and the value of learner time. I was repeatedly and helpfully given insights into the different expectations of newer generations of learners.

Mobilization depends on connectivity. Different designs require different levels of connectivity. It's a mundane issue, but nevertheless a critical issue on the path to m-learning success. It's also an issue that can be overlooked until in the throes of deployment.

Now that we're in touch with each other through our social connectivity, can we share responsibilities in different ways? Should we each specialize more and depend on our networks? Or should we become more generalized (and depend on our networks for specialized assistance)? Hmm.

We're starting to see that even little injections of simulation energize learning in extremely valuable ways. Simulation isn't just for NASA and hugely funded enterprises; it's really a cornerstone of experience-based learning. Authors and instructional designers need to embrace the fundamental concepts before hanging out their shingles.

And, of course, I was faced with tradeoffs that justify the professional status of instructional designers and strategists. Solutions have to be affordable. Regardless of the potential benefits of high-impact learning, organizations scrutinize their budgets not on the basis of return on investment, but rather in terms of absolute costs. Well, not all do. In fact, I'd venture to say that those organizations that tend to win over their competitors see learning more as a strategic investment and adjust budgets accordingly. But even there, and more certainly elsewhere, there are pressures to keep costs low and deliver training quickly. The quality issue, unfortunately, floats. I appreciate the many authors who have taken up the reality of this situation and given us survival maps, if not paths to certain success.

I've learned a lot, and I'm proud to share this compendium. I doubt not that every reader will find valuable and potentially career enhancing insights herein. Enjoy and be successful!

About the Editor

Michael W. Allen pioneered multimedia learning technologies, interactive instructional paradigms, and rapid-prototyping processes, bringing each forward into leading corporate enterprises. He is the chairman and CEO of Allen Interactions Inc., which builds universally acclaimed custom e-learning, provides strategic learning consulting, and trains e-learning professionals in collaboration with ASTD. With a Ph.D. in educational psychology from The Ohio State University, he is an adjunct associate professor at the University of Minnesota Medical School, a popular conference speaker, and a prolific writer.

Michael's Other Books

Michael Allen's e-Learning Annual 2008. Part of the *Pfeiffer Annual* series, first published in 1972, this edition presents a wide range of perspectives from some of the earliest and most renowned leaders in the field. This book frankly and objectively presents lessons learned and the critical steps to success. This important resource will help both educator and trainers create, purchase, and apply quality e-learning programs more effectively.

Michael Allen's e-Learning Annual 2009. This second edition of the *Pfeiffer Annual* series provides a compilation of the best current, truly up-to-date thinking in their respective topic areas. The book embraces controversy and a diversity of viewpoints. This is an essential reference for e-learning professionals who are interested in the most current thinking about instructional design and management.

Michael Allen's Guide to e-Learning. As an international speaker and consultant to virtually every business sector over his more than thirty-five years of research and development in technology-based instruction, Michael Allen speaks out about his frustrations with e-learning and brings fundamental issues to light. He shares specific, commonsense guidelines that reliably produce effective and practical learning solutions. From his pioneering work on learning management systems, to authoring systems, and now on instructional design, experts and buyers alike follow his leadership and respect his opinion.

Creating Successful e-Learning — For Getting It Right the First Time, Every Time. This is the first volume of six in Michael Allen's e-Learning Library — a comprehensive collection of proven techniques for creating e-learning applications that achieve targeted behavioral outcomes through meaningful, memorable, and motivational learning experiences. This book walks readers through the revolutionary processes of rapid prototyping and iterative design as a means of identifying the conflicting and hidden agendas of organizations, winning essential support, and generating creative learning solutions.

Designing Successful e-Learning — Forget What You Know. This is the second volume of six in Michael Allen's e-Learning Library. This book examines common instructional design practices with a critical eye and recommends substituting success rather than tradition as a guide. Drawing from theory, research, and experience in learning and behavioral change, the author provides a framework for addressing a broader range of learner needs and achieving superior performance outcomes.

Successful e-Learning Interface — Making Learning Technology Polite, Effective, and Fun. This is the third volume of six in Michael Allen's e-Learning Library. This book dives into the differences between and importance of learner interface design and user interface design. Using the structural foundations of interactive learning experiences—context, challenge, activity, and feedback—as organizers for the itemized and specific guidelines that have been effective in applications across significant varieties of content, time and time again, the author unwraps the true power in learner interface design.